How to Order:

Quantity discounts are available from the publisher, Prima Publishing, P.O. Box 1260IS, Rocklin, CA 95677; telephone (916) 624-5718. On your letterhead include information concerning the intended use of the books and the number of books you wish to purchase.

U.S. Bookstores and Libraries: Please submit all orders to St. Martin's Press, 175 Fifth Avenue, New York, NY 10010; telephone (212) 674-5151.

BLACK KNIGHT
Al Davis
and His Raiders

Ira Simmons

Prima Publishing
P.O. Box 1260IS
Rocklin, CA 95677
(916) 624-5718

Developmental editing by Dick O'Connor
Composition by Janet Hansen, Alphatype
Production by Carol Dondrea, Bookman Productions
Interior design by Judith Levinson
Cover design by The Dunlavey Studio

Prima Publishing
Rocklin, CA

Library of Congress Cataloging-in-Publication Data

Simmons, Ira Bruce.
    Black knight : Al Davis and his Raiders / by Ira Bruce Simmons.
      p.   cm.
    ISBN 1-55958-055-0
    1. Davis, Al. 1929–   .   2. Sports team owners—United States— Biography.   3. Los Angeles Raiders (Football team)—History.
    I. Title.
    GV939.D342S56   1990
    338.4'7796'092—dc20
    [B]   90-42251
                                     CIP

90 91 92 — 10 9 8 7 6 5 4 3 2 1

Printed in the United States of America

CONTENTS

FOREWORD

Since his emergence upon the national sports scene in 1963, when as coach and general manager of the Oakland Raiders, he nearly single-handedly turned a laughingstock professional football team into the winningest organization in team sports, Mr. Allen M. Davis has been revered by some and hated by others. As Commissioner of the American Football League, his strategy of signing National Football League veteran quarterbacks brought the older circuit to its knees with a merger proposal. But when the junior league won the war and subsequently bungled the peace, Al Davis was forced to return to the Oakland Raiders. He then built a colorful and successful team, highlighted by Super Bowl appearances in the 1960s, 1970s, and 1980s and three world championships. The battles of Al Davis have never really ended. In 1980 and 1981, Davis successfully defied the City of Oakland and both the commissioner and the other owners of the NFL with a controversial move to Los Angeles. And nine years later, unhappy with his present surroundings, Al had four cities bidding for the Raiders by offering inducements unheard of previously in municipal politics and sports. He finally selected Oakland and was immediately rejected by its partisan politicians.

The story and glory of Al Davis and the Raiders extends beyond Los Angeles and Oakland, as the famed "Silver and Black" have become a "dark" version of "America's team." NFL Properties report that Raider merchandise is now the top seller among all 28 NFL teams. The Raider emblem of a man wearing an eye patch with a knife clenched in his teeth has become world famous and even chic among many groups as an anti-establishment symbol of defiance and difference. This is indicated by such phenomenon as construction workers in New York City wearing the Raider symbol on their hardhats and gang members in Watts and other inner-city locales donning Raider jackets and sweatshirts. In popular music, the Raider presence ranges from the controversial Luther Campbell of the rap group 2 Live Crew wearing the Silver and Black to cute Donny Wahlberg of New Kids on the Block entertaining suburban girls in his Raider jacket. Not surprisingly, much of the Hispanic population throughout California has adapted the Raiders as "their team." It is not uncommon to observe buses at daybreak on a Sunday morning along Highway 99 carrying Hispanic Raider fans to Los Angeles from such far-off places as Turlock, Fresno, and Visalia. Discount the results of a 1990 *Los Angeles Times* public opinion poll; the Raiders, and not the Rams, are the most popular team in Southern California. If you don't believe it, just count all those silver and black jackets along Beverly Boulevard.

But Al Davis and the Raiders do not represent only fun and games. In 1980 through 1982, Al Davis tackled an entire league, unpopular public opinion, and many hostile politicians and won the right to move to Los Angeles by successfully challenging what the courts decided was an illegal rule concerning franchise shifts in the NFL. The Raiders also won $34,000,000 in damages from the NFL (later settled at $20,000,000) and $7,000,000 from the City of Oakland, the latter for attempting to invoke the power of eminent domain to stop their departure. They also helped the Los Angeles Memorial Coliseum Commission win $21,000,000 in damages and then were shockingly jilted when the LAMCC did not use the money to improve the Coliseum.

The Raider phenomenon has been reflected by a football team long composed of flamboyant, unusual, and often unpredictable characters such as Ben Davidson, George Blanda, Otis Sistrunk, John Matuszak, Ken Stabler, John Madden, Lyle Alzado, and now Bo Jackson. Of course, many of Al's players and coaches have become famous in their own right. Madden is the most popular football announcer on television and endorses everything—motor oil, hardware stores, computer games, and tractors. There have also been best-selling volumes written by Jack Tatum (two), Stabler, Matuszak, and Madden (three books). These men are interesting individual personalities, but they also represent parts of the larger story of Al Davis himself, because no organization in professional sports has had a more zany and colorful collection of players through the years than the Oakland/Los Angeles Raiders.

It is not surprising that many people both in and out of sports do not agree with the things that Al Davis has done and intensely hate the managing general partner of the Los Angeles Raiders. It sometimes seems as if everybody wants to "teach Al Davis a lesson." The animosity is reflected by the annual refusal of a small clique of sportswriters to vote Davis into the Professional Football Hall of Fame even though his credentials for enshrinement exceed many who have already been selected. But the detractors must grudgingly admit that Al Davis is unlike anybody else who has ever operated a sports franchise and that men like this must be appreciated for their genius, guts, guile, and willingness to take chances where others would not dare.

The story of Al Davis is really the story of professional football over the past 30 years because no one else has had a greater impact on the landscape of American sports than the managing general partner of the Raiders. His exact title is "president of the general partner." (What the hell does that mean?) The slogans such as "pride and poise," "commitment to excellence," and "just win, baby" are well known to football fans. But these are more than hollow phrases to encourage football players or parody material for use in beer commercials; they have been the Al Davis philosophy of life both in and out of football. Because his actions have had such a widespread impact in the political and municipal arenas of this country, the story of Al Davis and the Raiders extends beyond sports.

I am not your normal sports fan. While the New York Giants, led by Frank Gifford and Y. A. Tittle, were dominating the Big Apple pro football scene in the early 1960s, I was a Brooklyn teenager who somehow developed a perverse hatred of squeaky clean Pete Rozelle and his league and instead spent most of my Sunday afternoons watching the new American Football League games in black and white on ABC Television. I also occasionally made it out to the Polo Grounds and sat among the bird poop and the thousands of people disguised as empty seats to attempt to get enjoyment from Harry Wismer's dreadful New York Titans. It wasn't easy. Each December, while others were wrapping Christmas presents, I was deriving excitement by telling my friends that "Mickey Slaughter signed with Denver" or "the Chargers got Rufus Guthrie." And when Brooklyn-raised Al Davis took over the Oakland Raiders in 1963 and transformed them into instant winners, I had my hero for life. Even though other AFL originals such as Lamar Hunt, Bud Adams, and Ralph Wilson remain on the pro football scene, only Al Davis endures as the true essence of what the AFL really was, a bunch of brash but competent upstarts from the streets, who would "take no prisoners" in their successful attempt to equal, if not exceed, those cocky snobs who lived over in the good part of town. And they did. It took a mere nine seasons for the American Football League to be considered the equal of the bullies. And regardless of what the "NFL writers" said either then or now, the AFL played pretty damned exciting football.

Just read, baby!

ACKNOWLEDGMENTS

Many people helped in the preparation of this book, but some deserve a special mention. Don Maroney, the editor and publisher of *Sportspage News,* first let me use his paper as a forum for my peculiar Raider ideas and then provided unlimited access to a wealth of information. Harry Bruno is a good friend whose advice has proved to be invaluable. Richard Blech, a.k.a. "Rick in Riverside," provided much information and support. Bob Valli and Ron Reisterer and their staffs at the *Oakland Tribune* were most generous with their resources and their time. A doff of the old fedora to Ben Dominitz and Jennifer Basye of Prima Publishing for their willingness to publish the book. A special thanks to Bob Berger from the University of California, Berkeley Extension program for sharing his knowledge and for his encouragement. My appreciation also goes to Dick O'Connor for his review of my manuscript. And last but certainly not least, my wife Cheryl and our daughters Jana, Mindy, and Stacy have to be commended for putting up with all my gyrations and palpitations during the development of the project.

Chapter 1

"WE'LL GET
THIS THING
STRAIGHT AND
WE'LL BE ALL RIGHT"

"Many of us were closet Raider fans for many years . . . I always preferred the Raiders. They were rough, tough, rotten guys. The Niners were Mr. Clean. Bill Walsh is a rather God-like figure. John Madden and the Raiders were like the Grateful Dead."
—Herb Caen, San Francisco Chronicle

*I*t probably seemed like old times for Al Davis, the managing general partner of the Los Angeles Raiders, or more correctly, the president of the general partner. Both Al and his team were suddenly in the national spotlight again. During the last three seasons of losing teams and dwindling attendance at Los Angeles Memorial Coliseum, the national media had turned elsewhere for stories about professional football players and teams. The New York Giants, Washington Redskins, and San Francisco 49ers were the last three world champions, and the press was consumed with their players, coaches, owners, and fans. Everybody seems to love winners, and suddenly the Raiders were being grouped with other teams that had recently fallen from prominence such as the Dallas Cowboys, Pittsburgh Steelers, and Miami Dolphins. Another sour year and the Raiders could be in the same sorry class as the perennial losing clubs like the Tampa Bay Buccaneers, Detroit Lions, and Atlanta Falcons for the normal cursory preseason stories. No more spreads in *Gentlemen's Quarterly* or cover stories in *Sports Illustrated* for Raider players. But somehow this third week of August, 1989, was different.

Al Davis was doing something that had never been done in any sport before. After abandoning Oakland and moving his Raiders to Los Angeles in 1982, he was voluntarily agreeing to have his football team play an exhibition game at Oakland Coliseum, the stadium that was his former home. Nobody had ever come back voluntarily; the Brooklyn Dodgers never returned to Brooklyn, the Milwaukee Braves were gone and forgotten, and after an unannounced move on a snowy night in March 1984, the owner of the Indianapolis Colts would never dare set foot in Baltimore again. Franchises have moved in every major professional sport and never looked back. As usual, Al Davis was being unorthodox and unpredictable.

When they announced the game in March, nobody was really sure what to expect. Although radio and television ratings for Raider games broadcast into the Bay Area were good and there were still many Raider jackets and bumper stickers around the East Bay, some in the press were still skeptical. For example, the *San Francisco Examiner* did not bother to send a reporter to cover the press conference that announced the game. After all, with the San Francisco 49ers winning a Super Bowl only a few weeks before, who would be interested in the Los Angeles Raiders anyway?

Everybody. The 50,000 tickets that went on sale at 10 A.M. the following day were gone by 12:30. "We're talking total madness," said a ticket seller who found a long line of people at his window when he showed up for work. "Springsteen gets crowds like this. I hope we don't run out of tickets, because these are Raider fans, and I'm likely to get killed."

Smelling a good story, the press was looking toward Al Davis again. Both the *Washington Post* and *New York Daily News* had published lengthy interviews with Davis, *USA Today* ran two columns in the same week about the Raiders, and the television networks, who chose not to televise the exhibition game nationally, also pounced on the story of the return of the Raiders to the Bay Area. And rather than be hostile about his attempts to leave town, the Los Angeles media seemed to join in the gaiety. "We break up homes all the time out here" was how *Los Angeles Times* columnist Jim Murray viewed the on-again, off-again, Oakland–Al Davis relationship.

So Davis was being quoted again, just as in the good old days, although carefully avoiding all discussions of whether the Raiders would permanently move back to Oakland. And after being ignored for more than 11 years, Davis was also being asked again for his advice on the future of the National Football League. Not only by the press but by the other owners, the 27 people whom he opposed in courtrooms in the early part of the decade over the right to move his team without their permission. Davis was now being requested to serve on a committee that was suddenly created to break an impasse that had split the owners over the choice of a new commissioner. Al was also chosen as a member of the Board of Executives that was overseeing the establishment of an international spring league that the NFL was forming. Ironically, Davis had long been an advocate of a minor professional football league that would play its games in the spring, but his suggestions were virtually ignored by the other owners.

How things have changed. In 1978, after taking the Pittsburgh Steelers to court over statements concerning his players being called part of a "criminal element," Al Davis was ostracized by Commissioner Pete Rozelle and his fellow owners and was removed from serving on all committees in the National Football League. This included banishment from the Competition Committee, the most prestigious group in the league. Obviously, relationships were further exasperated by the move to Los Angeles, which was opposed by the league. They tried to stop him, sue him, and strip him of the Raiders, but they lost and lost big. A $20,000,000 settlement was given to Davis by the league after a larger award was made in court. Perhaps the owners appreciated that Al Davis was conciliatory in compromising the amount of the settlement. Maybe everybody in the NFL is now mellowing with age. In 1978, Al was 49 years old, but he still looked closer to the 33-year-old "boy wonder" who came out of nowhere to create the winningest team in professional sports. Or did the other owners see a 36-year-old Al Davis, who as Commissioner of the American Football League forced the National Football League into a merger in 1966? A few weeks ago Al had turned 60, and now he was older than many of the newer owners. Perhaps they suddenly viewed Davis as an elder statesmen, the way Al had viewed people like Sid Gillman and Carroll Rosenbloom 30 years earlier. Maybe they finally realized that the Raiders' move to Los Angeles in 1982 and Davis's later actions in trying to move in 1990 probably doubled the value of their franchises. Hey, this guy Davis who first started talking about luxury box seats years ago wasn't so goofy after all! Whatever the reason, the owners were willing to forgive and forget his past indiscretions and welcome him back as a full partner in the NFL.

So at least for the week preceding the exhibition game in Oakland, attention was on Al and where his team may be located in the 1990s. The current performance of the Raiders, who had lost two preseason games at the Los

Angeles Coliseum before the smallest crowds in their L.A. history, was being shunted aside. It was just as well. Al Davis had been nicknamed "The Genius" for fielding the most competitive team in professional football for 22 years. It seemed that everything the Raiders did was successful. They consistently produced the most colorful, most exciting, and most entertaining teams. And then suddenly it all seemed to go sour. The Raiders, who prided themselves on making wise draft choices of college talent or obtaining useful players who had been failures elsewhere, suddenly seemed to be doing everything wrong. For example, Marc Wilson, a shy, tall, and skinny quarterback from Brigham Young University and a top draft choice of the Raiders in 1980, later was given close to a $1,000,000 annual salary by Davis to keep him from the rival United States Football League. He never justified the high salary and was subsequently booed unmercifully by the usually passive Los Angeles crowds. And with good reason; Wilson had lost the 1985 playoff game against New England by suddenly getting confused and unnecessarily calling two timeouts that helped cost the Raiders the game and perhaps their fifth appearance in the Super Bowl. It was obvious to many football people that Wilson was not a worthy successor to Jim Plunkett, Ken Stabler, Daryle Lamonica, and George Blanda, who always seemed to pull victories from the jaws of defeat. But because of the large contract, Wilson was made the starting quarterback through the 1987 season. (Al could have saved his money: The USFL went out of business in 1986.) There were other personnel failures as the Raiders slumped to a 5–10 record in 1987, their worst season since 1962, the year before Al Davis arrived in Oakland. The Los Angeles media delighted in catching glimpses of Davis shaking his fist, screaming obscenities, or banging on the table in the press box when things went wrong.

The 1988 season had been a little better, but the team still missed the playoffs. Al Davis selected Mike Shanahan as his new head coach. Shanahan had been an assistant coach with the Denver Broncos, the Raiders' biggest rival of recent years. He was hired on February 29, 1988, the last day that NFL teams were allowed to hire assistant coaches away from other teams for the coming season. While the Raiders were losing, the Broncos finished in first place and went to the Super Bowl in both 1986 and 1987. It was the first time that Al Davis had ever brought in a head coach from outside the Raider organization. During Shanahan's first season with the Raiders, dissension surfaced between the assistant coaches who came from Denver and the holdovers from the regime of former coach Tom Flores. These things had never happened before to the Raiders, and the discord appeared to be continuing in the 1989 training camp. The problems now were accentuated by the absences of halfback Marcus Allen, the biggest star of the team, and Bo Jackson, who normally doesn't join the Raiders until after his baseball season with the Kansas City Royals. After Jackson had a mediocre 1988 campaign, Allen and some of his Raider teammates were openly questioning why Jackson was getting more money for playing half a schedule than they were making in a full season. The smallish Allen was also objecting to his new role of throwing his body into defensive linemen as a blocker for the speedier Jackson. Thus the holdout.

Although the national press didn't seem too interested in the 1989 edition of the Los Angeles Raiders, Al Davis was very concerned. Shanahan was the head coach, but Davis was always present at the training camp in Oxnard, California, watching every player and every play, perhaps silently plotting, scheming, and cajoling, but saying little to Shanahan and his assistants in front of the players. Shanahan was very uptight and the players knew it. The rumors were widespread that Mike had better get the Raiders off to a good start in 1989 or else he'd be fired. And Shanahan had better adhere to the Davis

philosophy of offense and defensive play or face the con-
sequences. Al was openly questioning Shanahan's use of
the "motion and scheme" type of attack that they use in
Denver. The Davis philosophy is to throw the ball long,
run off left tackle and just win, baby—the way the Raiders did it in their best years. Everyone had his chin up and
was publicly optimistic, but there was a lingering fear that
this team may have gotten too old too fast; that the defensive players who were signed as free agents after being
unprotected by other teams would not do the job; that
the offensive line was weak; that there was an unstable
quarterback situation; and that there was no Marcus
Allen or Bo Jackson on the scene to save the day.

Al Davis knew his team was in trouble. He knew that
the yardstick of success in football and in life is measured
in victories and defeats. Period. You are only declared a
winner if you have accumulated more victories than the
other guy. There is no second best in the National Football League and no consolation prize in the game of life.
Al Davis knew that. When he was the Commissioner of
the American Football League and engaged in a struggle
with the National Football League for survival, he de-
vised a plan for signing their best players who were already under contract. It may have seemed dirty and un-
ethical to detractors, but it led to the pro football merger
in 1966. When the other owners were opposed to the
transfer of his franchise to Los Angeles, he went to court,
hired the best antitrust lawyers, and fought to invalidate
their illegal rules on franchise transfers. He won the right
to move where he wanted and collected money from both
the NFL and the City of Oakland because of their attempt to stop him. When his wife had a severe heart attack and the doctors told him that she might never re-
cover, he kept a constant vigil at the hospital, brought in
heart specialists from all over the world, and battled for
the best care. And eventually Carole Davis recovered. Al
Davis has done whatever it takes to win and conquer his

environment and dominate the opposition, whether the foe has been another team, an entire league, an adversary in a courtroom, or the Grim Reaper himself.

Perhaps it is just as well that the media focus of the week was on the return of the Raiders to Oakland and not on the apparent deficiencies of the team. Al Davis knew that the sellout crowd in Oakland on this summer night would react fanatically to anybody wearing those silver and black uniforms, but how would Los Angeles in 1989 and perhaps Oakland or Sacramento in the future respond to a bad team? After a number of friends, mentors, players, and ex-players had died within a few months, Davis told the assembled press multitudes at Oxnard, "I can control this [the team]; I can't control death." As the writers from the *Los Angeles Times, Orange County Register,* and *Oakland Tribune* dutifully recorded every word, they must have wondered why this man with the ducktail haircut, receding hairline, and dark sunglasses, who had maintained such a hold on the sports world for so many years, was suddenly preoccupied with death rather than football. This wasn't the Al Davis that their editors had told them to expect. What was with this guy anyway? It didn't sound like the Boy Wonder whom the editors knew when they were beat reporters back in the halcyon days of the early 1960s, when Al Davis seemed to come out of nowhere and preached "pride and poise" and "commitment to excellence" to a ragtag football team that somehow bought the message.

Was this the same Al Davis from Oakland, circa 1963? Or had he gone Hollywood? Or senile? While Sacramento, Oakland, Irwindale, and Los Angeles engaged in a bidding war to obtain the Raiders, Al kept his future plans for the Raiders' next home a big secret and didn't discuss the topic with the press. Rumors abounded that Davis would announce a move to Oakland at halftime of the exhibition game. Or perhaps he would divulge his plans at a dinner on the eve of the game to be attended by ex-President Gerald Ford. Nope. Al said that he wouldn't do anything to detract from the game. Even an exhibition game.

It was wild in Oakland on the day of the game. The cars, trucks, and recreational vehicles began lining up outside the Coliseum parking lot as early as 2 A.M. The gates opened at 9:30 A.M. and the main lot was full by 2 P.M., five hours before the kickoff. The Oakland fans were partying with the fervor of the good old days. When his limousine arrived about 4 P.M., Al Davis was besieged with fans begging for his permanent return to Oakland. Much to the surprise of many in the San Francisco press corps, there was no hostility. Al flashed his three Super Bowl rings at the worshipers and smiled meekly as he entered Oakland Coliseum, a stadium that would probably never have been built without his presence back in the 1960s.

The game was somewhat predictable. The Raiders were decisively outplayed but trailed the Houston Oilers only 9–7 at halftime. The crowd was in a frenzy from their first glimpse of the Silver and Black in the opening warmups. There were some banners draping the stands that advocated Sacramento as the next destination for Al Davis's team, but the crowd was a typical Oakland throng: loud and perhaps a little rowdy. There were many wearing "Oakland Raider" garb, which had not been legally obtainable for eight years. A spectacular fireworks display at halftime honored the achievements of the old Oakland Raiders. The crowd reacted wildly. But nobody knew if Al Davis saw it. The Raiders scored two touchdowns in the second half but lost in the final seconds of the game when a reserve Houston quarterback fooled the Raider defense with a surprise running play. Nevertheless, the Oakland fans were thrilled to see the Raiders again and wondered if they were being teased by a mere carnival passing through town. Or perhaps this really was a prelude for the 1990s.

And to the surprise of the Bay Area media, the Raider

game scored the second highest television rating of the week. More people watched the Raiders play the Oilers on television than were tuned into the 49ers-Chargers game three days earlier. Only Roseanne Barr had more viewers than the Silver and Black. Maybe Barr could help solve the Raiders' linebacking problem.

After the game, Al Davis was asked again if he would move to either Oakland or Sacramento but begged off the questions. He said he had a timetable but "I'm not about to discuss it." Contrary to what his critics think, the man does have feelings. He told the assembled media, "I'm emotional and inspired; that's a lot for me to say." Later a black limousine took him away in the cool summer Bay Area night to the home he still owns in Piedmont, an exclusive community in the hills above Oakland.

Perhaps the decision concerning the future location of a football team is relatively trite. But keeping everybody in the dark is vintage Al. The unpredictable ways of Al Davis become only more so with the passing of time. Although the fans and media are somewhat frustrated with the absence of an answer to their biggest question, they are not surprised. He may be older, the face wrinkles are starting to show, the hairline may be receding, and the glasses are seldom detached from his nose. But neither age nor the Southern California sun has mellowed him. It's really the same old Al Davis.

Chapter 2

THE EARLY, EARLY SHOW

Al Davis attended Erasmus Hall High School in the Flatbush section of Brooklyn, New York. Then, after a brief fling at Wittenberg College in Ohio, he joined the big boys at Syracuse University. His first paying job was a football and baseball coaching stint at Adelphi College in Garden City, Long Island, New York. He next went into the army as a private and became head football coach at Fort Belvoir, Virginia. And there was that one year as an unpaid consultant with the Baltimore Colts. Or was it as a scout? Or was he an assistant coach? Two years as an assistant at The Citadel in Charleston, South Carolina, followed. Three years as assistant at the University of Southern California starting in 1957 and another trice as an assistant to Sid Gillman for the Los Angeles/San Diego Chargers before going to Oakland.

That's it.

Bring on the next chapter.

Not so fast, dude. In many sports books, the early years of the subject make for very boring reading. Something like: Gee, Mom, I always wanted to be a quarterback, or a center fielder, or another Magic Johnson. And of course, the star of the book could have been an all-star, all-American, *Parade* magazine scholastic, *USA Today* athlete of the decade and all that.

This story is very different.

Al Davis was not an all-American athlete. More specifically, he did not play sports at all for the high school team. Jim Brown, Floyd Little, and Ernie Davis were all-American football players at Syracuse University. Al Davis was not.

So how did this Jewish kid from Brooklyn, who really wasn't much of an athlete, become a brilliant organizer, an exceptional evaluator of talent, and a winning football coach? And later a club owner who became more famous than any of his athletes or fellow owners?

Al Davis was born in Brockton, Massachusetts, on July 4, 1929. His family, which consisted of a brother, mother, and father, moved to an apartment building off fashionable Eastern Parkway in Brooklyn when he was six. For those who have been infuriated by the Al Davis Brooklyn accent, which is sometimes accompanied by a southern drawl, just think how bad it would have been if the Davis family had stayed in Massachusetts!

His father was a manufacturer of children's clothing and was very wealthy. Jerry Davis, Al's younger brother, is in the retail shoe business in New York. Next year, when ESPN televises the NFL draft, take a good look at the Raider table in the hotel ballroom at draft headquarters. One of the people on the telephones will be Jerry Davis.

The mother of Al and Jerry Davis lives in Long Beach, Long Island, and has been there since the early 1950s.

The impression that the Raiders press guide gives of Al is of a high school letterman in baseball, football, and basketball. Kindly put, that impression is erroneous. This may surprise his adversaries, but Al was somewhat of a swinger during his Erasmus years in the middle of World War II. "He was a clown, full of the devil," recalled a female classmate at Erasmus. "He was one of the in crowd, a popular guy," said Larry Robbins, who attended high school with Al and is now the Erasmus Hall California Alumni President.

Today, fraternities and sororities are not permitted on most high school campuses in America. But in 1945 and 1946, Al Davis played football for the Rho Sigma Tau fraternity house. A friend recalled that "Al Davis was not a great player. He did not play for Erasmus." Davis also played softball and basketball for Rho Sigma Tau and served as student manager of the Erasmus basketball team, coached by Al Badain. When Badain passed away in 1989, Davis delivered the eulogy at the funeral. During his teen years, Davis developed an interest in coaching football and became fascinated with the strategic side of the game.

Barbra Streisand and Al Davis are arguably the most famous graduates of Erasmus, which is located in the heart of the Flatbush section of Brooklyn. Upon the 200th anniversary of the school in 1987, Davis was honored as the bicentennial man of the year. He has generously contributed funds to Erasmus, and the school gymnasium has been renamed the "Al Davis Gym."

The next stop for Al was Wittenburg College in Ohio for one semester. Davis then enrolled at Hartwick College in upstate New York but was only there for a few months before transferring to Syracuse University. He graduated in August 1950 with a bachelor of arts degree, majoring in English. He played football for the freshmen team but never the varsity squad. The records also show that Al was a member of the junior varsity basketball team. His interest in football was building, but he never played or coached for the Syracuse University team. Prior to 1949, Syracuse played a lesser schedule, but with the arrival of head coach Ben Schwartzwalder, the Orangemen became a powerhouse and won the national championship in 1959. There is no record of Al Davis making his mark in football at Syracuse.

After graduating from Syracuse, Al Davis returned to the New York City area to begin a coaching career. Ed Stanisek gave Davis a job as offensive and defensive line coach at Adelphi University, a school that did not admit men until 1947. Another assignment was as coach of the baseball team. In 1952, Davis coached the baseball team to an 11–5 record, their best season ever. He met and married his wife, Carole, at Adelphi. Al started attending annual football coaching clinics and conventions and achieved some national attention in May 1952 with an article in *Scholastic Coach* magazine. The story was called "Line Quarterbacking, Situation Blocking at Its Best," and it explained offensive line blocking assignments. An advocate of the T formation, which was starting to achieve prominence, Davis called his concept the "triple line quarterbacking system." After observing where the defensive linemen were placed, an offensive lineman would call signals for the blocking assignments. Twenty-two different formations were diagramed in the article. The blocking system story received widespread admiration within the coaching community. Among the early admirers of the young coach was Sid Gillman, head coach at the University of Cincinnati.

Next came a stint at Fort Belvoir, Virginia. Private Al Davis leapfrogged over holdover assistant Bill Everson and succeeded Captain James Talley as head coach of the service team in 1953. The 23-year-old coach had a car and driver at his disposal. In the days when almost all able-bodied men were drafted, the military bases fielded good teams augmented by college and pro stars. Among the players on the Fort Belvoir Engineers were quarterbacks Don Engles and Ed Kissel, and running backs Jim Leftwich, Hank Lauricella, Bob "Shoo-Shoo" Shemonski, Doug Eggers, Bob Langus, and Glen Smith. Davis led the Engineers to an 8–2 record. Although a loss to the Quantico Marines in the season finale cost Belvoir a chance to go to the Poinsetta Bowl in San Diego, Al Davis had enjoyed a great season in his first opportunity as a head coach.

At Belvoir, Al started making contacts with NFL and Canadian Football League teams, providing scouting information about his players. He required payment for the service. Davis also established a closer relationship with the Baltimore Colts, who were located about 60 miles from Belvoir and had just moved to Baltimore in 1953. Al worked a deal with Colts' coach Weeb Ewbank. He promised that he could help the Colts sign Belvoir's Doug Eggers and Bob Langus if Ewbank would pay his way to the annual NCAA football coaches convention in Cincinnati. Weeb agreed and the Colts had their players.

Upon his discharge from the army, Davis spent a year as an unpaid scout for the Colts. "Al had a lot of brass," recalled John Steadman, veteran columnist for the *Baltimore Evening Sun,* who worked in public relations for the Colts in those days. "He marched players into the Colts dining hall at the training camp in Carlisle, Pennsylvania, unannounced." Among the players that Al "discovered" was Philadelphia high school track star Angelo Coia, who later played for the Chicago Bears and now works in the player personnel department for the Raiders. Steadman added that "Al had entrée to the Colts office." It was in 1954 that Davis first met Colts owner Carroll Rosenbloom. Their lives would touch many times in the subsequent years.

At the next NCAA coaching convention, Al Davis was looking for a coaching position at a major college. He accepted a position as line coach on the staff of John Sauer at The Citadel in Charleston, South Carolina. General Mark Clark, who led Allied troops in the Italian Campaign in World War II, was the president of the private military university. Davis and The Citadel were a natural: Sauer was installing a straight T formation, and Al was the perfect assistant to implement the change. Among the players at The Citadel was Angelo Coia. In 1955 The Citadel improved from a 2–8 to a 5–4 mark, the first winning season since prior to World War II. During their two years at The Citadel, the Davises gave birth to a son they named Mark Clark Davis.

After two successful years as an assistant to Sauer, Al Davis next moved to the University of Southern California. Don Clark, 35, was the new head coach in 1957 and inherited a team coached by Jess Hill that was on NCAA probation for making illegal payments to athletes. Al was backfield coach in 1957–58 before adding defensive line chores to his assignment in 1959. Also on the staff at USC was Mel Hein, whom Davis would later name director of officials in the AFL. The Trojans had some pretty good players in those years: Willie Wood, who was on five championship Green Bay Packer teams and is now in the Professional Football Hall of Fame; tackle Monte Clark, who played for the Cleveland Browns and later was head coach of the San Francisco 49ers and Detroit Lions; running back Lloyd Winston, who played with San Francisco; and Don Buford, a running back at USC, who later starred in left field for baseball's Chicago White Sox and Baltimore Orioles. Angelo Coia was a transfer from The Citadel. The first season was a disaster for Clark; the Trojans plunged to a 1–9 record.

By Clark's third year, the Trojans had returned to prominence in what was then called the Pacific Coast Conference. In 1959, identical twins Marlin and Mike McKeever starred as linebackers, and Ron Mix was anchoring the offensive line. Southern Cal was 8–0 before losing to archrivals UCLA and Notre Dame. As an assistant, Davis was also involved in recruitment, a sensitive assignment at USC. In February 1959, Davis and Nick Pappas, who was field secretary of the general alumni, were accused of overly aggressive recruiting of quarterback Ben Charles and center Dave Morgan. Both Pappas and Davis were barred from further recruiting activities.

On December 15, 1959, with one year left on his contract, Don Clark unexpectedly resigned and was replaced by John McKay, who was a first-year assistant coach for USC. Despite the good season, Clark was criticized for not beating UCLA and Notre Dame. Clark was also blamed for an ugly incident in the game against California in which Mike McKeever, using his elbows, fractured the face of Cal halfback Steve Bates.

And then there was the recruitment incident of Pappas and Davis. It didn't help Clark and it presumably cost Al Davis an opportunity to coach the Trojans. Another factor may have been that Davis had the wrong ethnic background for what was then an extremely WASP private school in Los Angeles. McKay did not ask him to remain on the staff, so Al Davis was suddenly unemployed.

On the same day that Clark resigned, Sid Gillman also quit as coach of the Los Angeles Rams. The Rams had slumped from an 8–4 record in 1958 to a dismal 2–10 in 1959. Gillman was also caught in a bitter feud between co-owners Dan Reeves and Ed Pauley. A few weeks later, general manager Pete Rozelle hired former Rams star quarterback Bob Waterfield as the new coach. Rozelle was also going to be starting a new job soon. In January 1960 Rozelle, who was criticized and eventually repudiated by a judge for a premature contract that the Rams gave to Heisman Trophy winner Billy Cannon, became Commissioner of the National Football League. He was a compromise choice of the NFL owners to succeed Bert Bell, who had died of a heart attack a few months earlier. And oh yes, Billy Cannon was awarded to the AFL Houston Oilers.

Gillman was not unemployed for long. The American Football League was forming, and Barron Hilton, the son of hotel magnate Conrad Hilton, was awarded a franchise in Los Angeles. Hilton hired legendary Notre Dame coach Frank Leahy as his general manager. The Chargers were starting to make some news in Los Angeles with early signings of veteran players and rookies. Much ink was received when both the Chargers and NFL New York Giants signed Mississippi fullback Charlie Flowers. A court eventually awarded Flowers to Los Angeles. On January 7, 1960, the Chargers hired Gillman as head coach. Ironically, the very next day, a group of wealthy businessmen met in Oakland to prepare a bid for the eighth and last AFL franchise, which became available when Max Winter in Minnesota decided to join the NFL. Leahy resigned a few months later and Gillman also became general manager of the Chargers. On January 19, 1960, Gillman hired Al Davis as backfield coach. The two had first met back in 1952 at a coaches convention, and Gillman had been impressed. Jack Faulkner, who later coached for the Denver Broncos and is now director of administration for the Rams, was picked as defensive backfield coach. Two weeks later, Chuck Noll joined the Chargers as defensive line coach, completing the staff.

Gillman was considered one of the greatest organizers in football. The Chargers set up a vast information network, with 122 college coaches added to the payroll. Don Klosterman was hired as the chief scout and proved to be as aggressive as Al Davis. His cloak-and-dagger methods helped land Flowers. Also in the Los Angeles Chargers front office was Al LoCasale, who would later be director of player personnel when Klosterman was hired away by owner Lamar Hunt of the Dallas Texans.

Unshackled by some of the collegiate restrictions, Al Davis could now strut his stuff as an excellent evaluator and recruiter of talent. Davis went to work immediately to sign players for the new team playing in the new league and was credited with wrestling some of the best Chargers away from the NFL. Davis pulled off a major coup by signing Ron Mix of USC, who was the Number One draft choice of Carroll Rosenbloom, Weeb Ewbank, and the Baltimore Colts. In 1960, the Chargers also signed running back Paul Lowe of Oregon State, who became one of the first star players in the new league. The Charger publicists always delighted in describing Lowe as one of the greatest "climax" runners in football, whatever that means.

In 1961, Davis did even better. One of his prize catches was Keith Lincoln of Washington State. Lincoln proved to be an excellent runner and receiver out of the backfield. Thanks to Al Davis, the Chargers also "stole" defensive end Earl Faison of Indiana from the Detroit Lions. Defensive tackle Ernie Ladd was one of the first professional players ever signed from Grambling College. But the best was saved for the 1962 season. At the conclusion of the Bluebonnet Bowl in Houston, head scout Don Klosterman signed Kansas quarterback John Hadl on the field. Detroit had drafted Hadl in the NFL. A week later, immediately upon hearing the final gun at the Sugar Bowl game, Al Davis raced out on the field and signed Arkansas offensive end Lance Alworth to a contract under the goal posts. San Francisco 49er head coach Red Hickey could only look on helplessly in disgust as Davis stole his top draft pick and eventual Hall of Famer. "I knew it wasn't safe to let Alworth go to the dressing room," said Davis. "But I figured he could at least make it to the goal posts without being stopped." Al got to coach the prize rookie in 1962, and Davis was selected by Alworth to introduce him at Canton, Ohio, in 1978 when "Bambi" entered the Hall of Fame.

In addition to the recruiting and signing process, Davis was enjoying coaching the wide receivers for Gillman. Two early AFL stars who were catching passes for the Chargers were Dave Kocourek of Wisconsin and Don Norton of Iowa. In 1962, they were joined by Alworth and Reg Carolan. Kocourek would later play for the Raiders.

After incurring losses estimated at $900,000 from playing in the Los Angeles Coliseum in 1960, Barron Hilton moved the Chargers to San Diego in January 1961. *San Diego Union* columnist Jack Murphy played a match-

making role in mating Hilton with San Diego city officials. Although the disadvantages of playing before
sparse crowds in the cavernous Coliseum was a lesson
that somehow escaped Al Davis, the influence that Jack
Murphy had in San Diego did not. He would later become one of a small group of nationally known media
people with whom Al Davis would regularly share his in-
nermost football secrets.

In the first three years of the AFL, the Chargers probably had the most talented rosters but just couldn't win
the championship. In 1960, Los Angeles won the Western Division title but lost to Houston 24–16 in the first
AFL title game. George Blanda threw three touchdown
passes, including an 88-yard toss to Billy Cannon that
broke the game open. The inaugural season in San Diego
produced a 12–2 record as the Chargers won their first
11 games and looked as dominant as the Cleveland
Browns were in the old All-American Conference. But
the Chargers again lost to Houston in the championship
game. San Diego could not overcome penalties, fumbles,
injuries, and a 35-yard touchdown pass from Blanda to
Cannon.

In 1962, the San Diego team was decimated by injuries, plus a famous faux pas by Gillman. The Chargers
put injured starting quarterback Jackie Kemp on waivers. This was a common way to measure trading interest
around the AFL. When Buffalo claimed Kemp, Gillman
did not immediately rescind the waivers. With Kemp
gone, rookie John Hadl was forced into service, and the
Chargers struggled to a third place finish with a 4–10 record. Only 1–13 Oakland was worse.

Al Davis made many friends in San Diego and was impressed with some of his fellow Chargers. LoCasale
would eventually became his right-hand man in Oakland. Bob Zeman, a defensive back, was to be an assistant
coach for the Raiders. Sam Gruneison, who saw action as
an offensive guard and linebacker, also was later a Raider

assistant. And although Gillman and Davis were to become bitter rivals in future campaigns in both the AFL and NFL, and their personal relationship was often less than cordial, there has always been a healthy respect between the two men. Al Davis basically learned the lessons of an effective organizational setup from "the man with the bow tie," Sid Gillman.

In 1963, the San Diego Chargers finally put it all together. Veteran quarterback Tobin Rote was acquired from the Canadian League, and Alworth, Lincoln, Lowe, et al. stayed relatively healthy. The Chargers were 11–3 in 1963 with two of the losses coming to the Oakland Raiders. In the AFL championship game, Lincoln contributed 349 yards of total offense, including 206 yards rushing, and scored twice as San Diego demolished the Boston Patriots 51–10. It was the only time in 30 AFL/AFC seasons that the Chargers ever won a title.

When they played the 1963 championship game in San Diego, the assistant coach and talent scout who was responsible for so many of the championship players was not on the sidelines. Al Davis now lived in Oakland.

Chapter 3

THE RAIDERS B.A. (BEFORE AL)

"If we could only have our [owner] meetings in San Francisco, we would have sold more tickets than we were selling to the ballgames."
—Wayne Valley

While Al Davis was successfully recruiting and coaching players for Sid Gillman and the Chargers, the Oakland Raiders, the other AFL franchise on the West Coast, were playing out quite a different scenario up north. The fact that the Oakland club was not moved or did not fold in the years 1960–62 must be considered a major upset. They were a team without a home, with few quality players or coaches, and with too many owners who knew too little about football. They were the only AFL team in those first three seasons that did not play .500 ball in at least one season. The Raiders compiled only a cumulative 9–33 record in that period. The 1961–62 clubs won a combined total of three games. In their "NFL Theatre" program, ESPN frequently shows films of the 1952 Dallas Texans as an example of a collection of laughable losers. These Raiders would have made a better example. They probably don't have many films of the 1960–62 Oakland Raiders. It's just as well.

The Twin Cities of Minnesota were originally given an AFL franchise. When the NFL dangled an expansion franchise in front of owners-to-be Max Winter and William Boyer, Minnesota dropped out of the AFL. So a search was under way for the eighth AFL team. Los Angeles Charger owner Barron Hilton, one of the wealthier men who threw in with the new league, threatened to check out if another team wasn't placed on the West Coast. Enter Oakland.

In 1960, the Bay Area was starting to hit a period of unprecedented population and economic growth, most of it in the East Bay in and around Oakland. Three different groups of owners emerged, and on January 8, 1960, they consolidated into one force. Three weeks later, an eight-man group headed by Y.C. (Chet) Soda was formally awarded the Oakland franchise. The owners of the NFL San Francisco 49ers wished them well. Quarterback Joe Kapp, who led the neighboring University of California Golden Bears to a Rose Bowl appearance, expressed a desire to stay home and play for Oakland. George Jacopetti headed a task force of civic leaders that was investigating the possibility of building a multipurpose stadium. Everything sounded so promising.

Too promising. The new football team did not have a place to play. Joe Kapp's school did not want the pros playing in Berkeley. There were no other possibilities in the East Bay. There was only one place to play, dreaded San Francisco. For 1960, Oakland played most of its home games at Kezar Stadium in San Francisco, which was also the home of the 49ers. When there were scheduling conflicts with the 49ers, the final three home games were switched to the new Candlestick Park.

And what shall we call this team? Well, the *Oakland Tribune* and Junior Chamber of Commerce ran a contest to select the best name. The winner: the Oakland Señors. Somehow the name Señors did not exactly provide a rallying cry for anybody and did not exactly enthrall anyone except Soda, who usually called his close friends by that name. On April 7, 1960, *Oakland Tribune* columnist Ray Heywood "filed" a mock court petition to change the name. "Will the team band dress in serapes?" asked Heywood. "Will the club emblem be a tired man in a sombrero sleeping in the shade of a cactus?" The conclusion of Heywood: "Change the name to almost anything, but don't leave it Señors."

The contest was reopened. The second winner was "Raiders." Thank God. Oh yes, the woman who submitted "Señors" as the winning entry did receive her grand prize: a round trip to the Bahamas.

The new team also did not have any players. The other seven teams had been working off a college draft list since November and were also starting to sign free agents and Canadian Football League players. Oakland inherited the Minnesota list of draft choices but most of them were already committed to the NFL. In March, the AFL allowed the Raiders to select players from the other teams in a supplemental draft. Kapp signed with the Canadian Football League.

Out of the confusion and turmoil of the first year, General Manager Soda found three pretty good players. Center Jim Otto, a native of Wausau, Wisconsin, was drafted by his hometown Green Bay Packers. But Packer coach Vince Lombardi had the capable Jim Ringo at center so Otto signed with Oakland. He became a starter in the first preseason game and did not give up the position until he retired 15 years later. To label Otto as durable would be a gross understatement. His career has included 20 operations, 15 on his knees. His "double zero" jersey became well known throughout the football world. Otto was All-AFL in each of the 10 seasons for the junior league. In 1980, Otto became the first Oakland Raider to be admitted to the Pro Football Hall of Fame.

Another 1960 player who would become famous was College of the Pacific quarterback Tom Flores. Ignored by the NFL, Flores was a walk-on at the first Oakland training camp. He shared the signal calling with veteran Vito "Babe" Parilli in 1960 and became the starter in 1961 when the Babe was traded to Boston. After missing the 1962 season with a bout of tuberculosis, Flores was back at the controls in 1963 when the first Al Davis team raced to a 10–4 record. Tom was later traded to Buffalo and was the third-string quarterback for Kansas City on their Super Bowl IV championship team. In 1972, Flores returned to the Raiders as an assistant coach and in 1979 succeeded John Madden as the head coach. Under his tutelage, the Raiders won two Super Bowls. But that is getting way ahead of the story.

Wayne Hawkins also played his football at COP, now the University of the Pacific. The offensive guard also came into the first Oakland camp in Santa Cruz as an unknown. But he won a starting job and played alongside Otto for 11 seasons. Hawkins remains one of the more active Raider alumni from the early days and is still a favorite with the fans.

Jim Otto was a first-team All-AFL player, but the 1960 Raiders also had two second-team performers: guard Dan Manoukian and defensive back Ed Macon, another recruit from College of the Pacific. Macon had nine interceptions. Billy Lott was an effective halfback and was often paired in the backfield with Tony Teresa, who scored ten touchdowns. Teresa rushed for 141 yards in a game against Buffalo. Jack Larschied was the primary wide receiver and also fielded punts. Wayne Crow doubled as a punter and halfback. The first Raider roster was filled with players from Northern California; many had played in junior colleges. As was common with most AFL teams looking for talent in those early days, players were frequently shuttled in and out, making it difficult for the press and fans alike to figure out who's who. Tryout camps were frequently held, and unheralded players always had a better than even chance of making a ball club.

The Raiders hired Eddie Erdelatz as their first head

coach. A Bay Area native, Erdelatz had been a successful college coach at the Naval Academy. After being by-passed for the vacant University of California position in favor of Marv Levy, Erdelatz actively sought the professional job in Oakland. Soda hoped that Erdelatz, as a "name" coach, would give his new team some positive publicity and perhaps a touch of class.

With their late start as a franchise, nobody was too upset that the inaugural edition of the Oakland Raiders compiled a 6–8 record. They finished third in the AFL West behind the Los Angeles Chargers and Dallas Texans, two clubs with larger money bags and more talent than Oakland. The first Denver Bronco club was last. Erdelatz often referred to his underdog team as "Guys named Joe."

For the trivia buffs out there, Oakland lost its first pre-season game 20–13 to the Dallas Texans. Flores and Teresa were impressive. With many tickets given away, Soda expected more than the 12,000 who wandered into Kezar on a July night. Two weeks later, the Raiders beat the New York Titans 23–17 in Sacramento. Defensive end George Fields, former Los Angeles Rams linebacker Bob Dougherty, and defensive back Joe Cannavino helped stop the final Titan drive.

The first game that counted was a 37–22 defeat by Houston. George Blanda threw four touchdown passes for the Oilers. The initial touchdown in the franchise history was a 19-yard touchdown reception by Teresa. Although Babe Parilli hit two touchdown passes in the second game and the Raiders discovered an exciting running back in Jim "Jetstream" Smith, Dallas won the contest by a 34–16 count.

It would be a gross understatement to say that attendance that first year in San Francisco was disappointing. Although Soda expected 40,000 to see Billy Cannon and his teammates, the opening game with Houston at Kezar attracted an "announced" crowd of 12,703. It was all downhill from there, until a minuscule 5,159 attended the season finale at Candlestick, a 48–10 rout of Denver.

The first win was a 14–13 squeaker at Houston in week three. Blanda missed two easy field goals for the Oilers. Smith and tight end Gene Prebola scored for Oakland. Four turnovers helped lose a 31–14 game at Denver. In Dallas, Erdelatz gave an inspirational speech to the Raiders at halftime, a sort of "win one for the Soda," and Oakland responded with a 20–19 victory. Billy Lott rushed for 70 yards and end Alan Goldstein scored twice for the Raiders.

The record improved to 3–3 with a 27–14 decision over Boston. Little Jack Larschied, all 160 pounds of him, ran 87 yards for a touchdown on the second play of the game to set the pace. Flores completed 14 of 24 passes for 161 yards.

The first ever eastern trip for the Raiders began ominously with a 38–9 drubbing at Buffalo. The Oakland highlight was 153 yards of kickoff returns by Larschied on the muddy War Memorial Stadium turf. A come-from-behind 28–27 win at the Polo Grounds in New York was next. The Jetstream scored twice and Flores passed for the other two. At Boston Teresa scored three times, but the Raiders could not overcome a 34–14 Patriot lead. Final score: Pats 34, Oakland 28.

The stars of a 20–7 victory over Buffalo were running backs Teresa and Lott, defensive tackle Ramon Armstrong, and linebacker Riley Morris. But with a chance to get back in the title race, Oakland was mauled 52–28 at Los Angeles. Charger head coach Sid Gillman and assistant Al Davis smiled as their offense gained 529 yards and Paul Lowe and Jack Kemp made mincemeat of the Raider defense.

The Chargers traveled to Candlestick for a command performance and the results were similar: Los Angeles 41, Oakland 17. Four touchdowns in the fourth quarter helped the Chargers clinch the first AFL Western Division title. Four Raider turnovers undermined a solid performance by Tom Flores.

New York quarterback Al Dorow was the difference in a 31–28 Titans victory over the Raiders on December 11. Dorow connected for three touchdowns, two to New York split end Art Powell.

The 1960 season concluded on a positive note, a 48–10 thumping of Denver. The Raiders compiled 532 yards of total offense and scored 31 fourth-quarter points to gain their sixth win. On the other side of the field, Broncos quarterback Frank Tripuka became the first quarterback in history to pass for 3,000 yards in a season.

On January 17, 1961, Wayne Valley, Bob Osborne, and Ed McGah bought out Chet Soda and four others in an attempt to solidify the organization and reduce the embarrassing infighting, which became a running joke in the San Francisco press. Kezar Stadium was permanently left for the 49ers, and the Raiders moved to Candlestick Park for all seven home games of the 1961 campaign.

With Soda removed from the scene, Bud Hastings became the new general manager. But the previous disorganization during the Soda regime led to little or no help in the college draft. One name player who was signed was Number Two draft choice George Fleming, a running back and place kicker from the University of Washington. Lott, Macon, and Manoukian were traded. Alan Miller came from Boston to play fullback and Fred Williamson was a starting cornerback. Miller later became a practicing attorney. The "Hammer," as Williamson liked to be called, was eventually traded to Kansas City. The Hammer prided himself on being a hard hitter, but his football career is best remembered for being embarrassed by the Green Bay Packers in the first Super Bowl by getting knocked out on a block. Later Williamson became an actor and was to star in many "blacksploitation" movies in the 1970s. Bob Dougherty did a stellar job at linebacker and Clem Daniels played eight games at halfback. Daniels had originally signed with the Dallas Texans but couldn't move Abner Haynes from the starting halfback position. Jim Otto was the only Raider on the 1961 All-League team. Williamson earned a spot on the second squad.

In 1989, the Pittsburgh Steelers lost 51–0 and 41–10 in their first two games and everybody felt sorry for head coach Chuck Noll. The Steelers got off the mat and made the playoffs. Well, the 1961 Oakland Raiders lost 55–0 and 44–0 in the first two games. There was no getting off the floor for this team, which finished with a 2–12 record. The reason was simple: While the caliber of play in the AFL improved in 1961, the Oakland Raiders probably got worse. Erdelatz, who was famous for his "jitterbug" defenses at Navy, was yanked off the dance floor after the first two games and was replaced by Assistant Coach Marty Feldman. Not Marty Feldman the comic, but a real live football coach. It probably wouldn't have made a difference if Lombardi, Rockne, or Halas had coached this team. Or Peter Sellers.

Hurricane Carla was threatening the Texas Gulf Coast as the Raiders met the Oilers in the inaugural contest. Carla never struck but George Blanda, Charlie Tolar, and Don Smith of the Oilers did. "This is the worst licking I've ever taken as a coach or a player," said Erdelatz. The 44–0 crushing by the Chargers did produce some statistical bright spots for Oakland. Running back Charlie Fuller gained 69 yards and Tom Flores completed 14 of 23 passes. But the Chargers stole five passes. "I just don't know the answer," sighed Erdelatz. He received an answer immediately after the game when he was fired and replaced by Feldman, his offensive line coach. Two weeks later, General Manager Bud Hastings resigned and accepted a job in private industry. So much for the glamour of pro football!

The offense came alive in the home opener against Dallas, scoring five touchdowns, but the defense allowed

462 yards and six scores. Flores completed another 14 of 23 and defensive back Bob Garner ran an interception in for a touchdown. Dallas won 42–35. Feldman then tasted his first victory as the Raiders beat Denver 33–19. Fleming kicked a 54-yard field goal in that game, which is still a club record. Converted defensive back Wayne Crow rushed for 107 yards, and Flores passed to Alan Miller and rookie Bob Coolbaugh for touchdowns.

Oakland lost the next three games. After a 24–14 lead in the fourth quarter, two crucial fumbles by Fuller helped lose a rematch with the Broncos. The Raiders could only gain 22 yards net rushing in a 41–10 drubbing by the Chargers. In windy Candlestick Park, New York fullback Bill Mathis scored the only two touchdowns of the contest in a 14–6 Oakland defeat. "One of the worst games I've ever seen," said Feldman, who was beginning to sound like Erdelatz.

A 31–22 victory at Buffalo was achieved with a big third down reception by end Charlie Hardy. Alan Miller chipped in with a 55-yard run. It was to be the last game that Marty Feldman would ever win.

Turnovers and the running of Mathis made Oakland a 23–12 loser in New York. The turning point of a 20–17 defeat in Boston came when Wayne Crow attempted to punt out of the Oakland end zone. The ball accidentally hit the goal post and bounced back toward Crow. Patriot defense end Leroy Moore fell on the ball for a Boston touchdown. The fluke play ruined a good effort by Flores, who threw touchdown passes to Hardy and tight end Doug Asad. The fourth consecutive road game for Oakland belonged to Abner Haynes as the Texans' running back scored five touchdowns and gained 158 yards in a 43–11 pasting by Dallas.

The 1961 Raiders did no better at home, losing the final three games. Oakland failed ten times on third down conversions in a 26–21 setback to Buffalo. "It's the sign of an immature team when you constantly lose the

close ones," said Feldman, who could have substituted a
choicer adjective for "immature." Babe Parilli and Billy
Lott, who were traded to Boston in 1961, were a part of
all five Boston scores in a 35–21 loss. It ruined another
fine effort by Flores and defensive end Riley Morris, who
scored a touchdown. In the long-awaited season closer,
Houston scored 26 second-quarter points and gained
522 total yards as Oakland lost for the twelfth time in
1961. One Raider highlight was a 46-yard interception
return by middle linebacker Tom Louderback. "I wanted
to toss the ball in the stands . . . but there wasn't anyone in
the stands," said Louderback of his touchdown. The announced "crowd" of 4,821 people at Candlestick was
probably sitting in the other end zone, Tom.

In early 1962, Robert Osborne seemed to have made a
wise move by selling out and leaving the morass to Valley
and McGah. Buffalo owner Ralph Wilson quietly loaned
money to Valley and McGah to keep the ship afloat. The
first of many rumors started to surface about the possible
relocation of the Oakland franchise. Portland, Atlanta,
New Orleans, Kansas City, Cincinnati, San Antonio, and
Seattle were all to be mentioned as possible cities for the
Raiders over the next year. There was one certainty: The
Oakland Raiders could not survive either psychologically or financially by playing their home games in San
Francisco.

In early November, McGah and Valley went to Oakland Mayor John Houlahan and the city council and
asked for a place to play in Oakland. They threatened to
sell or fold the team if there was no response. Fortunately
it wasn't an election year in Oakland. The city responded
by constructing a temporary 15,000-seat stadium at a site
in downtown Oakland where Merritt College now stands.
Frank Youell Field was considered to be "temporary"
until the much-discussed Oakland Coliseum could be
built. But there was still the major question of whether
this team could survive in Oakland.

The 1962 college draft was another washout with center-linebacker Dan Birdwell the only signed player of any worth. General Manager Wes Fry furiously made trades to attempt to upgrade talent. Olympic sprinter Bo Roberson was acquired from San Diego. Defensive back Joe Cannavino, who led the Raiders in interceptions in 1961, was sent to Buffalo for DB Vernon Valdez. Wayne Crow and a draft choice were dealt to Buffalo for defensive tackle Chuck McMurtry and quarterback M. C. Reynolds. A good rookie find was linebacker Charlie Rieves of Houston. Rieves, defensive tackle Joe Novsek, and offensive tackle Charles Brown all became starters on this talent-starved club and made the All-AFL rookie team. Tommy Morrow, a second-year free agent, was second in the AFL with 10 interceptions. Morrow pilfered a pass in each of the last four games in 1962 and the first four contests of 1963 for an overall streak of eight. When the Dallas Texans signed quarterback Len Dawson, who was languishing on the bench of the NFL Cleveland Browns, they traded the incumbent, Cotton Davidson, to Oakland. Cotton became the Oakland starter when Flores missed the season with an illness. Davidson also doubled as the punter and took a turn as a place kicker. Cotton spent the next eight seasons with the Raiders, mostly as a backup quarterback. These days, Davidson is a cattle rancher near Waco, Texas. While in limbo, Flores was hired by the *Oakland Tribune* sports department and covered both the Raiders and 49ers. Williamson and Otto continued their excellent play and both were All-League performers.

The preceding paragraph gave the highlights of 1962. Oh yes, but what happened in the games? Well, the first three games were at home and the 12,893; 12,500; and 13,000 announced crowds must have seemed like Times Square on New Years Eve to Valley and McGah. But the Raiders lost all three. Newly acquired quarterback Lee Grosscup fired three touchdown passes for the

New York Titans, who scored a 28–17 victory in the season opener. Ancient Don Heinrich passed two yards to John White for an Oakland touchdown. Former Oakland prep and Stanford All-American receiver Chris Burford was the star the following week. But not for Oakland. Burford played for Dallas and caught three touchdown passes from Dawson in a 26–16 decision. Daniels and Davidson scored for Oakland. A 42–33 loss to San Diego was made closer by reserve quarterback Chon Gallegos, who had two fourth-quarter touchdown passes. Roberson returned a kickoff 86 yards earlier in the contest.

After two defeats against Denver, Feldman was replaced by Red Conkright, the defensive line coach. In a 44–7 shellacking by Denver, Gallegos had two passes returned for touchdowns by the Broncos. Tripuka and George Shaw, another name from out of the distant AFL past, quarterbacked Denver to a 23–6 win in the return match. Daniels scored the only Oakland TD. Four days later Feldman was fired. Because the Giants were playing the Yankees in Game seven of the World Series across the Bay, the event received little notice in the Bay Area media. Although the dismissal of a head coach is not a pleasant task, the firing should have been timed to generate interest in the fledgling team. It was a good example of the general ineptness of the Oakland organization in those pre–Al Davis days.

We now return to the season already in progress. Conkright would lose eight more times before the Raiders finally would win one for the redhead. The new coach spent three miserable weeks in the east and lost to Buffalo, Boston, and New York. Only Roberson scored for Oakland in a 14–6 loss to the Bills. The Raiders and Patriots were tied at 16–16 in the fourth quarter when Boston's Larry Garron broke free for a 41-yard touchdown run. And journeyman quarterback Johnny Green passed the Titans to a 31–21 win, which nullified two scores by Daniels and a 92-yard pass from Davidson to Roberson.

The 0–8 Raiders returned home and lost 28–20 to Houston. George Blanda wiped out a 20–7 Oakland lead, and linebacker Gene Babb's interception of Davidson ended the disappointment. Former Raider Wayne Crow scored the only touchdown in a 10–6 Buffalo win.

Three road games followed. Hunter Enis passed to Dobie Craig for a score for Oakland in the Cotton Bowl. Unfortunately the Texans had five touchdowns. The Raiders were trailing 28–7 at San Diego when Davidson suddenly found Dick Dorsey for 65- and 90-yard touchdown passes, but an Earl Faison interception ended the dream. At Houston, Daniels ran for 157 yards but Blanda and the Oilers still came out on top. Oakland was now 0–13.

A crowd of about 8,000 came out in a rainstorm to watch the season finale. And the Raiders escaped the ignominy of a winless season by beating Boston 20–0. Daniels capped a great campaign by scoring twice. Not to minimize Conkright's only victory as a head coach, but the dispirited Patriots had been eliminated from the AFL East race on the previous day when Houston routed the New York Titans and had little incentive to win. Otherwise, the Oakland Raiders of 1962 may have matched the 1976 Tampa Bay Buccaneers as the only 0–14 teams in pro football history.

The 1962 Raiders were simply awful. Of the 13 defeats, only the 10–6 loss to Buffalo could be considered a close game. Davidson completed a mere 37% of his passes and threw only seven touchdowns while being intercepted 23 times. Those numbers make even current quarterback Jay Schroeder's statistics look good. NFL and AFL reject Max Boydston led the team in receiving with 30 catches, *none* for touchdowns. In 1982, Denver hired Jack Faulkner off Sid Gillman's staff at San Diego and the Broncos became a contender, eventually finishing at 7–7. Oakland now had no competition as the ugly stepsister in the new league.

Although attendance increased with the move to Frank Youell Field, the fan base was still not solid. It was estimated that the Raiders had lost over $1,000,000 in the first three years. Late in the season, the *Oakland Tribune* and the mayor's office jointly launched a ticket campaign to keep both the Raiders and the American Basketball League Oakland Oaks afloat. The goal of Operation DRIVE (Damn Right I'm for Victory in East Bay) was to sell 7,300 season tickets to the seven Raider home games in 1963. The price: $31. (Munch on that one when you think of $45,000 luxury box seats in the 1990 Oakland-Raider deal.) The American Basketball League folded on December 31, 1962, and this version of the Oakland Oaks passed into sports oblivion. Would the Raiders be next?

Chapter 4

A MIRACLE IN
LITTLE OLD OAKLAND

*"They fear him in both leagues. As an assistant
with the Chargers and a talent man without
parallel in either league, they know this guy. They
fear him. He's moving up, wherever he goes, and
the football world knows it."*

—Don Clark, 1963

"**A**s 1963 began, Wayne Valley was seriously
looking for new blood to turn the Oakland franchise
around. Any blood. Among the names that surfaced as
head coaching candidates were Lou Agase, formerly with
Toronto of the CFL, Vince Lombardi (don't laugh too
hard), Green Bay assistants Bill Austin and Phil
Bengsten, and former Buffalo coach Buster Ramsey.
Valley and McGah had to clean house and do it quickly.

Somehow the search for a coach led the Oakland
Raider partners to Al Davis. Despite their 4–10 record in
1962, the San Diego Chargers were still the class organization of the AFL and Jack Faulkner's success in Denver
after being a Gillman assistant only made Davis more ap-
pealing to Oakland. Also, Lance Alworth had originally
been an Oakland draft choice whose rights were dealt to
San Diego. When Al Davis "stole" Alworth from Red
Hickey and the 49ers, Valley had to be impressed.

But did Al Davis want the job? Valley and McGah had spoken to Davis several times during the 1962 disaster but were rejected. They started a more serious recruitment of Al Davis during the last week of the year. Davis, who inherited a large sum of money when his father died in 1961, initially declined the Oakland job based on what was being offered. He wanted a large operating budget and a three-year contract as both coach and general manager. "What I want is enough time and money to build the Raiders into a professional football team" is what Davis told the Oakland people. At first Valley and McGah were reluctant but they eventually recanted. They knew the challenge of making the laughingstock of football into a winner would prove to be irresistible to Davis.

But Mrs. Davis did not raise foolish children. After observing the shenanigans that accompanied the Oakland franchise from afar, her son was not going to toil for Valley and McGah unless he was certain that the football climate was positive in Oakland. A few well-placed phone calls convinced Al that (1) the planned Oakland Coliseum was more than a mere pipe dream, (2) the politicians and important families that comprised the power base in the City of Oakland would support the Raiders, and (3) the *Oakland Tribune* had a positive attitude and wouldn't "rag" the team if its performance on the field or at the gate was disappointing. Davis was satisfied to hear that the Kaiser and Knowland families, who were both integral parts of the Oakland power base, were supporting both the Raiders and the Coliseum project.

Valley and McGah quickly learned that they were not dealing with Marty Feldman or Red Conkright. It took a total of 48 hours of numerous meetings over a three-week period to consummate the deal. On January 10, 1963, they met *five* different times. Davis and the Raiders agreed to a three-year contract at $20,000 annually. On January 18, 1963, Al Davis formally became head coach and general manager of the Oakland Raiders. In retrospect, January 18, 1963, was probably one of the three or four most important dates in AFL history. Maybe NFL history too. Three days earlier a little-noticed event occurred in New York when a group headed by David A. "Sonny" Werblin tendered an offer of $1,300,000 for the bankrupt New York Titans. The deal was later completed and the New York team, renamed the Jets, became the solid franchise that was so desperately needed in the largest media market. In 1964, Werblin helped negotiate the television deal with NBC that gave AFL clubs the infusion of cash needed to compete for players with the NFL. His signing of University of Alabama quarterback Joe Namath for $400,000 signified that the new league was here to stay.

Although his aggressive recruiting tactics had raised some eyebrows, the reaction to the hiring of Al Davis by Oakland was lauded in most circles. "Al is one of the brilliant young coaches in all football. He has an outstanding football mind and the potential to be one of the truly great coaches in the game," said Sid Gillman. Jerry Magee of the *San Diego Union* summed it up: "Glib Al Davis, whose flashing grin and fast talk make him one of professional football's most persuasive bargainers, is going to attempt the hardest sell in football—the Oakland Raiders."

And how did the 33-year-old Davis feel about ascending to a head coaching position? "I'm not interested in the job. I'm interested in whether I can do the job." Come again, Al? "I tell ya, Oakland don't need much. Forget the record books from now on. We're going to have them talking about us. You can bet on us."

The presence of the young coach was warmly received in Oakland and helped the efforts of Operation DRIVE. It also aided the new stadium project. On January 29, 1963, nine days after Al Davis was hired, the city council gave its approval for the eventual construction of Oakland Coliseum. Davis was pleased that his reconnaissance about Oakland was correct. "I came here from San Diego gambling on the development of a Coliseum and emergence of the Oakland area into the sports capital of the West," said Al.

Because the previous regime had traded away the first five draft choices for 1963, Al Davis was forced to actively pursue the trading market for players who would immediately improve the Raiders. Before opening day, Davis made 18 trades. Many were steals. Middle linebacker Archie Matsos was obtained from Buffalo for three second-line players. Guard Bob Mischak came from New York and was converted into a tight end. Defensive back and talented punt returner Claude Gibson followed Davis from San Diego.

Wes Fry, the 1962 general manager, was excused, and four new assistant coaches were hired. John Rauch handled the offensive backfield, Ollie Spencer coached the offensive line, Tom Dahms was in charge of the defensive line, and Charlie Sumner oversaw the defensive backfield. Not surprisingly, Spencer was pressed into service as an offensive guard in 1963. Dahms and Spencer remained Raider assistants through the 1970s. Sumner has had three different terms as a Raider assistant, and Rauch was later to succeed Davis as head coach when Al moved into the league office.

The day after the Oakland City Council gave its thumbs up on the new stadium, the Raiders signed free agent end Art Powell, who had played out his option with the New York Titans. Powell was impressed with Davis's theories of passing offense. He would come to admire Davis for his concern and respect for the welfare of black players. Davis wouldn't schedule exhibition games in cities that had stadiums with separate seating.

There were two 1963 rookies who made large contributions to Davis's first squad. Defensive tackle Dave Costa could be described as an early-day Lyle Alzado. Similar to Alzado, Costa was raised in Westchester

County, New York, and spent much of his youth running around with gangs. He eventually channeled his aggressions into high school football and attended the University of Utah. He was actually signed by the Raiders a few days before Al Davis arrived. Another good rookie find was Ken Herock of West Virginia University. Herock reported as a linebacker but was converted by Davis to a tight end. Herock played four years with the Raiders and then stepped into the front office, initially as a scout and later as director of personnel operations when Ron Wolf went to Tampa Bay. He is now director of player personnel for the Atlanta Falcons.

The new players were certainly an improvement, but nobody really expected much from this team. Davis hoped they would steal a victory or two along the way but was not thinking about championships. In fact, Davis was fearing the worst. It was in the 1963 training camp that "pride and poise" became a Raider motto. "No matter what the scoreboard says, keep your poise," Davis would tell his players.

Plans for the Coliseum were gathering steam. Operation DRIVE was a success, with 8,000 tickets sold. And September 5, 1963, is another significant day in Raider history. After playing five exhibition games with the gold and black uniforms of 1962, which were characterized by skinny but oversized numerals similar to the Chicago Bears, Al Davis changed the home attire to the silver and black that exists today. The 1963 road uniforms were white uniforms and silver numerals, which naturally proved impossible to read from the stands. They were eventually changed to black numerals. Davis patterned the uniforms after the West Point Army cadets, then coached by the legendary Earl "Red" Blaik.

The 1963 season opened on Saturday night, September 7, in Houston. The Oilers, Eastern Division champions in 1962, were shocked 24–13 by the Raiders. Houston suffered 10 turnovers. Tom Flores replaced

Cotton Davidson in the second half and marched Oakland 56 yards in seven plays for the go-ahead touchdown. Flores and Powell connected on an 85-yard score in the fourth quarter.

The fans and press reacted immediately to the victory. "If the Raiders had any tradition before, it was a ragged-tail tradition of failure and frustration. They were to the American League what the skinny guy on the beach is to the bully; kicking sand in his face and waltzing off with his doll. No more," noted George Ross of the *Oakland Tribune*.

A crowd of 17,568 "jammed" Youell Field for the home opener, and the Raiders responded with a 35–17 rout of Buffalo. This time Davidson was the passing star. There were heroes on defense too. Linebacker Clancy Osborne caused a Buffalo fumble, which was recovered by defensive end Dalva Allen. Tackle Chuck McMurtry also pounced on a fumble, and defensive back Jon Jelacic grabbed a deflected pass and scored a touchdown. The players tried to give the game ball to Davis, who declined. "Let somebody else get 'em," said Al, who added, "I'm not a sentimental guy. I only like to win." In Oakland, Davis was being hailed as the second coming of Jack London.

The Patriots beat the Raiders 20–14 at Youell the following week to break the overall three-game winning streak. It was 20–0 in the fourth quarter when Flores connected with Powell and Bo Roberson for touchdowns. A final scoring drive was stopped by an interception by Boston linebacker Nick Buoniconti. Oakland was held to 24 yards rushing as Daniels sat out the contest with a muscle bruise.

Oakland next headed to the East Coast for three consecutive road games. In those days, West Coast teams would live on the road for their eastern trips. With Daniels hurt, the Raider offense stalled and Oakland lost 10–7 at New York, 12–0 in Buffalo, and 20–14 at Fenway Park in Boston. Davidson and Flores were cumulatively 15 for 37 against the Jets. A Dick Wood fourth-quarter pass to Bake Turner was the margin of victory for New York. Jack Kemp passed to future Raider Bill Miller for the only touchdown of the Buffalo game. Daniels sat out the Boston game. Although defensive back Jim McMillin intercepted two Babe Parilli passes for Oakland, the Raiders couldn't hold a 14–3 third-quarter advantage. The road trip was a disappointment, but Davis was upbeat. "We're no longer a doormat. It wouldn't take much more to make this a good football team," said the coach.

Al Davis returned home with a 2–4 record, and some of the local optimism that was so prevalent after the first two games was gone. "Pride and poise, pride and poise, pride and poise," Davis told them over and over as the New York Jets came to town. Attendance dipped to 15,557. But the Raiders responded with a 49–26 victory. Daniels returned to the lineup and rushed for 200 yards, which stood as the team record until broken by Bo Jackson in 1987. Seventy-four yards came on one play. Dobie Craig caught a 93-yard pass from Flores and Alan Miller weighed in with two scores. The Raiders amassed 523 yards of total offense and rose from last to second place in the standings.

Next was a come-from-behind 34–33 win over eventual AFL champion San Diego, the only game that the Chargers lost at home in 1963. Davidson completed a second-half comeback with a 10-yard pass to reserve fullback Glenn Shaw in the final two minutes. Daniels gained 125 yards and wrestled the AFL rushing lead away from Paul Lowe. Bo Roberson returned kickoffs and punts for a combined 171 yards. A crowd of 600 was at Oakland airport to welcome the Raiders home.

Consecutive victories followed over Kansas City, the 1962 league champion. Claude Gibson's 85-yard punt return was the difference in a 10–7 win at home. Five days later, the boys raced to a 22–0 lead and held the Chiefs to only two yards at halftime. Daniels added 122 yards to his rushing stats and Flores and Powell connected for two scores. "We were pathetic," said Chiefs coach Hank Stram about their 22–7 defeat.

The Raiders did not play again for 20 days. After receiving a bye for November 17, 1963, they were scheduled to visit Denver on Sunday, November 24. After President John F. Kennedy was assassinated on November 22, AFL Commissioner Joe Foss postponed the weekend games.

The next game at Denver was played on Thanksgiving Day; the long layoff did not affect the Raiders. A 39-yard Davidson to Roberson pass put Oakland in the lead and they breezed to a 26–10 victory. Dalva Allen and Dave Costa harassed the Denver quarterbacks, and defensive back Jon Jelacic scooped up a fumble and went 99 yards for a touchdown. Another enthusiastic crowd was waiting at the airport.

After another week off, the Chargers came to town for a rematch. An overflow crowd of 20,249 saw San Diego jump to a 27–10 lead. The Raiders kept their pride and it was the Chargers who lost their poise. In an 11-minute, 47-second span during the second half, the Raider defense caused five turnovers, and the offense responded with four touchdowns and a field goal to beat back San Diego 41–27. Davidson fired two touchdowns and ran for a third. Daniels added 90 more yards rushing and overshadowed the vaunted San Diego tandem of Lincoln and Lowe, who had only five yards combined. "Fantastic," was Davis's reaction as the 8–4 Raiders pulled to within one game of the division-leading Chargers.

In week 13, the Raiders edged Denver 35–31 before 15,223 at Youell while San Diego was winning at Houston. Flores fired five touchdown passes, and Fred Williamson's interception with 32 seconds to play saved the day.

The Chargers smashed the Broncos in their closing game to win the division. The Oakland finale against Houston, played three days before Christmas, was one of the most exciting games in Raider annals and was the highest scoring game in AFL history. Nine other league records were set. In the first half, Houston's George Blanda and Oakland's Tom Flores matched pass for pass and the score was 35–35 at the intermission. Flores threw two more TD passes in the second half, but a 39-yard Mike Mercer field goal made the difference in the 52–49 victory. It was a career day for Flores, who fired six touchdown passes for 407 yards. Powell amassed 247 yards of receptions. The upstart Oakland Raiders finished 1963 with eight consecutive victories and a 10–4 record. It was one more triumph than the combined 1960–62 total. The Christmas card sent from the Raiders in 1963 said: "Happy holiday. [We're] dedicated to making the Oakland franchise a professional football power."

Davis was selected as Coach of the Year by *The Sporting News* and the wire services, and he was also honored as Man of the Year by the Oakland Junior Chamber of Commerce. But Davis deflected the praise toward his players. "Hey, you praise my players; they're terrific; they're the Raiders of Oakland," said Al. Four of those players—Otto, Daniels, Williamson, and Matsos—made the all-AFL team. The turnaround of nine games in the regular season is still the most in AFL/NFL history. Only the Baltimore Colts' improvement from 2–12 to 10–4 in 1974–75, the New England turnaround from 3–11 to 11–3 in 1975–76, and the San Francisco 49ers' jump from 6–10 to 13–3 in 1980–81 come close. "Al Davis, face it, is the best thing to come along in pro football, especially in the American League, in years," proclaimed George Ross of the *Tribune*.

From the edge of extinction, Davis single-handedly saved a dying franchise, assured that the new stadium would be built, and gave a city with a huge inferiority complex something to be proud of. Perhaps Al Davis surrendered his dibs on Oakland when he moved to Los Angeles in 1982. But without his presence and his miraculous work in 1963, there would never have been a Coliseum, an Oakland Athletics franchise, or many of the other sports and entertainment amenities that have filled the coffers and instilled civic pride. Another 1–13 or 2–12 season before average crowds of less than 10,000 and the Raiders either would have been moved or the padlock placed on the front office door of Valley and McGah. The millions of dollars that flowed into Oakland and Alameda County over the three decades as a boost to the economy would never have circulated. And both the name recognition and positive image that the area received from the Raiders led to companies' relocating to the East Bay, which brings jobs, jobs, jobs. That's Economics 101, folks. Give Al Davis an A+.

It was now time for the recruiting abilities of Al Davis to shine. From the college draft for 1964, Oakland beat the NFL to three blue-chip linebackers: Dan Conners of the University of Miami, Bill Budness from Boston University and Louisiana Tech's John Robert (J. R.) Williamson. Conners would spend 11 years with the Raiders as an all-pro middle linebacker, and he now works in the Raiders' personnel department.

From their 1963 "red shirt" or "futures" list of college players who stayed in school an extra year, the Raiders inked Arizona State defensive tackle Rex Mirich. A dispute arose between the Raiders and Carroll Rosenbloom's Baltimore Colts over Oakland's Number One draft choice: Arizona State halfback Tony Lorick. He signed with the Raiders a day before the NFL draft, and then a week later, with the help of a Los Angeles newspaper reporter, inked a pact with the Baltimore Colts.

Rozelle upheld the Colts' contract and Lorick played for Baltimore. He was the runner-up to Charlie Taylor as NFL Rookie of the Year in 1964, leading the Colts into the NFL championship game.

During the great turnaround of 1963, the Oakland Raiders were good, but lucky. Very lucky. Al Davis kept telling the audiences on the banquet circuit not to expect an immediate repeat of 1963 and instead emphasized the long-range outlook. "We're building the organization. As long as I'm here, we'll never stop working, never lose our sincere dedication to build Oakland into a top football power," said Davis. "We hope to continue to build an image people in Oakland and the world will be proud of. I hope the first step has been well taken."

A total of 4,600 seats were added to Frank Youell Field for the 1964 season. Funding for the Coliseum was approved by all parties, with construction set to begin in early 1965.

Davis's warning about a repeat of 1963 was right on target. The 1964 season began with five straight defeats. Flores and Daniels both got off to slow starts as the Raiders dropped the opener 17–14 to Boston before 21,126. Glenn Shaw scored the first Oakland touchdown of the season, but a key Daniels fumble in the fourth quarter cost the Raiders the old ballgame. On the last Raider possession of the contest, Coach Davis eschewed a tying field goal attempt and went for the win. It was unsuccessful. In the dressing room after the final gun, the demeanor of Davis was not pleasant. "How about that! We're down by 10 points, then come back and blow it on that damn fumble," said the coach.

The Davis disposition did not improve after the next contest, a 42–28 loss at Houston. Although Daniels scored three times for Oakland, the tandem of Flores and Davidson combined for five interceptions, and the Raiders could not stop Sid Blanks, the Oilers' rookie halfback, who ran for 127 yards. After the game, the buses that carried the Raiders to the airport left without Davis, who followed in a cab. "I don't like to lose. I'm not used to it. But we'll get it straightened out. I guarantee you. I haven't given up on this season," were Davis's remarks at the airport, which sound strikingly similar to what he said after the Raiders lost the first two exhibition games in August 1989. Nobody was certain if the bus drivers were fired.

Before the upcoming game against Kansas City, Al Davis signed Ben Davidson, late of the Washington Redskins. Employed at defensive end, Big Ben quickly became one of the better pass rushers in his eight AFL/AFC seasons. You have probably seen the colorful Davidson in those Miller Lite Beer commercials. Also acquired was defensive back Howie Williams, who was to be an occasional starter for the next six campaigns.

Against the Chiefs, the Raiders had opportunities to put the game away early. Three promising scoring drives ended with field goals. Trailing 9–7 entering the final period, Len Dawson led the Chiefs to two touchdowns and a 21–9 win. "We're just not ready for any championships," was the Davis assessment of his 0–3 Raiders.

Now for the 1964 version of *Nightmare on Elm Street,* also known as the Raiders' annual road trip east. In Buffalo, they played like champions and led in the fourth quarter only to taste a bitter 23–20 defeat. Davis raised the ire of the Bills before the game when the Raiders tried to claim injured cornerback Ray Abruzzese from the waiver wire. Cotton Davidson had a decent night for Oakland with 14 completions in 24 attempts, including a touchdown to reserve tight end Jan Barrett. From the sidelines, Davis watched Buffalo reserve quarterback Daryle Lamonica rally the Bills to the winning score and filed his impressions away for future reference. Newly acquired Billy Cannon committed a fatal mental error as the Raiders were moving toward the Buffalo end zone in the final seconds. Rather than get out of bounds to stop the clock, the tight end tried to gain a few extra yards and was tackled in bounds as the clock ticked away on the Raiders chances. Nevertheless, Buffalo Coach Lou Saban was impressed with the opposition. "There is too much talent on that club and they are too well coached to be 0–4," said Saban. "They'll start hurting people pretty soon."

"Pretty soon" was not the following Saturday night in New York. A 35–13 loss against the Jets was punctuated by five Oakland turnovers. Rookie New York fullback Matt Snell plowed the Raider defenses for 168 yards. A sixth straight loss was avoided in a Friday night game at Boston, but they didn't win either. After squandering a 34–14 lead, they needed Mike Mercer's last-second 43-yard field goal to salvage a 43–43 tie. In a passing duel between two old war-horses, Babe Parilli and Cotton Davidson combined for 737 yards through the autumn air of Fenway Park. Installed at fullback by Al Davis, Billy Cannon tallied 90 rushing yards.

The first victory was finally achieved with a 40–7 smashing of Denver. Daniels rushed for 167 yards and Cotton Davidson passed for 419 yards, still a team record, as the Raiders accumulated an astounding 628 yards of total offense, 199 in the first quarter. Powell had nine receptions.

But the glow of the initial win was short-lived as losses at San Diego and Kansas City brought the record to 1–7–1, reminiscent of the pre–Al Davis era. The Chargers picked off six Davidson passes in a 31–17 loss, as Lance Alworth burned Raider cornerback Fred Williamson for two touchdowns and 203 yards in catches. Before the game, Davis challenged Charger coach Sid Gillman about the eligibility of 47-year-old San Diego kicker Ben Agajanian, who played despite the protests of the Raiders. In the next contest, the Chiefs routed the Raiders 42–7, which was to be the biggest margin of defeat in the coaching career of Al Davis. "Awful, the worst game we've played since I've been here," said Al, who knew that he still didn't have the personnel to contend. "I still say that about four top players—not rookies—would really make the difference in our club," he added.

With Oakland out of the title race, the players could only play for pride and keep their poise. And they did. Oakland beat Houston 20–10, as a Ben Davidson sack of Oiler quarterback George Blanda produced a costly Houston fumble that was recovered by defensive end Dalva Allen. Cotton Davidson, who found Art Powell for two touchdown passes, also rushed for 44 yards. Coach Davis employed a three-man defensive front in a return match with New York and successfully stopped the Jets' ground game. Trailing 10–0, Cotton Davidson and Daniels combined for a 60-yard pass and run touchdown to put Oakland back in the game. Cannon then caught two touchdown passes as Oakland beat New York 35–26.

A holding penalty against Ken Herock nullified a Daniels score and cost the Raiders a win at Denver, but Mike Mercer kicked a 40-yard field goal late to salvage a 20–20 tie.

The Raiders successfully closed the 1964 season with victories over Buffalo and San Diego, who would soon meet in the 1964 AFL Championship game. With Buffalo safety Butch Byrd in his face, Art Powell caught a one-yard touchdown pass from Tom Flores on the final play of a 16–13 win. Defensive back Warren Powers had two Oakland interceptions. Today, almost all plays are sent in from the sidelines, but in those days, quarterbacks called their own plays. But guess who called the Powell touchdown? "Sure, I called that last play. I had to go to my man. Arthur gets the job done," said Coach Davis. It was the only play sent in from the bench during the entire game.

Flores fired touchdown tosses to Powell, Cannon, and reserve receiver–place kicker Gene Mingo in a 21–20 squeaker over San Diego. Daniels gained 129 yards in an incredible fourth-quarter performance. Warren Powers had two more interceptions. The win completed a five-game unbeaten streak and pushed the final record to 5–7–2, not as good as 10–4, but certainly better than 1–7–1.

There were some positive individual achievements. Cotton Davidson was second in the AFL in passing, and Daniels had a strong second half, finishing third in rushing among the running backs. Powell caught 76 passes for 1,361 yards and 11 touchdowns. Otto and Powell were All-League selections. "Well, we've narrowed the talent gap," was Davis's overall assessment of the season.

The college draft for 1965 was a smashing success. It was here that Al Davis and others around the AFL started employing "babysitting" tactics, en masse, to keep collegians away from the National League. The first four draft choices were all signed by Oakland. Bob Svihus of USC and Harry Schuh from Memphis State were two offensive linemen who would be solid contributors for the next six seasons. Schuh spurned the Los Angeles Rams to sign with Al Davis and would be the starting right tackle for the next six years. Svihus played on the left side. Gus Otto was converted from a fullback at Missouri to a powerful outside linebacker. And the Number two draft choice was a gem. Davis wanted a possession-type receiver to complement the speedy Art Powell. What he got was probably the best possession end who ever played the game: six-feet-one, 190-pound Fred Biletnikoff of Florida State. Another Floridian who was signed for delivery in 1965 was red-shirt draftee Carleton Oats of Florida A&M. Oats was an integral member of the defensive line for eight seasons and often played alongside colorful Ike Lassiter, who had bounced around the NFL and AFL before finding a home in Oakland. Running back Larry Todd of Arizona State was a 1965 rookie, who returned kickoffs and rushed for 149 yards in a win over Houston. Fred Williamson was dealt to Kansas City for defensive back Dave Grayson, who was to be All-AFL in

1965. He would be joined in the secondary by Kent McCloughan, a rookie from Nebraska. The Raiders obtained his draft rights from Houston. Amid rumors that he was committed to the Dallas Cowboys, the Raiders drafted Craig Morton of the University of California in the tenth round and promptly offered the quarterback a $200,000 bonus. Dallas matched the offer but the message was clear: Whether on the field or in the pursuit of collegians, Al Davis and the Oakland Raiders had "come to play," and the NFL had better beware. It is a message that would be learned repeatedly over the next 25 years.

The 1965 Oakland Raiders were somewhat more consistent than the 1964 model, finishing 8–5–1 and in second place behind San Diego in the AFL West. Any serious title chances were destroyed by the failure to win more than two games consecutively until the season was almost over. The Raiders won the first, third, fifth, seventh, ninth, eleventh, and thirteenth games of the season. A victory over Denver in Game 12 was their only win in an even-numbered week.

There would be no five-game opening losing streak in 1965, as the season began with an easy 37–10 triumph over Kansas City. Flores and Davidson were assisted by veteran quarterback Dick Wood, who was acquired from the Jets. Wood came off the bench against the Chiefs and connected with Powell for two scores. Fullback Roger Hagberg, who had previously played for the Winnipeg Blue Bombers in the Canadian League, gained 85 yards in his Raider debut. Claude Gibson added a touchdown on a 58-yard punt return.

The Chargers dominated the line of scrimmage in game number two and beat Oakland 17–6. The Raiders were held to 36 yards net rushing and the Chargers gained 207 yards on the ground. Two Gene Mingo field goals were the extent of the Oakland scoring. "We're just a year away," said Davis. Maybe two years, Coach.

The defense made life miserable for Houston quar-

terback Don Trull in a 21–7 Raider win. After a Trull
fumble was recovered by Oakland, Flores found fullback
Alan Miller with a five-yard pass for the clinching
touchdown. Daniels added 115 yards. "We needed this
one from an emotional standpoint," said Davis.

And now for the annual sojourn through the East. As
in 1964, it started with a tough 17–12 defeat at Buffalo.
Two Daniels fumbles nullified scoring chances. Howie
Williams had an interception and fumble recovery for a
stingy Raider defense that allowed the champion Bills
only 263 total yards.

After a cumulative 0–6–1 record on eastern trips, Al
Davis finally tasted a victory as Boston was upended by a
24–10 score. It was also the first win away from Frank
Youell Field in two seasons. There were many heroes including Flores and Powell, who produced two touchdowns, and Daniels, who gained 113 yards in a strong
performance.

A 24–24 tie in New York was a disappointment because mistakes cost Oakland a victory. Gene Mingo
missed two easy field goals and a poor snap on a punt led
to a Jets touchdown. Dave Grayson picked off a deflected
pass by rookie quarterback Joe Namath and returned it
76 yards. "If we were consistent, we'd be 5–1," said a disappointed Davis.

Returning home for a rematch with Boston, Flores
was knocked out of the game by Patriot defensive end
Larry Eisenhower. This time it was Dick Wood who
played an effective relief role, with two TDs to Art
Powell. Mike Mercer regained the place kicking job and
contributed three field goals. Gus Otto stole a Babe Parilli
pass and rambled 36 yards for a touchdown. The 30–21
win also featured the debut of flanker back Fred Biletnikoff, who caught seven passes for 118 yards.

"Overall, we didn't play well enough to win, that's all,"
said Davis after a 14–7 loss at Kansas City. He may have
added that two controversial "non-calls" by the officials,

of obvious pass interference on Raider receivers in the final minute, contributed to the defeat.

Larry Todd's 149-yard rushing performance followed in a 30–21 victory at Houston. Wood was 14 for 25 for 211 yards and three touchdowns in his best day as a Raider, as the Silver and Black had an early 20–0 lead and never looked back. Mercer chipped in with four field goals.

Buffalo quarterback Jackie Kemp enjoyed last-second heroics in the next Raider game. Kemp connected with fullback Billy Joe for a touchdown with seven seconds to go in a 17–14 Bills win. Daniels enjoyed a productive first half, accumulating 83 yards on a muddy field, but was held to four yards in the second half. Wood completed thirteen passes, ten to the Raiders and three to Buffalo.

At Denver, John McCormack would have enjoyed more success singing in the final act of *La Traviata* than trying to solve the Raider defense. The Bronco quarterback was intercepted four times in a 28–20 Oakland win. The steals by Gus Otto and Dave Grayson came in the fourth quarter and thwarted a Denver comeback.

After a week off, the Raiders beat Denver again. While Flores, Daniels, and Powell were producing three touchdowns in the 24–13 decision, the defense stopped the Broncos four times inside the Oakland 10-yard line. "They [the defense] were terrific, just fantastic," lauded Davis.

The Jets employed a triple-wing formation for much of their game in Oakland, but the Raiders adjusted to Joe Namath and his four receivers. As the Raiders were running out the clock with a slim 17–14 lead, Daniels suddenly burst through the New York secondary and scored on a 30-yard jaunt to ice the last contest played at Frank Youell Field. The Chargers clinched the AFL West in their game, so Oakland would have to be satisfied with a second-place finish.

The try for a ninth win was thwarted in the finale at

San Diego, won 24–14 by the Chargers. The Raiders blew a 14–0 advantage, and three Flores interceptions in the fourth quarter sealed the verdict.

So 1965 was a year of progress for the Oakland Raiders. Al Davis was gradually adding young talent, which was giving the Raiders the depth needed to contend for a championship. The new stadium was now under construction. Everybody was optimistic about 1966.

Although nobody knew it at the time, a brilliant coaching career had come to an end.

Chapter 5

"GO AFTER THEIR SUPPLY LINES": THE WAR WITH THE NFL

"When the time comes for the two leagues to sign players again, the AFL, for a certainty, won't be standing behind the door with Al, who knows a few things about recruiting."
—*Melvin Durslag*, Los Angeles Herald Examiner,
April 1966

*T*he most controversial and misunderstood part of Al Davis's professional football career was his role as AFL commissioner in the merger of the two leagues in 1966. Many of Al's detractors insist that the merger was nearly a done deal when Davis became the leader of the AFL on April 8, 1966. There are others who give Davis credit for forcing the amalgamation. The correct answer is that Al Davis did indeed force the merger. But the terms accepted by the AFL probably could have been negotiated without the brief, albeit secret, signing war waged by Al Davis and company.

By early 1966, the AFL was improving both at the gate and on the field. From the somewhat crude beginnings in 1960, characterized by a sea of red ink, all the franchises were now in decent financial shape. After the Chargers moved from Los Angeles to San Diego in 1961 and the Dallas Texans found happiness as the Kansas City Chiefs in 1963, there were no franchise shifts. Unlike the All-American Conference, which challenged the NFL in the late 1940s, nobody ever went out of business. Some clubs were beginning to approach profitability. But in the battle for players, many of the teams in the junior league were still losing to the NFL. While the Raiders, Kansas City Chiefs, New York Jets, and Houston Oilers were able to regularly beat the NFL in signing quality talent, some of the other teams were falling behind. The extinction of the AFL still seemed to be the ultimate goal of the NFL. Joe Foss had been hired as AFL commissioner in 1960 to help the new league obtain some prestige. Foss was a World War II hero and a former governor of South Dakota. But the AFL decided it was time for a change. Author Bob Curran accurately portrayed the situation: "The [AFL] owners knew they were in an alley fight and they wanted an alley fighter representing them. Joe Foss didn't qualify and, in their books, Al Davis did." Jack Murphy in the *San Diego Union* also saw the need to wave bye-bye to Foss. ". . . everybody loves good old Joe. But they had heard all his war stories and it was time to hire a working commissioner."

Al Davis had just completed three successful years as coach and general manager of the Oakland Raiders and the team was approaching title contention. The Raiders would also be playing in the brand-new Oakland–Alameda County Coliseum in 1966. So the call to arms from the AFL owners was answered with some reluctance. "I'm a football coach first" was the Davis reply. But the kid from Brooklyn could not refuse the challenge. Addressing the media when Davis was selected, Buffalo's Ralph Wilson spoke for the other owners. "He has gained a reputation as a coaching genius and an astute business-man. I realize we are putting a permanent crimp in a brilliant 16-year coaching career which has elevated Al Davis to the pinnacle of the pros, but I'm certain he is embarking upon a career as commissioner which will be even more illustrative." The stated goal of Al Davis: "My job is to make the AFL the best league in pro football. They'll get my body. I'll work at this job day and night and do the best I can." For his troubles, Al was given a five-year contract at $60,000 annually and an expanded budget for the league office. Nobody knew it at the time, but as successor to Joe Foss, Al Davis would serve the AFL for only four months and his actions would significantly alter the course of professional football history in America. Ed Levitt of the *Oakland Tribune* accurately looked into his crystal ball and saw the future. "The skirmishes that are bound to pop up between Davis and NFL commissioner Pete Rozelle should make things lively in the football front for some time. . . . Davis is 36 and Rozelle is 39. So the antagonists are youthful and determined, careful and calculating. They rarely make mistakes."

There were actually two factions present within the AFL. Led by Lamar Hunt and Ralph Wilson, six of the owners (including Joe Robbie of the new Miami Dolphins) would have given their quarterback and a defensive end to have the opportunity to join the NFL. However, the Houston, New York, and Oakland clubs saw no need for a merger. Wayne Valley, the co-owner of the Raiders, was aware of the merger talk and wanted his own man, Al Davis, in charge. Valley also knew that the NFL wanted the Raiders and the New York Jets out of their territories. An anonymous AFL owner correctly analyzed the Oakland participants. "If we're going to have a war, just don't count Wayne Valley out. He sent Al Davis to New York to run the league, but Oakland is tough and the NFL knows it."

Al Davis was formally named commissioner on April 8, 1966. The owners had first met with him about the commissionership on March 31, 1966. On Sunday, April 6, 1966, Kansas City owner Lamar Hunt and Dallas Cowboys president Tex Schramm had their first "cloak-and-dagger" meeting in Dallas. They were feeling each other out about the prospects of a merger. Al Davis, who was basically opposed to a possible merger, was aware of the talks but took the job anyway.

And the new commissioner got off to a good start in reorganizing the AFL hierarchy. Val Pinchbeck, Irv Kaze, and Mickey Herskowitz were brought into the league office as publicists. Kaze was to rejoin Davis in Los Angeles in the 1980s and is presently Commissioner of the Continental Basketball Association. Pinchbeck stayed on after the merger and is still in the NFL office. Herskowitz was a sports columnist for the *Houston Post* and later returned to that position. As a coach, Al Davis certainly knew how bad the officiating was in the AFL. Mel Hein, who had served as an assistant coach with Davis at USC, was hired as director of officials.

Just as Al Davis was getting organized, a bomb dropped. On May 18, 1966, the New York Giants signed Pete Gogolak, who was the first successful soccer-style kicker in pro football. A marquee name in the AFL, Gogolak had played out his option with the champion Buffalo Bills. Before Pete Rozelle approved the action of the Giants, the two leagues had an unwritten agreement not to touch veterans who had played out their option. Scotty Stirling, who succeeded Al Davis as Raider general manager, sounded the warning. "Dealing with optioned players is a two-way street. While we haven't talked to optioned players in the past, we will now." The NFL had stepped over the line, and Al Davis would make them pay the price.

On May 20, Dave Dials of WXYZ-TV in Detroit unveiled the "secret" strategy of the AFL. They would sign NFL veteran players to future contracts after they played out their options, primarily concentrating on players who would be available in 1967. Davis was to say later that "it was a declaration of war all right. And we had to do what the generals do in a way. Go after the supply lines. Hit the enemy where it hurts most." During the next two weeks, Don Klosterman of the Chiefs, Al LoCasale of the Chargers, Scotty Stirling of the Raiders, baseball pitcher Don McMahon and former Charger linebacker Maury Schleicher, among others, were sent out into the field to obtain signatures. They concentrated on the premier quarterbacks of the NFL. Al Davis later claimed that seven of the fourteen starting quarterbacks agreed to switch leagues. Houston signed John Brodie of the 49ers, and Oakland inked Roman Gabriel of the Rams to a three-year deal. The signing of Gabriel by the Raiders pleased Davis, who delighted in hurting Rozelle's old team, the Rams. Although Chicago Bears coach Mike Ditka currently gives the impression of intense loyalty to his team and seems to delight in trading his holdout players, in 1966 tight end Mike Ditka agreed to jump the Bears for the Houston Oilers. Oakland was looking at All-Pro cornerback Mel Renfro of the Dallas Cowboys. The New York Jets were talking to running back Paul Hornung of Green Bay. That apparently infuriated Packer coach Vince Lombardi, who in 1966 was an intimidating force both on and off the field. George Halas of the Chicago Bears and Lombardi of the Packers were livid with Rozelle for approving the Gogolak signing and threatened to find a new NFL commissioner, pronto, if the AFL didn't cease and desist.

Al Davis also had plans for the AFL to expand into Los Angeles and Chicago in 1967. It was a good idea. After winning the NFL title in 1963, the Bears quickly faded from contention. The Rams were perennial losers and the Los Angeles Coliseum was rarely filled. These cities looked like good places to challenge the NFL on its own turf and were the two largest media markets that did not have AFL clubs. Eventually Al wanted to expand the AFL to 14 teams. It was obvious that Davis was not interested in an amalgamation but instead wanted to make the American Football League superior to the NFL.

As details of the veteran signings began leaking, the press had a field day with Rozelle. Syndicated columnist Larry Merchant accurately described the generals in the war. "Davis doesn't fool around. He's a gutter fighter with guts and gall from Brooklyn. This is what Pete Rozelle, a public relations man from Madison Avenue, is up against. Davis versus Rozelle, despite the prestige of the NFL, is a mismatch. Davis is [Rocky] Marciano, coming at you from all angles and not especially grief-stricken if a stray blow hits below the belt; Rozelle is Wally Cox with a briefcase. Now the Giants, Rozelle, and the NFL have played right into Davis's strength. By signing Pete Gogolak, they have brought the level of the war down to a level that Davis can't be beaten at."

The signing war was not all one-sided. Raider center Jim Otto admitted that he was approached by Lombardi and the Packers. Other AFL stars were listening to offers, although no one other than Gogolak ever signed with the NFL. The battle was seemingly getting out of hand. Just the way Al Davis wanted it to be.

During this short but turbulent period in pro football history, there were three secret meetings that have become somewhat infamous. Besides their April 1966 meeting, Lamar Hunt met with Tex Schramm again and outlined specific terms of the merger. In late May, after the Gogolak signing, there was a larger meeting with Schramm, Baltimore owner Carroll Rosenbloom, and Cleveland's Art Modell on the NFL side and Wilson, Hunt, and Boston owner Billy Sullivan bargaining for the AFL. Pete Rozelle was also present. Agreement was reached on the basic terms of the merger.

Apparently Al Davis was not aware of any of the secret powwows. On Sunday night, June 4, 1966, Davis was invited to a meeting at the Manhattan apartment of New

York Jets president David "Sonny" Werblin. Werblin was ill and not present but Sullivan, Wilson, and Hunt were there. Davis was informed of the merger terms that would be announced a few days later. Al had assumed that any merger scenario would have Rozelle in charge of the NFL, Davis leading the AFL, and a separate commissioner as head of the overall organization. That was the way major league baseball existed. But the AFL negotiators sold him out. With Tex Schramm successfully running interference for him, Rozelle would direct the merged league, which would be the NFL. When the current television contracts for both leagues expired after 1969, the AFL would go out of business. Although Davis won the battle, the despised Rozelle won the war. Was it really a defeat for Davis? Columnist Jimmy Cannon thought it was: ". . . While Davis was scheming to grab players away from the Nationals, Rozelle stole his league away from him. The people who represented the Americans didn't even bother to advise Davis what was going on. It has to be the most embarrassing defeat in sports since the last time Sonny Liston dumped Floyd Patterson."

If the preference of Rozelle over himself was a blow to Al Davis, he was also not enthralled with what was decided for the New York Jets and the Oakland Raiders. The AFL clubs were going to collectively pony up about $26,750,000 for the privilege of sharing a football with Pete Rozelle's league, but the Raiders and the Jets each had to pay a special indemnity of $2,000,000 to the 49ers and Giants respectively for "invasion" of their markets. Later it came out that the original NFL merger proposal discussed by Schramm and Hunt featured a "one team, one market concept." This meant that both the Jets and Raiders would move and leave New York and the San Francisco Bay Area exclusively for the NFL. Wayne Valley, who once tried to buy the 49ers before the AFL came along, was understandably bitter. So was Werblin, who was one of three AFL owners to oppose the amalgamation. Disputing Rozelle's claim that all 24 professional teams unanimously supported the merger, Werblin told *New York Post* columnist Milton Gross that "there is absolutely no reason why the AFL should be paying the NFL anything. . . . Wayne Valley, Bud Adams [Houston], and I were not in agreement because of the terms. We were the only ones to spend money on players last year, but what can we do? Under league rules, a two-thirds majority carries and everybody is bound." (The AFL admitted Miami as an expansion club in early 1966 and the vote was 6–3 in favor of the merger.)

The NFL owners were required to vote unanimously to approve the merger. Both New York and San Francisco refused to ratify the deal until the bounty was increased. The original terms were revised and the Giants received $8 million and the 49ers $6 million for their positive votes. The 13 other NFL franchises each received a comparatively paltry $307,000. The NFL side of the house also raked in the money received from the expansion New Orleans and Cincinnati teams, even though the Bengals were placed in the AFL.

Werblin had every right to be angered. After signing Joe Namath and other high-salaried rookies, he had a better team than the New York Giants and was now receiving as much media attention as the NFL club. The Jets were starting to sell out Shea Stadium with the largest crowds in the AFL. Over in the Bronx, the Giants had rapidly fallen from contention and had the worst record in the NFL in 1964. There were many other indignities that the Jets suffered at the hands of the Giants. Frank Gifford, who in those days was doubling as a CBS analyst for the Giants and doing a nightly sports report on WCBS-TV in New York, caused a furor one Sunday night in 1964 when he refused to give the Jets (and other AFL) scores. Werblin had a team, led by the colorful Namath, that was to win the Super Bowl three years later. By 1966, the Jets were far ahead of the Giants in many ways, so the payment of indemnity money to the Mara family was a bitter pill for Werblin to swallow. Less than two years later, Werblin sold his interest in the Jets to his partners, led by local oilman Leon Hess. Ironically, Hess later hired Rozelle crony Jim Kensil to run the team, and the Jets were among the clubs most loyal to Rozelle during the next two decades, especially when Al Davis moved to Los Angeles. But on the playing field, the Jets have usually been one of the worst teams. They have not gotten back to the Super Bowl since 1969 and have been mostly losers for the past 20 years. Incongruously, Sonny Werblin became the chief operator of the Hackensack Meadowlands complex in nearby New Jersey. His first major tenant was Mara's New York Giants. Later the Meadowlands enticed Hess's Jets. So after their rivalry in New York City in the 1960s, both New York football teams now play their home games out of state.

If Al Davis hadn't been recruited into the AFL office, the Raider franchise probably would have floated into the Bay and washed ashore in Puget Sound. But Davis and Valley proved to be tough enough to prevent the NFL San Francisco 49ers from entirely taking over the Bay Area. The 49ers were playing in ancient Kezar Stadium and were an also-ran team in the 1960s. Average attendance was about 30,000. It would be another five seasons before the 49ers moved into an expanded Candlestick Park. In the East Bay, the Raiders were about to christen the new 50,000-seat Oakland–Alameda County Coliseum. The Raiders were improving on the field and were about ready to embark on an unprecedented 20-year period of being the most consistent winners in football. Under the original merger proposal, which had the Raiders moving to Seattle, the 49ers were planning to play half of their home games in the new Oakland stadium.

Most pro football fans do not relate to indemnity payments and reparations. The biggest news of the merger was the creation of a world championship game, later to be called the Super Bowl. This was advantageous to the AFL, because a victory on the field over the NFL would give the American League instant credibility. Now everyone would know how good these guys really were (or weren't). And beginning in 1967, each AFL team would play one exhibition game against an NFL opponent. So starting in 1967, the Raiders played the 49ers in the summer (they lost 13–10). The series continues to this day. Strangely, the Jets played the Philadelphia Eagles and not the New York Giants in 1967, as the two organizations in the Big Apple remained hostile. The Jets and Giants finally met for the first time in the 1969 preseason. The Jets won that night, but when they met for real in 1970, the Giants came away with a 22–12 victory at Shea Stadium.

The most interesting result of the 1967 preseason interleague games was the Kansas City Chiefs' 66–24 rout of the Chicago Bears. The Chiefs were defeated in Super Bowl I by Green Bay. Three years earlier, Kansas City lost local hero and superstar running back Gale Sayers of Kansas to Chicago in the football signing war. So the Chiefs took out their frustrations on the poor Bears. But Kansas City paid a price for the win over Chicago. The emotionally drained Chiefs were flat through much of the regular season and quickly fell out of contention in the AFL West during 1967.

Another big "winner" that emerged from the joining of the leagues was NBC. Using contacts from his days in the entertainment business as head of the Music Corporation of America, Werblin had helped the AFL negotiate a five-year, $34,000,000 agreement with NBC in 1964. The AFL games were on ABC from 1960 to 1964. However, ABC did not always provide the regional coverage that is common today; in 1960 it was contractually obligated to televise only four of the seven road games of the clubs. Not broadcasting road games back to the local fans certainly did not help the gate in those early crucial AFL days. In 1960, ABC was decidedly the "number three" network in the ratings and still had many UHF stations in its lineup. Also, ABC was not televising games in color. This was before the advent of cable television and even before UHF channels became mandatory for all TV sets. The infusion of NBC money allowed the AFL to successfully compete with the NFL for college players. Art Rosenbaum of the *San Francisco Chronicle* calculated just how profitable the merger was for NBC. "The National Broadcasting Company's contract with the AFL has three more years to run. As each of those years arrives, the sponsor worth of an AFL game will increase and may even approach that of an NFL game, which will sell next season for $110,000 a sponsor minute, at 18 commercials a game. Maybe NBC made $10 million—oh call it $20 million—on the merger." The marriage between NBC and AFL/AFC clubs, wed in 1964 with Sonny Werblin as the justice of the peace, has successfully continued into the 1990s.

What was Al Davis's reaction to the terms of the merger? Two days before the agreement was announced, Davis told Billy Sullivan, "You abandoned me. You sold me out. We had it won and you gave it away. I was the general who won the war." He could have said the same thing to Hunt and Wilson, of course. It may be coincidental, but the relationship between Davis's Raiders and Sullivan's Patriots was especially stormy during the next two decades. Billy Sullivan was especially close to Valley and had little use for Davis after Valley sold his interest in the Raiders in 1976. Davis later claimed that the Raiders wanted to trade for Jim Plunkett in 1976 but Sullivan wouldn't talk to him. Plunkett was traded to San Francisco instead. In the playoff of 1976, with the help of a controversial roughing-the-passer penalty, the Raiders beat the now New England Patriots 24–21 in a hard-fought playoff game in Oakland. The Raiders then won the AFC Championship game and their first Super Bowl.

Two years later in a preseason game, a hard but clean hit by Raider safety Jack Tatum on Darryl Stingley of the Patriots left the New England receiver permanently paralyzed from the waist down. Not surprisingly, much controversy was to follow, especially over Tatum's alleged failure to visit Stingley in the hospital. And in 1986, after New England had knocked the Raiders out of the playoffs with a 27–20 victory in Los Angeles, Raider linebacker Matt Millen went charging after Pat Sullivan, Billy's son, who was heckling Howie Long from the New England bench. After the game, the tasteless Sullivan remarked that the New England victory was revenge for the Stingley incident.

But as usual, the last laugh belonged to Al Davis. Most football scouts agreed that the Patriots usually possessed the most talent in the NFL, but except for their dismal Super Bowl appearance in 1986 when they were massacred by the Chicago Bears, New England rarely produced a winner. When the Patriots finally won a division title in 1978, head coach Chuck Fairbanks left New England for a college job. However, the Patriots regularly led the league in contract holdouts. Mike Haynes, one of their best players, held out for much of the 1983 season. He was finally traded to the Raiders and helped the Silver and Black win Super Bowl XVIII. The relationship continued to sour when Sullivan testified against Davis during the trials of 1980. Davis returned the favor by testifying against Sullivan in a lawsuit brought against the Patriots by some season ticket holders in 1982. After nearly going bankrupt in 1988, the Sullivan family sold its majority interest in the Patriots to Remington Razor Company president Victor Kiam.

So was Al Davis instrumental in bringing about the merger? Definitely yes. The merger talks were hastened by the "signing all the veterans" tactic of the AFL commissioner. It must be remembered that the NFL was trying to put the AFL out of business in the early 1960s. An obvious example of this intention was the way the NFL added expansion teams. After admitting four members from the defunct All-American Conference in 1950, the NFL did not expand again until the AFL was formed. Applicants for new franchises like Hunt, Wilson, and Adams were regularly rejected. Not coincidentally, after the AFL was organized the NFL placed a team in Dallas to compete with Hunt's Texans and then located a franchise in Minnesota, which led to the AFL withdrawing its proposed team in the Twin Cities and later giving the franchise to Oakland. In 1965, the NFL awarded Atlanta a franchise to thwart the AFL, which was considering the Georgia capital. So the older league definitely was aware that the AFL was in its face.

Some of the terms that were accepted were particularly galling to Davis and other AFL partisans. Besides the indemnity payments forced upon Oakland and the New York Jets, it was decided that all future contracts for veteran NFL players that had been engineered by Al Davis were to be declared null and void. (However, the Pete Gogolak deal with the Giants was honored.) The NFL players who signed lucrative AFL contracts, such as John Brodie, threatened legal action and were eventually paid off. If Al Davis had been negotiating merger terms for the AFL, those contracts would have certainly been honored.

The complete amalgamation of the leagues is another term that enraged Davis. It could be argued that the AFL was playing more exciting football in 1966 than their NFL counterparts because passing-oriented teams are always more exciting than running clubs. So the personality and flavor unique to the AFL would eventually be lost. Led by Lombardi's Packers, the NFL was a running league, primarily playing "three yards and a cloud of dust" type football. The AFL was also moving into more modern stadiums than the senior league. In addition to New York and Oakland, San Diego opened a new

stadium, the Oilers were going to play in the Houston Astrodome, and Denver was expanding Mile High
Stadium.

In 1970, Al Davis did receive some revenge. During
endless meetings that were called to decide realignment
of the merged league, Davis's leadership held the 10 AFL
teams together (Cincinnati joined the league in 1968) as a
block. Eventually Baltimore, Cleveland, and Pittsburgh
combined with the 10 AFL clubs to form the American
Football Conference, which continues to this day. For
their "sacrifice," the Colts, Browns, and Steelers were
given $3,000,000 each to switch, rather than fight.

A common college player draft was another striking
feature of the merger agreement. That would end the
signing war and save everybody money. It would also ensure that in time, both leagues would be equal on the
field. This certainly would help some of the NFL weak
sisters, such as Pittsburgh and Washington, that were getting clobbered by the AFL teams in the battle for talent.
But despite the funds expended for signing players, all of
the AFL teams were now financially healthy. It appeared
that Oakland, New York, and Kansas City were developing superior teams in the signing wars. In fact the Chiefs,
Raiders, and Jets were the AFL representatives in the
first four Super Bowls. So it seemed that the AFL could
have continued without a common draft.

Al Davis was emphatically against a common draft. "A
common draft is the worst thing that could happen to our
league. We almost got twice as many draft choices as the
other league because we have 9 teams and they have 15;
we shouldn't lose that advantage." The common draft
didn't prevent the Raiders from acquiring talented
rookies. In the first two years after the merger, the Raiders selected offensive linemen Gene Upshaw and Art
Shell, who are now both in the Pro Football Hall of Fame.
Another jewel from the 1968 common draft was Alabama quarterback Ken Stabler.

In summary, the AFL really didn't need the merger under many of the terms given. But don't blame Al Davis. His tactics won the war, but Sullivan, Hunt, and Wilson and the owners of Miami, Denver, and San Diego (where a deal for Barron Hilton to sell out to Gene Klein was in the works) bungled the peace. Davis painfully learned that while he was a genuine football man who would sacrifice anything, including profits, in a battle to produce a quality team or league, most of the owners in both leagues had a different view of the world. They were more concerned with profitability than fielding winning teams. Look at the record. In the 20 seasons since the two leagues combined, the Raiders remain the only original American Football League team to win a Super Bowl. And they have done it three times. Denver has been embarrassingly chewed up and spit out four times in the championship game, and New England's only appearance was a similar disaster. Buffalo, San Diego, New York, Kansas City, and Houston have never made it since the merger. Not once.

Although you can bet that owners such as Ralph Wilson and the Hunt family were relentless in their pursuit of success in the business world, they were uneasy about the "take no prisoners" approach used by Al Davis to sign players in the football war. It caused uneasiness and mistrust that simmered over the next decade and finally exploded when the Raiders attempted to move to Los Angeles. So it was not surprising that two months after the merger was announced, Al Davis resigned as AFL commissioner and returned to the Oakland Raiders, not as coach and general manager but as managing general partner under a 10-year contract that gave him nearly total autonomy. Based on the book value of the Raiders in 1962, Al was able to buy a share of the team equal to what Wayne Valley and Ed McGah had. So for a grand total of $17,500, Al Davis was roughly a one-third owner in the Raiders. What was Valley's reaction to the return of his new partner? "We're glad to have Al back. We know Oakland agrees." The local press was equally ecstatic. George Ross of the *Oakland Tribune* summed it up: "His success, immediate and brilliant in football and in management from the outset, zoomed the franchise into an orbit of excitement." That orbit was to rise in altitude for the next decade as the Oakland Raiders were then to become the most consistent winner and colorful team in football.

Chapter 6

"I WANT TO BE THE MOST FEARED"

"Before the merger, it was a fight for survival. Now it's a relentless fight to be Number One. And any member of the Raider team who isn't in that fight, and doing his best to win it, doesn't belong in our organization."

—Al Davis, 1969

*B*efore accepting the position of AFL commissioner, Al Davis had been busy preparing the Raiders for the 1966 season. And beyond. The AFL draft provided defensive back Rodger Bird of Kentucky and halfback Pete Banaszak of Miami University, who once considered entering the priesthood. Although not particularly flashy or powerful, for 13 seasons the dependable Banaszak was always there when a key first down or touchdown was needed. He led the NFL with 16 touchdowns in 1975. His 47 career touchdowns rushing is topped only by Marcus Allen in the Raider record book.

An interesting draft pick was tight end Tom Mitchell of Bucknell, the Number Three selection. Mitchell was drafted by the Baltimore Colts in the NFL but signed with the Raiders. He played with Oakland in 1966 and caught 23 passes, including one for a touchdown. Mitchell was waived the following summer and then signed with Baltimore. He became an integral part of the Colts' 1968 Super Bowl team. During those halcyon days of the pro football war, it was common for many writers who followed the National League to derisively label players who are cut from the NFL and join the AFL as "NFL rejects." For AFL fans, the tables were finally turned; Mitchell was a genuine "AFL reject" who made good in the senior league.

The starting tight end for the 1966 Raiders was Billy Cannon, who was acquired from Houston in 1964 for draft choices. Davis had been patient for two years as the former Heisman Trophy winning halfback was learning the nuances of the tight end position. Over the next four seasons, the Raiders would be rewarded with excellent production from Cannon. Billy was also helping the Raiders recruit some of the 1966 draftees.

Two other good trades were also made. Completing an earlier deal with Buffalo that sent Bo Roberson to the Bills, the Raiders received guard George Flint and defensive tackle Tom Keating. Flint was cut in training camp, but Keating was a stalwart in the defensive line for the next seven seasons before being traded to Pittsburgh. With the emergence of Dan Conners as a middle linebacker, the Raiders traded Archie Matsos to Denver for tight end Hewritt Dixon. Davis converted the Florida A&M grad into a hard-driving fullback. Before the opening game, tackle Dave Costa was sent to Buffalo for Bill Laskey, a strong outside linebacker.

John Rauch succeeded Al Davis as head coach, and Scotty Stirling, who once was the beat writer of the Raiders for the *Oakland Tribune,* became the general manager. When he returned following the merger, Davis was complimentary about his successors: "John Rauch is a close friend of mine and I would not have taken this job (AFL commissioner) without a clear understanding that he is to remain as head coach of the Oakland Raider football team. I am equally impressed with Scotty Stirling over the months as general manager." With Al Davis really calling the shots, Stirling resigned following the 1967 season and would spend most of the next 20 years as a general manager for teams in professional basketball. Stirling is currently a scout for the NBA Sacramento Kings.

A new assistant coach was Bill Walsh, who had been an assistant at Stanford. Walsh spent only one year with the Raiders and then became head coach of a semi-pro team in 1967. After John Madden resigned as Oakland coach following the 1978 season, Walsh, who was then head coach at Stanford, was mentioned as a possible candidate for the Raider job. After telling friends he was not interested in working for Al Davis, Walsh accepted the vacant San Francisco head coaching position. Salivate over how things might have been if Walsh had joined the Raiders instead of the 49ers. Two "geniuses" on one team may have been one too many.

The 1966 Raiders matched the 1965 edition with an 8–5–1 record. Kansas City won the AFL West as the Chargers skidded to third place. Helping Miami launch their new franchise, the Raiders beat the Dolphins 23–14 in the Orange Bowl. Tom Flores found Art Powell and Mitchell for touchdowns in the third quarter to give Oakland the lead. A giant goose egg was laid in Houston in a 31–0 rout by the Oilers. George Blanda connected for two Houston touchdowns, and Cotton Davidson spent most of the evening running for his life.

After splitting the first two games on the road, the Raiders christened Oakland Coliseum with a 32–10 loss to the Chiefs. Three blocked kicks and two interceptions in the second half by the Chiefs made the difference. The only Raider touchdown was a 22-yard touchdown pass from Davidson to Clem Daniels. Attendance was 50,746. The Chargers then handed the Raiders their third straight defeat, 29–20. Rauch was criticized for not trying for a first down on a fourth-and-one and taking a field goal. San Diego then scored two touchdowns. Flores returned to form with three touchdown passes and 261 yards in a 21–10 decision over Miami. Powell, Biletnikoff, and Roger Hagberg were the touchdown scorers.

Two road wins were next. The Raiders avenged their earlier defeat by KC with a 34–13 trouncing of the Chiefs. Tom Flores threw a 75-yard touchdown to Cannon and a 76-yarder to Hewritt Dixon as part of a 301-yard afternoon. In New York, Flores led a late 83-yard, 11-play drive into the end zone. With two seconds to play, Dixon scored the decisive touchdown in a 24–21 upset. The Raiders were back in the Western Division race.

Patriot fullback Jim Nance shredded the Raider defense for 206 yards and two scores in a 24–21 loss at Boston. Daniels scored all three touchdowns for Oakland. Next were wins over Houston, San Diego, and Denver. On a muddy field, Flores connected with Biletnikoff for 78 yards on the third play of the game, and the Raiders never looked back in their 38–23 thumping of the Oilers. Against the Chargers in a 41–19 rout, Flores was brilliant early, and 219 yards were gained on the ground, mostly in the second half. Defensive back Kent McCloughan starred at Denver with two interceptions and Cannon had two long receptions. Raiders 17, Broncos 3.

The Raiders turned into a turkey in a Thanksgiving home game by committing four turnovers in a 31–10 loss to Buffalo. Fullback Wray Carlton scored twice as the Bills were headed toward the AFL Championship game. The loss virtually finished off Oakland's title chances for the 1966 season.

The following Saturday, Oakland settled for a 28–28 tie against Joe Namath and the Jets. Mike Eischeid was the goat, missing three field goals and shanking a punt that gave New York good field position for their tying touchdown. Dan Conners stole a Joe Namath pass for one Oakland score and Art Powell had two more for the Silver and Black. The Raiders closed with a 28–10 victory over the Broncos, which featured three more touchdown passes for Flores, who finished the season with a career high 24. "If we can just get off to a good start next year, there's no telling what may happen," lamented Rauch after the final game.

Daniels, Otto, and Grayson were again recognized for their solid play and were chosen on the official All-AFL team. Some other polls also included Wayne Hawkins and Kent McCloughan.

Davis had built well in his four years in Oakland, and the Raiders had reached title contention. The offensive line was young, they had good running backs and receivers, and the defense was solidifying. What they were lacking was a quarterback who could match up with Len Dawson and Joe Namath, who were the best signal callers in the league. Flores had a good year in 1966 but was immobile and seemed to get hurt easily when sacked. He was really not the long passer that Davis coveted. Davidson was a good veteran, who relied more on experience and guile than a strong arm. The Raiders had signed Roman Gabriel during the war between the leagues, but the contract was nullified in the merger. In the first common AFL/NFL draft, Bob Griese and Steve Spurrier, the two best college quarterbacks, were chosen within the first four picks, long before Oakland made its first selection.

Daryle Lamonica was a good but not great quarterback at Notre Dame. He was drafted by both Buffalo and Green Bay in 1963 and signed with the Bills. Jackie Kemp was the starting quarterback for Buffalo. Coach Lou Saban wanted Lamonica to play. What to do? Lamonica became the baseball equivalent of a relief pitcher, coming into ballgames in the fourth quarter, often regardless of the score. This combination helped the Bills win three division titles and two AFL Championships. Al Davis apparently saw more of a future for Lamonica than being Kemp's caddy in Buffalo. In March, the Raiders obtained Lamonica and wide receiver Glenn Bass. The price was high: quarterback Tom Flores, wide receiver Art Powell, and two draft choices. Because he wanted to be closer to his home in Toronto, it was Powell who requested a trade to Buffalo. Years later, Flores admitted that he drove past Oakland Coliseum with tears flowing down his cheeks on the day of the deal. Although both Powell and Flores were popular with Oakland fans, Davis realized that the Raiders could not advance into the upper echelons of pro football without a good young quarterback. The trade was a gamble, but Lamonica seemed to be the best prospect available. To replace Powell, the Raiders eventually signed free agent Warren Wells of Texas Southern. He had been cut by both the Detroit Lions and Kansas City Chiefs in the 1967 training camps. The fleet-footed and sure-handed Wells would eventually become one of the most feared receivers in the AFL.

In two other seemingly unimportant deals, the Raiders acquired two players who would someday find their way into the Pro Football Hall of Fame. Oakland and Denver made numerous trades in those days, with the Raiders usually being the benefactors. One of those trades gave the Raiders cornerback Willie Brown. For the next 12 seasons Willie Brown was a fixture in the Oakland secondary, and opposing quarterbacks usually directed their attack elsewhere.

In Houston, ancient quarterback and place kicker George Blanda had clearly worn out his welcome. After leading the Oilers to the first two AFL Championships, Blanda had become very inconsistent and the fans were yelling for some fresh blood. They got such memorable names as Jackie Lee, Pete Beathard and Don Trull. After Blanda was released by the Oilers, he was signed by the Raiders, mostly for field goals and extra points. Blanda would play with the Raiders through the 1975 season, when he was 48 years old. In 26 seasons as a professional, Blanda set career records for field goals and points scored that will never be broken. More about ol' George later.

And then there was the draft. From the red-shirt list of the previous year came wide receiver Rod Sherman of USC. Sherman spent 1967 with Oakland, went to Cincinnati in the 1968 expansion draft, but was reacquired in 1969 and gave the Raiders three more seasons. From the first common draft came Dwayne Benson of obscure Hamline College, who was a tough outside linebacker for five years. But the Number One pick was a jewel. Gene Upshaw had played offensive guard and tackle at Texas A&I. In head-to-head games against Kansas City, Chiefs defensive end Julius "Buck" Buchanan had destroyed the Raider blocking scheme and ate Oakland quarterbacks for lunch. The Raiders inserted Upshaw at left guard and ceased to worry about Buchanan or many other defensive lineman for the next 15 years. The durable Upshaw missed only one game in his entire career and also gave the Raiders superb leadership. Currently the president of the National Football League Players Association, Upshaw was admitted to the Pro Football Hall of Fame in 1987.

With Bill Walsh departing, the Raiders brought in two new assistants. John Polonchek was in charge of the backfield, and an obscure college assistant from San Diego State was hired by John Rauch to coach the linebackers. His name: John Madden.

So with the additions of Lamonica, Brown, Upshaw, Blanda, and Madden, how could this team miss? They didn't. The Raiders compiled a 1967 record of 13–1, the best in AFL history. They smothered Houston 40–7 in the championship game. The lone loss to the Jets was followed by 10 consecutive wins.

The Raiders got off to a fast start at home, destroying Denver 51–0. There were many heroes, including defensive back Warren Powers, who returned a Steve Tensi

pass 30 yards for a touchdown, and newly acquired Warren Wells, who caught a 50-yard touchdown pass from
Blanda. Rodger Bird returned nine punts for 143 yards
and the defense held the Denver offense to a net of five
yards. Boston was then humbled 35–7 as Daniels gained
95 yards and Lamonica scored the final touchdown on a
21-yard scamper. A key Lamonica-to-Cannon screen
pass in the fourth quarter broke the game open in a 23–
21 win over Kansas City.

The annual eastern swing started badly but ended
OK. It started with a 27–14 loss at New York before
63,106 on a Saturday night. Lamonica suffered four interceptions and the Jets accumulated 151 yards on the
ground. The defense was the story in a 24–20 win at Buffalo. Dan Conners and defensive back Howie Williams
had important interceptions of Jackie Kemp. A game in
Boston was broken wide open when a Dan Birdwell sack
of Patriot quarterback Babe Parilli caused a fumble that
was recovered by Willie Brown. Hagberg and Wells both
found the end zone twice as the Patriots were burned by a
48–14 count.

The next game was against undefeated San Diego at
the Coliseum before a record 53,474 fans. Dave Grayson,
subbing for the injured Willie Brown, intercepted three
John Hadl passes to turn a 16–10 Oakland lead into a
51–10 rout. "We're still in the race," said a brave Sid
Gillman after the carnage was complete. Clem Daniels
became the first AFL runner to gain 5,000 yards. Daniels
retired after the 1967 season and is now co-owner of a
sports bar in Oakland with former Kansas City defensive
end Marvin Upshaw, Gene's brother.

Denver, Miami, and Kansas City were the next three
victims. Eleven sacks of Bronco quarterbacks and two
Lamonica-to-Bill-Miller touchdowns made the difference in Denver. The Raiders struggled against Miami
until Bill Laskey recovered a fumble in the fourth quarter. Lamonica then hit Cannon with a 47-yard touch-

down, the third of the game for the tight end. In Kansas City, the Raiders reversed their 1966 Thanksgiving setback with a 44–22 beating of the Chiefs. Powers and Brown both stole Len Dawson passes for touchdowns. Subbing for an injured Daniels, Pete Banaszak gained 81 yards on 13 carries. Up next: a rematch in San Diego as the 9–1 Raiders would meet the 9–2 Chargers.

It was no contest. Lamonica threw four touchdown passes as the Raiders rolled over the Chargers again, 41–21. Larry Todd contributed a 62-yard run. A 19–7 win at Houston the following week clinched the AFL West title. Dixon swept 27 yards for the only touchdown and Blanda added four field goals. In the jubilant Raider locker room, Coach John Rauch and managing general partner Al Davis were both given a shower by the players. Fully clothed.

In a game punctuated by penalties and fighting, revenge was heaped upon the Jets by a 38–29 score. Linebacker J. R. Williamson made numerous big plays for the Raider defense, and Lamonica matched Namath with three touchdown passes. The regular season ended with a 28–21 win over the Bills. Defensive end Carleton Oats and Conners scored touchdowns for the defense, but it was a Hewritt Dixon run in the final three minutes that completed the thirteenth win of the season.

The Raiders were ready for their first AFL Championship game. Over the next 11 seasons, they would participate in nine AFL or AFC title games. They would lose seven times, but not on December 31, 1967.

The 1967 championship game against the Oilers started close and turned into a rout. After Blanda kicked a 37-yard field goal, Hewritt Dixon swept around left end 69 yards into the end zone for a 10–0 Oakland lead. In the closing seconds of the first half, the Raiders faked a field goal attempt. Lamonica, who was the holder for the play, fired a 17-yard touchdown pass to reserve tight end Dave Kocourek. The rout was on. Lamonica and end

Bill Miller both scored in the second half and Blanda added two more field goals. Final score: Oakland 40, Houston 7. It was quite a New Year's Eve celebration in Jack London Square.

Super Bowl II found the Oakland Raiders against Green Bay in what would be Vince Lombardi's final game as Packer coach. Three plays swung the contest toward the NFL. Leading 6–0 in the second quarter, Bart Starr found wide receiver Boyd Dowler all alone for a 62-yard touchdown completion. Lamonica answered with a 23-yard strike to Miller. But just before halftime, good Oakland field position was nullified by a Rodger Bird fumble of a punt which Green Bay recovered. Don Chandler kicked a 43-yard field goal for a 16–7 Packer halftime lead. Critical play Number three occurred in the third quarter. Starr faked a run on a third down and found the unguarded Max McGee with a pass at the Oakland two. Donny Anderson then ran into the end zone. Hall of Fame cornerback Herb Adderley later intercepted Lamonica and ran 60 yards for another six points. Another 23-yard touchdown pass from Lamonica to Miller completed the scoring.

Final score: Green Bay 33, Oakland 14. Sure it was disappointing, but the Raiders played a better game than Kansas City in Super Bowl I. With this young, multitalented team put together by Al Davis, many fans thought that Oakland would play in many more Super Bowls. But it would be nine seasons before they would return.

Nobody could deny the Raiders their 1967 post-season honors. Rauch was AFL Coach of the Year. Lamonica was Player of the Year. Cannon, Schuh, Upshaw, Jim Otto, Lamonica, Dixon, Keating, Ben Davidson, Conners, and McCloughan made one or more of the various All-League teams.

The 1968 college draft would be one of the most fruitful in Raider history. But the top pick, quarterback Eldridge Dickey, did not pan out. Controversy ensued among the Black Panthers in Oakland and various other radical groups in Berkeley when the Raiders tried to convert the black college quarterback to flankerback (wide receiver). In 1968, there were no starting black quarterbacks in the pros. Dickey played four seasons as a wide receiver but never was a starter.

Ralph "Chip" Oliver, a linebacker from USC, proved to be another unusual choice. Oliver was impressive on special teams and as a reserve and had won a starting position when he quit after two seasons to live in a commune. Really.

The Number Two pick was quarterback Ken Stabler of Alabama. A knee injury kept Stabler away in 1968. After prematurely retiring in 1969 and returning the following season, he was brought along slowly until he became the starter in 1973.

And the round 3 choice was an offensive left tackle. He won a starting job in 1970 and did not permanently relinquish his position until the Raiders were playing in Los Angeles. Art Shell played his college football at Maryland State, a small black school far from the beaten path on the eastern shore of Maryland. But the Raiders found him. Teamed with Upshaw, the left side of the Raider line became so hard to penetrate that defensive linemen would have better luck trying to shoot spitballs through a missile silo.

From the University of Utah came versatile running back Charlie Smith, who was adept both as a receiver and running back. Smith played seven seasons in Oakland.

George Atkinson was a defensive back out of Morris Brown College. He played cornerback in 1968, but was later to star at strong safety. Atkinson also returned kicks and punts in his 10 years with the Silver and Black. Following retirement, Atkinson settled in the Bay Area and now operates a real estate appraisal firm. He would become intimate friends with Lynn Swann of Pittsburgh, as we shall see later.

And how did the Raiders ever find their eleventh draft choice, fullback Marv Hubbard of Colgate, the college, not the toothpaste? Like Stabler, Hubbard sat out 1968 but replaced Dixon in the backfield in 1969. He gave the Raiders seven productive years, before being succeeded by Mark van Eeghen, another Colgate running back.

Entering the 1968 season, it was obvious that the three best AFL teams were playing in New York, Kansas City, and Oakland. The games between the three teams would be the most eagerly anticipated contests of the season. In 1968, the Raiders played five games against the Jets and Chiefs, all of them memorable.

The Raiders opened with four relatively easy wins, including three on the road. Buffalo, Miami, Houston, and Boston were the victims. In his first professional game, Atkinson ran wild as a punt returner, gaining 205 yards in a 48–6 annihilation at Buffalo. Buffalo punter Paul McGuire was often the only defender who could stop Atkinson. It was enough to put McGuire in the broadcast booth and also proved too much for Buffalo coach Joel Collier, who was fired after the pasting. The Raiders next accumulated 542 combined yards in a 47–21 rout at Miami. Lamonica gained 306 yards through the air in a first half punctuated by four touchdowns. Dixon gained 187 yards against the Oilers but his three fumbles kept the game close. But touchdowns by Wells and Cannon iced the 24–15 decision. A 41–10 trouncing of Boston featured a game-breaking 41-yard reverse run by Wells.

The only two losses of the season followed. San Diego upset the Raiders 23–14 at home and then the Chiefs burned Oakland 24–10 in KC. The Raiders couldn't stop Lance Alworth, who had nine receptions for the Chargers. Five Oakland turnovers didn't help. Kansas City used a full house backfield with two tight ends and the three running backs amassed 294 yards. Len Dawson attempted only three passes, completing two.

The Raiders won the last eight regular season games to finish 12–2. Led by the passing of Lamonica, they scored more than 30 points in 10 of their victories. In their first ever meeting with Cincinnati, the Raiders overcame bad officiating and an 87-yard run by rookie Paul Robinson to win 31–10. They rushed for 265 yards and had an overwhelming 26–8 advantage in first downs over the Bengals. The next visitor was the Chiefs and the Raiders avenged the earlier loss with a 38–21 win at the Coliseum. Oakland had a 38–7 lead in the third quarter and coasted to victory. Warren Wells, in a preview of things to come, burned Chiefs' cornerback Willie Mitchell for 11 receptions.

In the exciting 43–32 win over Joe Namath and the Jets, Charlie Smith scored a touchdown in the last 75 seconds to finally put Oakland in the lead of this seesaw battle. When the Jets fumbled the kickoff, Preston Ridlehuber recovered the ball in the end zone. Unfortunately, both of those scores came after 7 P.M. Eastern Standard Time, when NBC cut off the end of this game to show *Heidi,* a children's movie.

NBC should have preempted the dull rematch in Cincinnati the following week instead. The Raiders piled up 604 yards in a 34–0 rout. On Thanksgiving Day against Buffalo, George Atkinson was the hero. He scored the only touchdown with a 33-yard interception and then caused Bills quarterback Ed Rutkowski to fumble late in the game, setting up a field goal. Charlie Smith opened the scoring in a 33–27 decision over the Broncos, but the defense starred with four interceptions of Denver quarterback Marlin Briscoe. And at San Diego, Lamonica connected for three touchdowns and Rodger Bird intercepted John Hadl for a touchdown.

The 34–27 win over the Chargers gave the Oakland Raiders a 12–2 record, but the Chiefs also finished at 12–2, which necessitated a special playoff game. Having teams with the same record decide a title race by a playoff game is the better way to settle ties, rather than the complicated formulas of division records, conference records, common opponents, number of cheerleaders, etc., that the NFL instituted after the merger. The television networks, who seemingly make up their schedules 20 years in advance, wouldn't like the idea of unscheduled playoff games, but the fans would love it. Wonder who runs this country anyway?

The Chiefs had a powerhouse team in 1968 but they were weak at one position. And Lamonica knew where it was from the earlier meeting at the Coliseum. Once again, left cornerback Willie Mitchell was picked clean by Lamonica in a 41–6 Oakland triumph. The Mad Bomber fired five touchdown passes, three to Biletnikoff and two to Warren Wells, to send the Chiefs home for the winter.

The following Sunday it was the Raiders at Shea Stadium against the Jets for the AFL championship. Lamonica amassed 401 yards through the air, but George Atkinson was unable to defend effectively against wide receiver Don Maynard, who caught two touchdown passes from Joe Namath. Late in the game, New York linebacker Ralph Baker recovered an errant lateral pass from Lamonica to ensure the 27–23 Jets win.

A few weeks later, Rauch unexpectedly resigned as head coach of the Raiders to assume the same position with the Buffalo Bills. "I really wasn't surprised. . . . I can't blame anyone for trying to branch out," was Davis's response to the media. But why would anyone leave a team like Oakland that had a 12–2 record for a 2–11–1 mess in Buffalo? "A conflict between Davis and Rauch was the apparent reason for John's desire to switch to the Bills," reported Bob Valli in the *Oakland Tribune*. No foolin', Bob!

Valli was right. With Scotty Stirling gone, Al was the obvious general manager and was also sort of a coach emeritus. The specter of Al was always present, and Rauch was peeved over the lack of recognition for his coaching. But at least Rauch was a winner at 35–10–1 for his three seasons. Twenty years later and with a lesser record, Mike Shanahan was beset by many of the same problems. He should have consulted with Rauch.

The press reported the situation but declined to take sides. "As his [Davis's] employee, you do things his way or no way," said Ed Levitt of the *Tribune*. "Who is right and who is wrong? In this case perhaps it isn't a situation where someone is right or wrong. Al Davis is handling the Raiders the only way he knows how. And that has proven to be just about the most successful system in football."

After two terrible seasons in Buffalo, Rauch probably wished he were still toiling for Al Davis back in Oakland. Despite the presence of blue-chip rookie O. J. Simpson, the Bills had a combined 7–20–1 record in 1969 and 1970. Rauch was fired and replaced by Harvey Johnson, the same man he replaced.

On February 4, 1969, Al Davis surprisingly chose John Madden, his 33-year-old linebacker coach, to succeed Rauch. Davis was asked why he picked an unknown field general. "So were Don Shula, Weeb Ewbank and Vince Lombardi unknowns when they got their first head coaching job . . . The big thing in coaching is not the name. The big thing is winning. John Madden has a fine football mind. I think he'll do an outstanding job."

Madden proved to be a great choice by Al Davis. The players loved big John and the team kept winning. The image of his arms flailing from his huge shoulders along the sidelines as Madden screamed at referees quickly became a familiar sight in saloons and living rooms across America.

The 1969 cast of characters inherited by Madden was similar to the previous model. Only the Number One draft pick, Art Thoms, defensive tackle from Syracuse and the second choice, offensive guard George Buehler of Stanford, would prove to be of much help. Thoms was a regular contributor until a 1976 injury knocked him out of the starting lineup and ended his career. Buehler became the starting right guard in 1971 and basically stayed there until being traded to Cleveland in 1979. Thoms and Buehler have good reasons to be close friends. Both Thoms and Buehler now jointly operate five laundromats in Hayward, California. And the women they married are sisters.

It was difficult for many rookies to make the Oakland roster. The Raiders of 1969 were a collection of talented young veterans who would compile a flashy 12–1–1 record for the rookie head coach.

The season began with two close victories at home against Houston and Miami. Lamonica found Wells for a 64-yard score that won a 21–17 encounter with the Oilers. Blanda won the Miami game with a 47-yard field goal in the final 10 seconds. Dave Grayson helped beat the Dolphins with a 68-yard touchdown interception. Against the Patriots, a 13–0 deficit was converted into a 38–23 victory at Boston when Lamonica threw four touchdown passes. In week four, the stubborn Dolphins tied the Raiders 20–20. A brilliant interception by linebacker Bill Laskey set up the tying Oakland touchdown. The defense sacked Bob Griese six times. With his two field goals and two extra points, George Blanda set an AFL record by scoring in 46 consecutive games.

A 24–14 win at cold and snowy Denver was cinched on a two-yard touchdown reception by Billy Cannon. The Raiders then crushed Rauch's Bills 50–21 before 54,418 at the Coliseum. Two items of significance: Lamonica fired six touchdown passes in the first half, and the sell-out started a string of SRO crowds that continued into 1980, when Al Davis already had his telescope aimed at Los Angeles.

Lamonica came out of a sickbed at San Diego to add three more touchdown passes to his total. Dave Grayson had three interceptions to tie for the AFL career record. In Cincinnati, the Raiders quickly fell behind 31–3 and were upset 31–17. Rookie quarterback Greg Cook threw two TD passes for the Bengals, who stopped the Oakland 15-game unbeaten streak. Not to worry. The Raiders rebounded with a 41–10 beating of Denver. The rout was on when a 53-yard touchdown pass to Biletnikoff erased a 7–7 tie. A dull game with San Diego was won on an 81-yard Lamonica-to-Wells pass. Dan Conners stole the football out of the hands of Charger tight end Willie Frazier and rambled 25 yards into the end zone. Conners then scored another touchdown in Kansas City, and Dave Grayson pilfered two Dawson passes to set a career AFL mark as Oakland won, 27–24.

A penalty-marred 27–14 win at New York in their only 1969 meeting against the Jets was followed by a 37–17 victory over Cincinnati. Lamonica outgunned Joe Namath by hitting Wells for two more touchdowns. The win over Cincinnati was accentuated by 309 yards rushing. In the season finale against the Chiefs, both teams played it cautiously. A Charlie Smith eight-yard run was the only touchdown as the Raiders won 10–6. Booming Mike Eischeid punts continually gave the Chiefs poor field position. Both teams stuck to the ground as Dawson attempted a mere six passes. The win gave the 12–1–1 Oakland Raiders the title over the 11–3 Kansas City Chiefs.

In 1969, Commissioner Pete Rozelle changed the playoff scheme in the AFL. The Raiders met the Houston Oilers, the second place team in the AFL East, while the New York Jets, winners in the East, entertained Kansas City. At 6–6–2, the Oilers were hardly a playoff team. The result was predictable: The Raiders overwhelmed Houston 56–7. The game was over very early: Lamonica threw three touchdown passes in the first period, and George Atkinson intercepted a Pete Beathard pass for another score. Rod Sherman, who was injured during the regular season, celebrated his return to action by catching two touchdown passes. The 56 points in one game is still a team record. In New York, the Chiefs upset the Jets, so Kansas City and Oakland would meet for a third time to decide the AFL champion and representative for Super Bowl IV.

The Raiders should have saved some of their points from the Houston game in a cookie jar for the following Sunday. The visiting Chiefs beat the Raiders 17–7. For Raider fans, this was known as "the Aaron Brown game." Lamonica injured his passing hand when it hit the helmet of the Chiefs defensive end in the second quarter. Neither Lamonica nor his replacement Blanda was effective, and the Chiefs had four sacks of the Oakland quarterbacks.

For the Raiders, it was another disappointing finish to what had been a great regular season. Lamonica was again named Most Valuable Player and was among ten Raiders on the final All-AFL team. There would be a few more heartbreaks along the way before the Oakland Raiders would conquer all.

1970 was the first year of a merged NFL. No more AFL, no more two-point conversions. It was the beginning of "Monday Night Football" and overhyped Super Bowls. Pittsburgh, Cleveland, and Baltimore moved into the newly-named American Football Conference. Cincinnati, which played in the AFL Western Division in 1968 and 1969, joined Houston, Cleveland, and Pittsburgh in the AFC Central, so the AFC West was reduced to four originals: Oakland, Kansas City, Denver, and San Diego.

Despite the win of two previous Super Bowls, 1970 was not a memorable season for the AFL representatives. In interleague play, the NFC drubbed the AFC 27–12–1. The Raiders were the only original AFL team to make the playoffs, and Baltimore, an old NFL club, won the AFC Championship and the Super Bowl. Of the original eight teams, the Raiders' 8–4–2 mark was the best record. Kansas City was 7–5–2 and none of the other six AFL brethren won more than five games.

With the Raiders a contending team, Al Davis's job was simple: To maintain the "commitment to excellence," gradually replace aging players by bringing in quality talent to keep the Raiders in contention. Don't permit more than one area of the team to get too old at the same time. Draft choices from the first two or three rounds should eventually become starters. For the next 16 seasons, that formula worked to perfection as the Raiders constantly stayed in title contention.

The Raiders' first draft pick of 1970 was another plum, again taken from a small black school. Morgan State College in Baltimore was the alma mater of tight end Raymond Chester. He quickly became a starter and gave the Raiders a solid pass catching and blocking tight end. Chester was All-AFC in 1971 and 1972 before being traded to the Colts for defensive end Bubba Smith. It was not one of Al Davis's better trades. Smith was over the hill and contributed little to Oakland. Al atoned for his trading error by reacquiring Chester in 1978. Ray was the starting tight end on the Super Bowl XV team.

Defensive help from the 1970 draft was supplied by defensive end Tony Cline and linebacker Gerald Irons. Defensive back Jimmy Warren was obtained from Miami. George Atkinson was moved to safety and Nemiah Wilson played cornerback opposite Willie Brown.

The opening game of the 1970 season was a 31–21 loss at Cincinnati. Reserve quarterback Sam Wyche was in charge of the Bengals' passing attack, and the current Cincinnati coach probably played his best game as a pro. Jess Phillips, who would later play for Oakland, had a 78-yard touchdown run which counteracted a 63-yard punt return by the Raiders' Alvin Wyatt. At San Diego, the Raiders couldn't hold a 27–13 fourth quarter advantage and settled for a tie when George Blanda missed a 32-yard field goal with nine seconds to go. A 20–14 Saturday night loss in Miami was a strange game; the Raiders made 183 yards rushing and the Dolphins could garner only seven first downs. But Bob Griese connected with newly acquired Paul Warfield for two touchdowns as torrential rains made the field conditions treacherous. After three games, the Raiders could only show two losses and a tie. The long-term outlook for the 1970 season was looking disastrous. Were the Raiders an overrated AFL team that would get its comeuppance in the National Football League?

No way. The Raiders rebounded with a vengeance, going undefeated in the next seven games. Lamonica regained his AFL form in Denver, firing four touchdown passes in a 35–23 triumph. Then the Raiders met the Washington Redskins, their first time on "Monday Night Football." Lamonica eclipsed Sonny Jurgensen with three more touchdown tosses in a 34–20 victory. Dixon rushed for 164 yards and Charlie Smith added 61. The Raiders won 31–14 the following week when Blanda replaced an injured Lamonica and peppered Pittsburgh with three touchdown passes. The game was the start of a run of five memorable games for the veteran quarterback and place kicker.

The Raiders next traveled to Kansas City for the first of their two annual grudge matches against the Chiefs. Rookie Raymond Chester snagged two touchdown passes, but Blanda kicked a 48-yard field goal on the last play of the game to salvage a 17–17 tie. But the game was more memorable for a sequence that occurred late in the game. On a third down play, Chiefs quarterback Len Dawson scrambled to a first down that could have put the game away for Kansas City. Raider defensive end Ben Davidson hit Dawson after the whistle had blown. As the referee was about to assess the Raiders an unsportsman-like conduct penalty, Chiefs receiver Otis Taylor jumped on top of Davidson and a brawl ensued. Taylor was thrown out of the game but no penalty was called against Kansas City. John Madden and defensive captain Dan Conners argued and convinced the officials that a penalty would have to be called on the Chiefs if Taylor was ejected. The result was offsetting penalties for unsportsmanlike conduct, which nullified the gain by Dawson. The third down play would have to be repeated. Kansas City coach Hank Stram was furious. The Chiefs were then stopped on third down and had to punt, which led to Blanda's tying field goal. The following season, a rule change was made which would have allowed Dawson's scramble for a first down. But not in 1970.

At home against Cleveland with the Raiders behind 20–13 late in the fourth quarter, Blanda passed the Raiders into a tie with a 14-yard touchdown toss to Wells. An interception by McCloughan then gave the Raiders the ball at midfield, and after a short pass from Blanda to Dixon, there were only seven seconds left. Ol' George did it again: a 52-yard field goal for a 23–20 win. Raider announcer Bill King, who judged the odds of a successful Blanda kick to be "76 million to one-half," proclaimed Blanda as "king of the world." The difference in a 24–19 victory at Denver was a Blanda-to-Biletnikoff pass, and his toe provided the winning margin in a tight 20–17 decision over San Diego. A clutch interception by Bill Laskey set it up for George.

On Thanksgiving Day in Tiger Stadium, two early Lamonica-to-Biletnikoff connections gave the Raiders a 14–0 lead, but the inspired Lions prevailed 28–14. Another miracle finish occurred the following week in the cold of Shea Stadium. With the Raiders trailing the Jets 13–7, Willie Brown intercepted quarterback Al Woodall at the New York 33. With eight seconds remaining, Lamonica was forced to try a "Hail Mary" pass. He threw it into the New York end zone where Warren Wells was covered by two defenders. The Jets foolishly tried for an interception. Wells somehow stole the ball away for a 14–13 win.

A 20–6 decision over Kansas City gave the Raiders the title at 8–3–2. Defensive end Tony Cline made life miserable for Len Dawson. A Lamonica-to-Biletnikoff touchdown clinched the contest. The final game was against San Francisco. The 49ers needed the game to win their first ever division title. The game was a sellout, but Al Davis refused to lift the television blackout in the Bay Area, which in those days was in effect for all home games in the NFL. The blackout policy would be changed in 1973. Earlier in the 1970 season, the New York Jets removed the blackout for their game against the Giants. Bay Area football fans would have no such luck.

Perhaps the football gods punished Al Davis and the Raiders for the blackout. It was a cold, rainy day in Oakland and the Raider performance matched the elements. The 49ers crushed the Silver and Black 38–7 in this meaningless game for Oakland as Lamonica, Blanda, and young Stabler were all ineffective.

Post-season game Number one found the Raiders at home against the upstart Miami Dolphins who were the "wild card" team under the new playoff format. The Dolphins won the last six games under new coach Don Shula to finish at 10–4. It was a muddy field in Oakland and the defenses dominated. An 82-yard touchdown pass from Lamonica to Rod Sherman was the pivotal play as Oakland beat Miami, 21–14. Willie Brown also contributed by returning an errant Bob Griese pass into the end zone.

The 1970 AFC championship game was the old versus the new: The Baltimore Colts, owned by Carroll Rosenbloom, against the Oakland Raiders, managed by the younger Al Davis. The 34-year-old John Madden was opposed by the much older Don McCafferty. It was Johnny Unitas against Daryle Lamonica and a veteran defense of Baltimore playing against the young offensive line of the Raiders.

The old guys carried the day. Baltimore defensive end Bubba Smith knocked Lamonica out of the game, but Blanda was unable to pull off another miracle. A Unitas touchdown pass to Ray Perkins broke open a tight game and the Colts prevailed 27–17. While Baltimore went on to win its only Super Bowl, Oakland had lost its third straight AFL/AFC championship game.

Chapter 7

WAYNE VALLEY, THE CRIMINAL ELEMENT, AND OTHER ASSORTED AL DAVIS BEDTIME STORIES

"[Davis] is like his team: tough, aggressive, somewhat ruthless, fearless, crafty, unpredictable. No man to get into a card game with on a boat. Or a fight in a dark alley."
—*Jim Murray,* Los Angeles Times

During the trial that decided the Raiders' move to Los Angeles, Al Davis said that he had a boyhood dream to own a pro football team. Apparently Wayne Valley was unaware of such a goal.

When he returned to the Raiders as managing general partner in 1966, Al Davis was legally given the right to call most of the shots for the Raiders, both on and off the field. Only the team budget was exempt from his perusal and approval. Davis had become an equal partner to Valley and McGah, but there was no question of who was *really* in charge. The general partnership rules allowed a positive vote of two out of the three major owners to decide matters. If things got sticky, the inactive and aloof McGah could be counted on to side with Davis. The year 1966 began a 10-year process that would eventually see Davis rid himself of Valley and become the most dominant and feared owner in team sports.

Al Davis had exhibited a lack of respect for Wayne Valley from the beginning. Viewing the Oakland fiasco of 1960–62 from San Diego, Al perceived that the Raider owners didn't have the foggiest notion of what professional football was all about. Davis was not impressed with either Valley or McGah during the interview process in early 1963. Although he was less than enamored of his new bosses, Davis kept his mouth shut and took the job because of the challenge.

Al Davis is a quick study, and knew that McGah was basically a silent partner. If he would ever ascend to the total management of the Oakland Raiders, he would first have to topple Wayne Valley. In 1966, he set out toward that goal.

Wayne Valley was later to say that the Al Davis who returned home from the pro football wars was not the same person who was coach and general manager. When Davis became managing general partner, he started keeping his distance from Valley. There has also been talk that Valley was slow in using his influence to have Warren Wells released from prison in 1971. Wells missed the entire season, the only one in an 11-year span that the Raiders missed the playoffs. Racism (Wells is black) was inferred. By the end of 1971, there was definitely a coolness between Valley and Davis, and two distinct factions were developing at Camp Silver and Black.

In July 1972, Al signed a new 20-year contract that gave him total control of all Raider decisions, which would ultimately include where the team should be located. In addition to his profits gained from a 16% ownership in the Raiders, Davis was also to be paid $100,000 a year. Ed McGah, who owned 23% of the Raiders, closed the deal with Al while Valley was attending the Summer Olympic games in West Germany. It was later alleged that neither Davis nor McGah bothered to tell Wayne Valley or anyone else in the organization about the contract. They certainly did not have Valley review, discuss, or sign it. In December 1972, Douglas Sargent, Valley's auditor and a Raider limited partner, discovered the contract during a routine inspection of the financial books. Valley was furious. He was basically told by Davis to like it or lump it. In 1973, Valley dumped the problem in the lap of Commissioner Pete Rozelle, who declined to become involved. During the meeting with the commissioner, Valley is alleged to have told McGah, "You never signed a fucking contract in your life." The next step for Valley was to go to court to break the deal. Valley was blunt when he announced his lawsuit to the media: "I want Al Davis out of this organization because he's not fit to live with."

The trial began in May 1975 and included an interesting array of witnesses. John Madden, George Allen, and Philadelphia owner Leonard Tose were among the advocates for Davis. It was disclosed in testimony that the Rams, Eagles, and Houston Oilers had all made employment offers to entice Al to leave Oakland. That was the excuse for Davis to talk McGah into a new agreement.

If Al and his friends were playing hardball during the trial, so was Valley. On June 1, 1975, the *Oakland Tribune* broke a story that Al Davis was a business partner of Las Vegas casino owner Alan Glick, who was being investigated by the federal government for a possible link to organized crime. Although Al shared an interest in an Oakland shopping mall with him, Glick's association with the mob was later proven to be more accidental than deliberate. "He [Davis] is extremely reluctant to discuss his business affairs with anyone," said a team representative. The feeling around Oakland was that Al should have known better than to become involved with Glick. Although he may have been dreaming of Al Davis going to jail, Pete Rozelle declined comment.

The timing of the story suggested that the hand of Valley had to be involved. As a millionaire home builder, Wayne was still regarded as somewhat of a hero in the East Bay. Although the Raiders were winning, Davis with his Brooklyn accent was still considered someone who could not be trusted. *Tribune* sports editor George Ross denied that the timing of the story was related to the trial. But it did seem mighty suspicious.

Fortunately for Al Davis, the Alan Glick story had no bearing on the trial. Much of the testimony seemed to suggest that there were enough hints dropped to Valley about the contract that he should have known what was coming. In October 1975 the judge upheld the validity of the contract but threw out the expanded powers portion of the agreement.

Knowing that he had not legally rid the Raiders of Al Davis, Wayne Valley sold his stock back to the partnership in February 1976. Al Davis's share of the Raiders was now estimated at 25.65%: 19.5% general and 6.15% limited holdings. Douglas Sargent, who was brought aboard by Valley in 1960, wisely held on to his share. When Sargent died, his holdings were passed on to his colorful wife, Gladys.

The bylaws of the Raiders franchise always gave the existing partners the opportunity to buy any stock that became available when a partner either sold out or died. So the original roster of 37 general and limited partners has gradually been reduced. When Ed McGah died in 1983, most of his limited partnership holdings were snapped up by the other partners. The remainder was passed on to his son. Today there are seven limited partners with you-know-who the remaining general partner. In fact, Al's formal title is president of the general partner. Ironically, limited partner Jack Brooks, who has spent much of 1989 and 1990 negotiating to return the team to Oakland, was originally brought on board by Valley.

Wayne Valley was out of the ownership scheme but would later come back to haunt Al Davis again. Both living and dead. When Valley tried to buy the San Francisco 49ers in 1977, Al Davis convinced Franklin Muelli, who was handling negotiations, to delay the sale. It was postponed and Valley eventually lost interest. The following year Al Davis received a finder's fee for helping Eddie DeBartolo, Jr., buy the 49ers. In January 1980, when the Raiders were teetering between Oakland and Los Angeles, Valley was mentioned as a buyer of the bankrupt Oakland Athletics baseball team. The thought of sharing the Oakland Coliseum with his former boss was probably enough to push Davis to Los Angeles. Also, Jack Maltester, who was president of the Oakland Coliseum Board during that turbulent period in 1980, had once been a political lobbyist for Valley. The acrimony between Maltester and Davis helped grease the skids for Davis's departure from Oakland.

Valley died in 1985. Family members were pleased when Mrs. Al Davis attended the funeral. Valley's will may have contained a hint at getting even with Al Davis. Whether it was civic-mindedness or that Valley sensed Al Davis may have wanted to return to Oakland will never be known. But part of the Valley estate was allocated to help procure an expansion team for Oakland. When Raider interests put out feelers about returning to the East Bay in 1988, Oakland Coliseum officials were not originally interested. They were more committed to expansion. Public pressure from Raider fans eventually forced Coliseum president George Vukasin to start negotiations with Al Davis.

The name of Ed McGah is shown as "In Memoriam" within the list of partners that is printed in the annual Raider media guide. And in the Historical Highlights section of said guide, there is no mention of the original owner. He may not have been a great football man, but if not for his presence or his money, there would never have been an Oakland/Los Angeles Raiders team today.

And the bitterness lingers on the other side too. In a 1989 interview, Gladys Valley, the widow of the former owner, could not hide the lingering resentment toward Davis. "We were not forced out. We sold the team because he [Davis] is too disgusting to work with."

*   *   *

Did you know that Al Davis once was interested in owning a baseball team?

The twelve years that Charles O. Finley owned the Oakland A's were filled with acrimony, confrontation, and mostly empty seats. Following the advent of free agency in baseball, Finley lost many of his star players. Attendance in Oakland, which was never overwhelming during the championship years, plummeted during the latter part of the 1970s. Finley was looking to get out. Furniture store owner Sam Bercovich, a good friend of Davis, was being mentioned as a possible buyer of the Athletics. Al Davis would come on board as a "consultant."

It was a good newspaper story but it never came to pass. The NFL had a rule that forbade their owners from holding a financial interest in other sports franchises. Perhaps already eyeing Los Angeles, Davis probably didn't want to go to the mat with Rozelle over the Oakland A's. There would soon be bigger fish to fry.

What if Al Davis had become a part owner of the Athletics? It is interesting to speculate on how Davis would have reacted as an owner to some of the bigger issues of recent years. For example, would Al have consented to the "collusion" of salaries among the owners that was later found to be illegal? Would Davis have abided by the "voluntary" 24-man roster when 25 was allowable? And what would have been the reaction of Bay Area fans if the

Raiders had moved to Los Angeles and the A's stayed in Oakland with Davis as owner? Interesting food for thought.

*   *   *

As many people know, the Raiders do not belong to NFL Charities with the other teams. Al Davis takes his $\frac{1}{28}$ share of the proceeds and distributes the money to many worthy causes. It is also known that Al has quietly paid medical bills of many former players and employees who can't afford it.

The Raiders have always gone far beyond the $\frac{1}{28}$ obligation. An example of this generosity is an annual golf tournament at the Riviera Country Club in Los Angeles that is cosponsored by the Raiders and the Boy Scouts of America. The tournament helps handicapped boy scouts. From 1983 to 1990, the joint effort has raised more than $1,000,000. Current players and former Raiders also participate in many charitable basketball games and autograph sessions in both Northern and Southern California for charitable causes.

Al Davis visited the late Tony Conigliaro in the hospital after he suffered a massive heart attack. He tried to encourage the baseball star by relating the courage of Carole Davis, who had a similar heart attack. And Al tried to save the late sports columnist Wells Twombly, who needed a liver transplant to survive. When former 49er defensive end Bob Hoskins died, the family couldn't afford to transport the body home for the funeral. Al Davis paid the freight.

There are many more similar stories of the Davis generosity, but they are buried within the immediate family or the Raider organization and shall stay there. It is a reminder that a man who has been widely characterized as greedy by his critics is probably one of the most generous owners in sports, and his players also share in the unselfishness.

*   *   *

The following is for those who have just graduated and are entering the working world and are asking the proverbial question: What is it like to work for Al Davis? "He wants your loyalty and he wants disciples," said a friend. Obviously, Al LoCasale and Ron Wolf, as evidenced by their longevity, have fulfilled the requirements. Others such as Scotty Stirling and Wayne Valley could not adhere to the Davis way of living. Friendships with Al Davis are based on respect and are not close. "Al is not a warm human being," said a sportswriter. If Al is working late at night, his staff hangs around, just in case.

Keep sending those resumés to the Raider offices in El Segundo, California.

*   *   *

How did Al Davis ever become entangled in the lawsuit of the United States Football League against the NFL? When the USFL filed its antitrust suit in 1984, it named the other 27 teams as the perpetrators. Because the Raiders had filed and won a similar suit against the NFL in Los Angeles, they were omitted from the USFL suit.

But many of his fellow owners were peeved when Davis testified at the trial against the NFL and described secret meetings that discussed strategy for handling the USFL presence. The reporters covering the trial in New York were kept busy; Davis and Howard Cosell took the witness stand on the same day.

When Al Davis recommended that the NFL merge with the World Football League in 1975, he was dismissed as an eccentric. Ditto the USFL in the 1980s. Davis has also long advocated the formation of a spring football league that would serve the NFL as a farm system and also develop new markets for future expansion. Well, lo and behold, the NFL has now formed a new World

League of American Football, which includes teams in Europe and the United States. Al Davis is a member of the Board of Directors of the WLAF.

It is never too late to teach the new dogs old tricks.

*   *   *

Then there was the "criminal element" story. The Raiders opened the 1976 season against their hated rivals the Pittsburgh Steelers. It was a hard-hitting, typically tough Raiders-Steelers game. The Raiders rallied for 17 points in the final three minutes for a 31–28 victory.

After the game, both Jack Tatum and George Atkinson of the Raiders were accused of taking cheap shots at Pittsburgh wide receiver Lynn Swann. Repeated television slow-motion replays turned an Atkinson hit on Swann into a violent scene from "Miami Vice." The headline "Swann Fears for His Life" appeared in newspaper descriptions about the game. In the Steelers' dressing room, coach Chuck Noll reported that "Swann got hit several times with forearms and elbows. It's a shame something like that clouds Oakland's performance." When the Steelers returned to Pittsburgh, Noll was more blunt. "You have a criminal element in all aspects of society . . . We presently have it in the NFL too. Maybe we have a law and order problem. It's been going on for a long time, last year's playoff game and before that. . . . You can defend yourself head-on, but not when it's with intent to maim."

As the story was unfolding, the Raiders were stunned by Noll's allegations. Wasn't Noll aware that Steeler cornerback Mel Blount ferociously slammed Raider wide receiver Cliff Branch into the Coliseum turf in the game? Nobody on the Raiders complained. In his first book, Tatum wrote, "Maybe we were [criminals], but the only difference between the Raiders and Steelers of the '70s was the color of the uniforms. The Steelers punched, kicked and gouged every inch of turf and so did the Raiders and make no mistake about it, when the Championship games begin, the nice guys and true sportsmen of football are usually on vacation."

Of course, Al Davis's dander was also being raised. "No one was killed. Why get excited?" he told Ed Levitt of the *Oakland Tribune.* Davis then decided that the press was to blame. "You guys are the problem. You want us to win. You want us to be tough. But when we're in a vicious game with the Steelers, a team that is notorious for busting up opponents, you seize on an incident involving one of our men and you hammer away. Do you realize what would happen now if we went back to Pittsburgh for one more game?"

Later that week, the commissioner fined Atkinson $1,500 and Tatum $750. Noll was fined $1,000. Steeler president Dan Rooney was furious that the penalty levied against the Oakland players wasn't more severe. The whole incident quickly mushroomed into a Steelers versus Raiders controversy. More specifically, it was Al Davis against the NFL establishment of Dan Rooney and Pete Rozelle.

George Atkinson soon hired flamboyant California State Assemblyman Willie Brown to represent him and subsequently filed suit against Chuck Noll. They were asking for $2,000,000 for damages from the "slanderous" comments.

"Criminal element" was an odious comment for Atkinson, who had been previously accused of embezzlement and larceny. He was acquitted of all charges. But the stigma remained.

Dan Rooney, probably after conferring with Rozelle, turned down a recommended settlement of $50,000 to Atkinson. They wanted to teach the Oakland Raiders a lesson.

The trial lasted a week. Noll was forced to admit that he had a "criminal" on his team: cornerback Mel Blount.

The lawyer representing Noll interjected Atkinson's prior arrests into the proceedings. Rozelle and Rooney took the stand on July 19. Next day, NFL supervisor of officials Art McNally testified that Atkinson's blow was deliberate. Commissioner Rozelle, retired referee Norm Schacter, former Steeler Andy Russell, and quarterback Terry Bradshaw all testified on behalf of Coach Noll. Bradshaw pointed out that "Atkinson's reputation is not exactly clean. I guess the word is dirty."

After deliberating for only four hours on July 23, 1977, the judge found Chuck Noll innocent of the charges. Al Davis had no comment.

Rozelle did punish Al for the indiscretion. He removed Davis from the NFL Competition Committee, the most prestigious extracurricular assignment in the league and a natural for football people like Davis. It would be 11 years before Rozelle would ask Al Davis to perform any other league service. And speaking of the commissioner . . .

*   *   *

Many of his detractors have claimed that Davis harbored a strong dislike of Rozelle, which originated in the early 1950s when Al was coaching at Fort Belvoir and Rozelle was the public relations director for the Los Angeles Rams. It was his disdain for Rozelle, they claim, that really fueled the feud of the two men when the Raiders attempted to move to Los Angeles.

That is not exactly true.

Sure, Al was upset when he was left out in the cold after the two leagues merged. Al was obviously peeved when Rozelle became commissioner of an enlarged NFL and Al returned to Oakland. And there was some resentment of Rozelle, mostly because Pete was involved in the merger talks and Al was not. But Davis really knew that the AFL owners who negotiated the merger were at fault, not Rozelle. The disdain was not personal. It was Rozelle, not Davis, who brought it to a personal level during the court trials.

Al has two sides. There is a business Davis and a personal Davis, and really, the twain rarely meet. Art Modell, the owner of the Cleveland Browns, has often disagreed with Davis at league meetings, especially when the Raiders tried to move from Oakland. But when Modell suffered a heart attack in Los Angeles, Davis was among the first to arrive at the hospital. It was not a publicity stunt. The "criminal element" episode certainly left bad feelings in Pittsburgh, but Al Davis was sitting in the first row at owner Art Rooney's funeral. There was never a great deal of love between Al Davis and Miami owner Joe Robbie, but again Al was there for the funeral. When he heard that Gene Klein died on March 12, 1990, a distraught Al Davis called Howard Neal, general manager at KFI radio in Los Angeles, to confirm the story before the public knew. It was Klein who took his dislike of Davis to an extreme level of personal hatred.

Al doesn't take it personally, but the other side does.

*   *   *

As the years have passed, Al Davis has gone from a renegade to a respected senior citizen within the NFL. The NFL roster of owners now includes many men (and one woman) who are younger than Davis. Two recent changes in ownership have come within the AFC Western Division. California developer Alex Spanos bought the Chargers from Gene Klein, and the tandem of Bay Area millionaires Ken Hoffman and Ken Behring purchased the Seattle Seahawks from the Nordstrom family of department store fame. Both men are friendly to Al. Another ally is Edward DeBartolo, Jr., of the San Francisco 49ers.

After Rozelle announced his retirement and the NFL went hunting for a new commissioner, two distinct factions emerged among the owners. The "old guard" of the NFL, wanting to maintain the status quo established by Rozelle, supported New Orleans Saints general manager Jim Finks as the new commissioner. A group of the "young turk" owners eventually came to prefer attorney Paul Tagliabue for the job. After being placed in nomination, Finks received 16 votes, including the one from the Los Angeles Raiders. But 19 were needed. Did I hear that right? Al Davis voting with the old guard?

Eventually Finks lost some support and Tagliabue inched closer to the 19 votes. But it was a stalemate. The outgoing Rozelle swallowed his pride and selected Davis as part of a committee of six to help break the deadlock. A compromise that would allow old guard owner Art Modell to maintain his power in the television negotiating committee was arranged by Al Davis. The skillful piece of negotiating broke the impasse as Modell and the old guard voted for Tagliabue.

So Al Davis has become an elder statesman in the National Football League. A part of the establishment. With Halas gone, Davis is the only pure football man among the 28 owners. So they listen. It really isn't that strange. Didn't political radical Tom Hayden get elected to the California State legislature? Don't Elton John and Rod Stewart now dominate the easy listening and not the rock music charts? The rebels of the 1960s have become mainstream in the 1990s.

In 1972, when he was asked about his relationship with Rozelle, Davis replied, "We've become good friends in recent years. We have no problems. Of course, it takes a long time to heal wounds. But there is no lack of respect, only a lack of camaraderie. . . . Remember during the war between the leagues, we weren't in the back room. We were in the front lines. It makes a difference."

When Rozelle announced his retirement in 1989 at the owner's meetings in Palm Springs, he tearfully embraced Al Davis. Many in the media thought it was an unspontaneous act between the slick public relations oriented commissioner and his biggest adversary. But Al was genuinely surprised and moved by Rozelle. Yes, they faced off in the courtrooms, at many NFL meetings, and behind the scenes, but Al respects and feels deeply about Pete.

Let it be.

Chapter 8

THE BRIDESMAID FINALLY GETS THE GUY

After losing to Baltimore in 1970, all Al Davis and John Madden could do was try to keep improving the team and hope for a few lucky bounces. After Unitas and his relatively slow receivers riddled the Oakland defense, the Raiders hoped the 1971 number one draft choice would help solidify the secondary. Learning hard-nosed football from coach Woody Hayes, Jack Tatum of Ohio State became one of the fiercest safeties ever to play the game. In nine Raider seasons, his pass coverage was usually superb. He was traded to Houston in 1980 and soon retired. People know that Tatum has written two best-selling books about his football days. Tatum has also received a bad reputation because of his vicious hit of New England's Darryl Stingley in a 1978 exhibition game, which left the receiver paralyzed. What people don't know about is the time Tatum has spent working with teenagers on drug awareness programs.

Madden added an interesting group of assistants to his staff for 1971. Former Denver head coach Ray Malavasi was hired to handle the defensive line. He would later coach the Los Angeles Rams into a Super Bowl. Former Boston Patriots coach Mike Holovak also

111

joined the Silver and Black. Holovak is now general manager of the Houston Oilers. And Bob Zeman, who played defensive back with the Chargers when Al Davis was an assistant, started the first of two long tenures with the Raiders.

Attempting to rebuild the right side of the offensive line, the Raiders acquired veteran All-Pro tackle Bob Brown from Los Angeles. Given to the Rams were Harry Schuh and Kent McCloughan. Rod Sherman, who was a rare contractual holdout the previous season, was later traded to Denver. Also obtained was tackle Ron Mix of the Chargers, who once upon a time was recruited by Al Davis. A rookie find was halfback Clarence Davis of USC. Ditto defensive end Horace Jones of Louisville and tight end Bob Moore of Stanford. From Bowling Green, a school more famous for academics, came linebacker Phil Villapiano, who was a mainstay on defense for nine seasons. Villapiano would finish second in the Rookie of the Year voting in 1971.

With all this talent, the Raiders thought they had a good chance for the Super Bowl. Instead they finished with the same 8–4–2 record as in 1970. This time Kansas City finished 10–3–1. Baltimore was the wild card team at 10–4, so the Raiders finished out of the money. Over a span of 11 seasons, 1971 was the only campaign in which the Raiders missed the playoffs.

For the first 10 weeks of the season, the 7–1–2 record for Oakland was as good as any in the NFL. On opening day, the star of the game was rookie Jim Plunkett. Not for the Raiders but the New England Patriots. The bumbling Raiders missed an extra point, a 20-yard field goal, and mishandled a punt in the 20–6 loss. Oakland then rebounded nicely with a 34–0 whitewashing at San Diego, as the defense thoroughly confused Charger quarterback John Hadl. Daryle Lamonica's 36-yard touchdown pass to Fred Biletnikoff in the third quarter started the rout. Tatum had his first big league interception.

In a 34–20 Monday night pasting of Cleveland, the Raiders recovered from a 20–10 Cleveland advantage with three fourth-quarter touchdowns. A George Atkinson interception was followed by a Clarence Davis touchdown run that put the game away. A 55-yard interception by Jimmy Warren was the highlight in an otherwise dull 27–16 decision at Denver.

Returning home, the Raiders beat Philadelphia 34–10 and Cincinnati 31–27. Stabler started against the Eagles but was ineffective and was replaced by Lamonica in the second half. Daryle threw four touchdowns, two to Biletnikoff. It was Blanda's turn to be the hero against the Bengals. The Raiders squandered a 17–0 lead and needed George to march the boys down the field on the final drive, which culminated when Marv Hubbard scored.

A 20–20 tie against Kansas City was followed by another tie against the lowly Saints before 83,102 in New Orleans. First, Blanda rallied the Raiders vs. KC. Eschewing a try for a touchdown on a fourth-and-inches late in the game, Madden had Blanda kick the game-tying field goal. Both the Raiders and Chiefs were now tied with 5–1–1 records. Against the Saints, the Raiders couldn't hold a 21–7 advantage, and the game was tied when New Orleans quarterback Ed Hargett hit Dave Parks in the end zone with eight seconds to play.

After a 41–21 win over a Houston team coached by Sid Gillman and a 34–33 squeaker over the Chargers, the Raiders were looking like a sure playoff team again. The Raiders moved to a 38–0 halftime lead against the Oilers as the defense picked off three Houston passes. The scoring opened with a 63-yard touchdown pass from Lamonica to reserve wide receiver Drew Buie. An interception of a Hadl pass by middle linebacker Dan Conners cinched the San Diego game. After the Raiders trailed the Chargers 24–10 at halftime, they rallied to assume a 34–24 lead. On a fourth down deep in their own territory, Madden had punter Jerry DePoyster run into the end zone for a safety to end the game.

The next week was an unmitigated disaster for the Silver and Black. Johnny Unitas made his first appearance at the Coliseum and picked Oakland clean in a 37–14 walloping. Lamonica threw four interceptions, but two slipped from the fingers of Raider receivers into the hands of Colt defenders. The Raiders then wasted 208 rushing yards, including a career best 143 by Marv Hubbard, in a 23–14 loss at Atlanta. The Falcons picked off Lamonica twice near their goal line to put the capper on a sloppy game.

A Jan Stenerud field goal with 1:34 to play gave the Chiefs a 16–14 triumph and the AFC West title in the Raiders' final appearance at Municipal Stadium. Two key plays that went against the Raiders were a 37-yard Blanda field goal attempt that was partially blocked and an apparent George Atkinson interception that was ruled a "trap" by the officials. The 21–13 win in the finale against Denver was for pride only.

The Raiders passing attack sputtered throughout 1971. Warren Wells spent most of the year in prison on a rape charge. A year in the pokey robbed Wells of his skills and he was waived the following summer. Bothered by both injuries and the increasing use of zone defenses in the NFL, Lamonica slumped to a 48.8% completion rate in 1971 and matched his 16 touchdown tosses with 16 interceptions.

Attempting to juice up the passing attack, the Raiders made wide receiver Mike Siani of Villanova the top draft choice. Siani would play six years with the Raiders until he was traded to Baltimore in the same deal that returned Raymond Chester to Oakland in 1978. But the real find in 1972 was Cliff Branch of Colorado University, who by 1974 would become the breakaway pass catcher whom Al Davis coveted. Branch was a major contributor in three

Super Bowl victories and played with the Raiders through the 1984 season.

Offensive lineman John Vella of USC was the second pick in the draft. Vella played both guard and tackle on the right side of the line until a shattering knee injury in 1977 curtailed his career. Vella now operates both a travel agency and a Raider souvenir store in Northern California and has been among the more active Oakland alumni in the movement to entice the Raiders back to their origins.

As 1972 began, Jim Otto was still solid as a rock as the Raiders center. Looking toward the future, the Raiders selected Dave Dalby of UCLA as a high draft choice. After seeing some action at right guard, Dalby became the starting center when Otto retired in 1975. Dalby played center with distinction into the 1985 season.

Because he shaved his head, it was alleged that defensive end Otis Sistrunk came from the University of Mars. He was actually acquired from the Los Angeles Rams. The colorful Sistrunk, who did not attend college on any planet, also played defensive tackle in his eight seasons with Oakland.

The Raiders still had a deficiency at the cornerback position opposite Willie Brown. An unheralded 1972 rookie quickly converted a weakness into a plus. Skip Thomas of USC liked to call himself "Dr. Death." The receivers that he covered in seven campaigns called him other names.

Tom Flores returned to the Raiders in 1972 as a quarterback coach. He would serve as an assistant under Madden for seven years before becoming head coach in 1979. After winning two Super Bowls and coaching the Raiders for nine seasons, Tom "retired." After assuming the figurehead position of "director of special projects" in the Raider front office, Flores answered the call of Seattle owner Ken Behring by becoming general manager of the

Seahawks. His team beat former boss Al Davis twice in 1989.

The changes of 1972 *did* make a difference, because the Raiders improved to 10–3–1 and won the division title. And yet the 1972 season is remembered for one flukey play that will never be forgotten by anybody who saw it. Or thought they saw it. More on that later.

The season opened with a 34–28 loss in an exciting game at Pittsburgh. The Raiders came from far behind and almost won. Lamonica replaced an interception-prone Stabler and had three touchdown passes in the fourth quarter, including a 70-yarder to Siani. The first ever visit to Green Bay was triumphant for the Raiders, with Hubbard gaining 125 yards and Tatum scampering 104 yards with an interception.

The home opener produced a 17–17 tie with the Chargers as an early 14–0 Oakland lead did not last. Blanda missed a 37-yard field goal that could have won it, and then San Diego, satisfied with a tie, ran out the clock. In a 34–0 Monday night shellacking of Houston, the Oilers were held to 89 yards rushing, and quarterback Dan Pastorini was a miserable 3 of 21 passing. The Raiders then overcame a 13–0 deficit to score a 28–16 victory over Buffalo. Hubbard, who rushed for 1,100 yards in 1972, gained another 122 yards against the Bills. A 55-yard touchdown pass to Ray Chester and a tackle of Buffalo running back O. J. Simpson on a third down rush by defensive end Horace Jones were the pivotal plays of the day. "Oakland had the class, but we just couldn't do it," said the Juice after the game.

On the day that the Oakland A's won the World Series in Cincinnati, the Raiders were upset 30–23 at home by Denver. Veteran quarterback Charley Johnson riddled the Raiders defense for 20 completions in 28 attempts for 361 yards. The first ever meeting with the Rams, now owned by Carroll Rosenbloom, was a 45–17 bashing by Oakland. The Raiders ran effectively behind the block-

ing of Upshaw and Shell and assumed a 28–0 first-quarter lead. Villapiano scored the final touchdown with an
83-yard interception.

The largest crowd that has ever seen a game in Arrow-
head Stadium, 82,704, watched the Chiefs score a 27–14
victory. Kansas City defensive end Aaron Brown manhandled Shell. The Raiders were now 4–3–1 and out of
first place.

The Raiders rebounded from the poor start and
rolled to the AFC West title by winning six straight
games. The victims were Cincinnati, Denver, Kansas
City, San Diego, the Jets, and the Bears. Charlie Smith
rushed for a career best 146 yards against the Bengals
and Hubbard added 98. Lamonica peppered Cincinnati
with short passes. The 37–20 thumping of Denver featured two Lamonica-to-Biletnikoff touchdowns with
Smith and Hubbard also reaching the end zone.

The earlier loss at Kansas City was more than avenged
with a 26–3 decision in Oakland. Lamonica hit 12 of 16 in
the first half, and a touchdown to Chester just before
halftime was too much for the Chiefs to overcome. A
Charlie Smith score with 1:18 to play gave the Raiders a
21–19 win at San Diego, which clinched the division
championship.

Hubbard had his third 100-yard game of the season
against the New York Jets as the Raiders withstood a
spectacular 403-yard passing evening from Joe Namath
to prevail 24–16. The loss knocked the Jets out of the
playoff hunt. The season concluded with a 28–21 victory
over Chicago. Running quarterback Bobby Douglas was
allowed to gain 127 yards, but Clarence Davis answered
back with a 45-yard run for the decisive score.

It was a typically frosty December Saturday in
Pittsburgh when the Raiders met the Steelers in a first-
round playoff game at Three Rivers Stadium. Led by
rookie fullback Franco Harris, the Steelers won the AFC
Central and were appearing in the first playoff game in

their history. The offenses of both teams were hampered by the slippery Astroturf. After a scoreless first half, Roy Gerela kicked two field goals as the Steelers took a 6–0 lead into the fourth quarter. Madden replaced the ineffective Lamonica with Ken Stabler. With 1:13 to play, the Raiders moved to the Steeler 31-yard line from where Stabler suddenly kept the ball and ran around left end for a touchdown. Oakland was now ahead 7–6. Following an 18-yard kickoff return, Pittsburgh quarterback Terry Bradshaw tried three passes, all of them incomplete. Time was running out on the Steelers fairy-tale season. On fourth and 10, Bradshaw threw a 15-yard pass toward halfback John "Frenchy" Fuqua. What happened next has never been totally resolved. The ball caromed off Fuqua, may have hit Jack Tatum, may have nicked a Steeler lineman, but bounced in the direction of Franco Harris, who was at the Raider 35-yard line. Harris caught the football and ran along the sidelines toward the Oakland goal line. Somewhere nearby was Raider defensive back Jimmy Warren. Warren had a decision to make: If he knocked Harris out of bounds, it would stop the clock and the Steelers would get an opportunity to kick a game-winning field goal. If he could somehow tackle Franco inside, before Harris reached the end zone, the clock would run out and the Raiders would win. Warren was not really in position for the latter but tried anyway. He missed and Harris scored a touchdown. But was it a legitimate play? If Tatum didn't touch the ball, it was illegal because two Steelers (Fuqua and Harris) could not consecutively touch the pass. There was no formal instant replay rule in those days, but the officials checked the NBC tapes anyway. Because they could not confirm whether Tatum touched the ball, the touchdown call was upheld and the Steelers won, 13–7.

Never has a football game ended with such an unexpected dramatic suddenness. Oh sure, Dallas's Roger Staubach threw a last-second bomb to Drew Pearson to win a playoff game in 1975, and Minnesota's Tommy Kramer somehow found Ahmad Rashad in the end zone with a "Hail Mary" against Cleveland in 1980 to alter that outcome. But the Franco Harris "immaculate reception" somehow equals the baseball home-run heroics of Kirk Gibson in the 1988 World Series and Bobby Thompson in the 1951 playoffs, and the Larry Bird steal of an Isiah Thomas pass in the 1987 NBA basketball playoffs, among the most amazing finishes ever to occur in team sports. And like the Oakland Athletics, Brooklyn Dodgers, and Detroit Pistons, the Oakland Raiders were on the wrong end of the fickle finger of fate. "I felt we had it won," said Madden. "I won't forget it for a long, long time."

So how do you make things better? You draft a punter on the first round in 1973, of course. It had never been done in the NFL or AFL before, but in 1973 Ray Guy of Southern Mississippi was the Raiders' No. 1 draft choice. A good pick, to be sure. Guy kicked the air out of the pigskin for 14 seasons, rarely had a punt blocked, and was a master at placing the ball in the "coffin corner" to deny the opposition good field position.

With the trade of Raymond Chester to Baltimore for defensive end Bubba Smith, the Raiders acquired tight end Warren Bankston from the Steelers as a possible replacement. Besides Bubba Smith, the only other newcomer of note was linebacker Monte Johnson of Nebraska who intermittently was a starter for the next eight seasons, eventually replacing Dan Conners. Don Shinnick joined Madden's staff as linebacker coach. Another new assistant was one of Al Davis's original 1963 tight end projects: Bob Mischak.

Oakland again was the best in the AFC West with a 9–4–1 record, finishing ahead of both Kansas City and Denver by 1½ lengths. The season opened with a 24–16 loss at Minnesota. George Atkinson scored the lone Oakland touchdown on a punt return. The Raiders returned home to meet the Miami Dolphins who had won 18 straight games. Because the Oakland Athletics were playing at the Coliseum, the game was moved to Berkeley, which had refused to take in the Raiders in 1960 (remember?). Blanda kicked four field goals to offset a late Griese-to-Jim Mandrich touchdown, as the Raiders broke the Miami winning streak with a 12–7 victory.

Phil Villapiano made 11 unassisted tackles, but the offense was nonexistent in a 16–3 loss at Kansas City. With no offensive touchdowns in three games, some changes were in order. Madden announced that Stabler would replace Lamonica as the starting quarterback. It was probably time. Lamonica was no longer the Mad Bomber of the AFL days. Stabler had been brought along slowly since 1968 and was getting older and wiser and certainly ready to play. And what's wrong with a southpaw quarterback anyway?

Lamonica was a reserve for the remainder of 1973 and all of 1974 before getting his release and joining the Southern California Sun of the World Football League in 1975. When the WFL expired, so did Lamonica's career.

And Stabler? Only injuries would keep him out of the lineup for the remainder of the decade. The colorful "Snake" soon came to be associated with clutch passing and last-second heroics. He was also known as a high-living party guy in the grand tradition of the late Bobby Layne. But somehow he was always ready to play on Sunday. And Monday night. Davis traded the Snake to Houston for Dan Pastorini in 1980 and later Stabler rejoined Bum Phillips, his Oiler coach, in New Orleans. But he will always be remembered as a Raider. Ken now does color commentary for CNN. Perhaps appropriately, he is also a national spokesperson for Southern Comfort and is involved in real estate development. Stabler and his third wife have settled in his native Alabama.

Stabler won his first two games as the starter: 17–10 at St. Louis and 27–17 at San Diego. Charlie Smith's two-yard run to pay dirt in the third period at St. Louis was the first Oakland offensive touchdown in 216 minutes, 12 seconds of play in 1973. Stabler hit 19 of 32 passes for 207 yards. At San Diego, Lamonica and Johnny Unitas sat on the bench as Stabler dueled Charger rookie Dan Fouts. A potent ground game assisted Stabler in the win.

Although sacked six times, the Snake had his first 300-yard passing performance in a 23–23 Monday night tie at Denver. The Raiders thought they had the game won when Blanda nailed a 49-yard field goal with 36 seconds left, but the Broncos quickly moved into field goal territory, and Jim Turner salvaged a tie for Denver with a 35-yarder with three seconds to play.

Stabler was on fire in Baltimore, completing 25 of 29 passes for 304 yards, and outpassed Colts quarterback Marty Domres in a 34–21 victory. Clarence Davis's 32-yard touchdown run put the game away. The Raiders finally played a home game in Oakland in week eight and destroyed the Giants 42–0. The average gain per offensive play for Oakland was an overwhelming 6.5 yards, and the Giants didn't cross midfield until the final four minutes of the contest.

After scoring 76 points in two victories, the Raiders could only amass 12 in home losses to Pittsburgh and Cleveland. The Raiders shot themselves in the foot against the Steelers, committing five fumbles and four interceptions. Stabler left the game early with a sprained knee. He returned against Cleveland but was ineffective in a boring 7–3 loss. There were 11 punts in the game. A seven-yard pass from Mike Phipps to Fair Hooker won it for Cleveland.

The Raiders woke up and reeled off four victories to win the division. The defense dominated the Chargers in a 31–3 victory. George Atkinson had a 58-yard touchdown interception in the game. In Houston, Dan Pastorini was sacked five times and Villapiano made 12 unassisted tackles in a 17–6 Raider win. The offense returned to life as the Raiders trampled Kansas City, 37–7. Hubbard paced a 259-yard ground attack.

The Raiders faced Denver in the finale with the AFC West and a playoff berth hanging in the balance. The difference in the 21–17 Oakland victory was a botched reverse on a fake punt attempt by the Broncos. Siani, Charlie Smith, and Clarence Davis scored for the Raiders.

Revenge for the "Immaculate Reception" game was exacted with a 33–14 win over the Steelers in a first-round playoff game in Oakland. Clarence Davis, Marv Hubbard, and Charlie Smith collectively gained over 200 yards, and Willie Brown converted a Bradshaw pass into a Raider touchdown to set the pace. The offensive line of Shell, Upshaw, Otto, Buehler, and Vella did a number on Joe Greene and his friends. The defense held Pittsburgh to 65 yards rushing. Blanda booted five field goals.

Next was the championship game in Miami. The Raiders were down only 17–10 at the beginning of the fourth quarter, but a Larry Csonka touchdown run and a Garo Yepremian field goal put the game out of reach. Don Shula played it close to the vest with Bob Griese throwing only six passes. Both Mercury Morris and Larry Csonka were unstoppable on the ground, as guard Larry Little and tackle Norm Evans blew away the Raider defensive line. With the score 20–10 in the fourth quarter and the Raiders moving down the field, Hubbard fumbled on a fourth down run, which ended all Oakland hopes of a championship. Two weeks later, the Dolphins would win their second consecutive Super Bowl by decisively beating Minnesota. The Raiders again were one game short and, for the fourth time since 1967, lost the AFL/AFC championship game to the team that eventually won the Super Bowl.

There was no question of who the Raider quarterback would be in 1974. Stabler had completed 62.7% of his passes in 1973, the highest in Raider history. The Snake was also gaining a reputation as a fourth-quarter performer who always made the big play when the game was in the balance. It would remain that way for the next four seasons, as the Raiders would continue to be in the upper echelon of NFL teams.

The 1974 draft was productive. Offensive tackle Henry Lawrence of tiny Florida A&M was the top pick. Lawrence played 13½ seasons at right tackle and usually gave the Silver and Black solid play. A member of three world championship clubs, the likable Lawrence is now the head of a Los Angeles company that sells computer goods, fax machines and other high-tech equipment.

Receiving help was provided for Stabler by the Number 2 choice: tight end Dave Casper of Notre Dame. Casper, who also played tackle in college, was a superb receiver who put the oomph in the attack that was lost in the trade of Ray Chester. After a slow start, Dave gave the Raiders many big games over the next few years. Casper was traded to Houston in 1980 but returned to the Silver and Black as an understudy to Todd Christensen in 1984.

The Number 3 guy from the 1974 draft was fullback Mark van Eeghan of Colgate, who eventually succeeded fellow Colgate alumnus Marv Hubbard as the Raider fullback. Legend has it that Al Davis "discovered" van Eeghan working out in a gym rather than on a football field and was impressed by the size of his legs. The Raiders were to be settled at fullback for their remaining eight years in Oakland. Another useful performer from the class of '74 was Ohio State wide receiver Morris Bradshaw, who also served as an effective special teams player.

The 1974 Oakland team soared to a 12–2 record, the best in the National Football League. One of the losses was the opening game, played on a Monday night in Buffalo. Three touchdowns were scored in the last three minutes, two by the Bills, which made the difference in a 21–20 game. Buffalo quarterback Joe Ferguson hurled two touchdown passes to Ahmad Rashad in the fourth quarter; the second TD followed an Art Thoms score on a fumble recovery for Oakland. It was the first time the Raiders lost a game in front of Howard Cosell and the Giffer. They would not be defeated again on a Monday night until the last game of the 1981 season.

Oakland won the next nine games. It was a balanced and potent offense combined with a tight defense that usually made the difference. The Raiders cruised past Kansas City 27–7 in the home opener. The Chiefs futilely tried a five-man defensive front but they couldn't stop Stabler or Dave Casper.

The Raiders went to Pittsburgh and, behind a potent ground game, shut down the Steelers 17–0. Steeler starting quarterback Joe Gilliam completed a measly eight passes in 31 attempts. Clarence Davis then rushed for 116 yards in a 40–24 triumph at Cleveland. The defense added five interceptions.

Touchdown passes to Branch and Bob Moore provided the points in a 14–10 victory at San Diego. A last-minute march down the field that was culminated by a Clarence Davis two-yard run lifted Oakland past Cincinnati 30–27.

Next the Raiders avenged their 1970 defeat to San Francisco with a 35–24 decision at Candlestick Park. Stabler passed 64 yards to Branch and a last-play fumble recovery by Harold Hart clinched the game. Stabler had four touchdown passes against Denver, including an 81-yarder to Branch. Final score: Raiders 28, Broncos 17. In a 35–13 romp over Detroit, Branch caught two more touchdown tosses.

Against the Chargers, it was Cliff Branch again with seven catches including a touchdown. When Denver lost to Kansas City the following evening, the Raiders clinched the AFC West title.

Not unexpectedly, the Raiders were flat the following Sunday when Denver beat them 20–17. Madden rested many of his starters. The season closed with victories over New England, Kansas City, and Dallas. Against the Patriots, Stabler added four more touchdown passes to his total as he outpitched Plunkett in a 41–26 win. Skip Thomas returned one of Plunkett's passes for a TD. The defense carried the Raiders to a 7–6 win over Kansas City. Otis Sistrunk saved the game with a sack of Dawson and a recovered fumble. And in their first-ever meeting with Dallas, Blanda had a 1–2–3 night: one touchdown pass, two field goals, and three conversions. The season-ending 27–23 Oakland victory knocked the Cowboys out of the playoffs.

Miami, seeking its third straight Super Bowl victory, was 11–3 in 1974. The Dolphins would travel to Oakland for the first round of the playoffs. Throughout the week before the game, there was unusual anticipation about this match. The newspapers (and the scalpers) called it Super Bowl IX½. The expectations would prove to be justified; it would be a classic confrontation that was more exciting than any of the previous eight Super Bowls.

The game opened with Miami's Nat Moore returning the opening kickoff 89 yards for a touchdown. Stabler brought the Raiders back and found Charlie Smith for a 31-yard tying touchdown. The lead seesawed all day. Miami was ahead 26–21 in the fourth quarter when, slowly but surely, Stabler marched the Raiders down the field. The Raiders moved to the Miami eight. There were 35 seconds left and Oakland was out of time-outs. Stabler went back to pass and was looking into the end zone for someone, anyone to get open. As he was being hit by Miami defensive end Vern Den Herder, Stabler fired the ball. Amid a "sea of hands" and with linebacker Mike Kolen clutching at his jersey, Clarence Davis grabbed the pigskin for the go-ahead score. When Villapiano intercepted Bob Griese at midfield with 13 seconds remaining, the Raiders had their 28–26 victory.

Pandemonium engulfed the Coliseum and the

players were ecstatic. Many remembered the frustrations of previous seasons. "It was about time something like that went our way in the playoffs. Usually that's the kind of thing that goes against us," said Gene Upshaw. "I hope Oakland goes all the way," remarked a spent Don Shula.

It was a great win, but the Raiders may have forgotten that there was another game to play. Pittsburgh was coming into the Coliseum for the AFC Championship game. And for the second straight year after a smashing victory in round 1, the Raiders came up flat at the wrong time. The Pittsburgh pass rush overwhelmed Stabler, the Raiders could not stop Franco Harris and Rocky Blier, and the Steelers started their run of four Super Bowl wins in six years. The sluggish Raiders could not hold a 10–3 lead as the Steelers scored three times in the fourth quarter. Final score: Pittsburgh 24, Oakland 13.

What could anyone say? It was easy. "Just use the same quotes from last year. And the year before that," said Marv Hubbard. "Every damn year it's like this. We had everything in our favor. We had them in our stadium, in front of our fans, on grass, coming off that great game last week. It just wasn't in the cards this year, again. When will it be?" asked Hubbard. Madden used only four words to utter the same sentiments: "Defeat is a bitch."

By now the talk that Oakland can't win the big one had reached a national crescendo. While the Raiders had remained the constant, a solid contender, teams like the Jets, Chiefs, and Colts had slipped. But before they became mediocre, these clubs had taken their turn at beating Oakland to advance to a Super Bowl victory. The Raiders sat home. Then the Dolphins and Steelers had become powerhouses. And they *also* used the Raiders as a stepping-stone. Oakland had beaten Miami and Pittsburgh at the wrong time in the wrong year, that's all.

In 1975, Oakland put almost the same team on the field as the 1974 collection. The Raiders dreamed of an all-Ohio-State defensive safety tandem of first-draft

choice Neal Colzie and veteran Jack Tatum that would
destroy enemy receivers. Tatum was fine, but for a top
draft choice, Colzie was a bust. In four years with the
Raiders, his main contribution was as a punt returner.

The most useful draft choices of 1975 were players
who provided depth. David Humm, a quarterback from
Nebraska, and Steve Sylvester, a guard from Notre
Dame, were mostly reserve players in their Raider years,
which stretched into Los Angeles.

There were two tall veteran "Teddy boys" who joined
the Raiders in 1975. Ted Kwalick, an All-American at
Penn State, was acquired from San Francisco to challenge
Bob Moore, Warren Bankston, and Dave Casper at tight
end. The other Ted cost the Raiders two number one
draft picks but the price was probably cheap. Ted Hendricks, all six-feet-seven-inches of him, was originally
drafted by Baltimore in 1969. The "Mad Stork" was a
mainstay on the good Baltimore teams of that era before
being traded to Green Bay in 1974. Hendricks was unhappy with his latest contract offer from the Packers and
was a free agent. Because of the so-called "Rozelle Rule,"
teams in the NFL rarely signed veteran free agents because the commissioner determined the "compensation"
that is given to the club that loses a player. Usually two
number one draft choices were awarded. After the Raiders signed Hendricks, Rozelle gave the Packers the Oakland No. 1 picks of 1976 and 1977.

It was a bargain. After being second string in 1975,
Hendricks played in three Super Bowls and was a leader
who excelled as a pass defender and always seemed to
make the big play. In 1990, Hendricks became the seventh Oakland/Los Angeles Raider to be inducted into the
Pro Football Hall of Fame. Other valuable veteran additions to the defense for 1975 were tackle Dave Rowe and
linebacker Willie Hall.

An interesting newcomer to the coaching staff was
John Robinson, who had been a boyhood buddy of John

Madden. Robinson coached the running backs for one season before leaving for USC. He eventually coached Heisman Trophy winners Charles White and Marcus Allen for the Trojans before ascending to the Los Angeles Rams in 1983.

The biggest change of 1975 was the retirement of Jim Otto. Except for Blanda, Otto was the last of the 1960 AFL originals still active. After thousands of snaps of the football, accompanied by many knee operations, "Double Zero" had finally called it a career. He started nearly every game for 15 years. Dave Dalby spent the next 11 seasons as a competent successor to Otto.

The 1975 Raiders were another powerful team and the result was an 11–3 regular season record. It started impressively with wins in Miami and Baltimore. Against the Dolphins, Harold Hart returned a kickoff 102 yards and the ground game was dominant. A 55-yard Stabler-to-Branch pass was the turning point of the Colts' game. Art Thoms registered nine tackles for the defense.

Trivia question: Who was Larry Lawrence? Answer: He was a Canadian Football League refugee who played as a backup Raider quarterback in 1974 and 1975. His only start in 1975 was a 6–0 squeaker over San Diego. This was followed by the first loss, a 42–10 beating by Kansas City. David Humm, the other reserve QB, hit Branch with a fourth-quarter touchdown pass against the Chiefs. A fifth straight road game was a 14–10 loss in rainy Cincinnati. Bengal linebacker Jim LeClair intercepted Stabler in the final minute to end a last-gasp Raider threat.

Nothing like good home cookin'! The Raiders won the next seven games, including five at the Coliseum. Two safeties were scored in a 25–0 shutout of the Chargers, and the defense held San Diego to a meager 157 total yards. Then the offense shifted into high gear: The next three scores were 42–17, 48–10, and 38–17; and the victims were Denver, New Orleans, and Cleveland.

Overcoming a 17–7 deficit, the Raiders chalked up 35 points in 24 minutes to beat the Broncos. New Orleans was overcome by an offensive avalanche of 34 first downs, 280 yards rushing, and 263 yards passing. Clarence Davis scored two touchdowns and gained 120 yards against the 0–9 Brownies.

1975 was the year the NFL started playing overtime games in the regular season. The Raiders' initial extra period games came in the next two weeks and they were both wins. Blanda, who had missed a 33-yard field goal with eight seconds to go in the fourth quarter, atoned in the overtime period with a winning 27-yarder against Washington. The Raiders rolled up more than 550 yards of offense against Atlanta but needed an 18-yard field goal with three seconds remaining to tie the game and a 36-yarder to beat the Falcons. With their 9–2 record, the Raiders had clinched another division title.

The season concluded with another win over Denver, a one-point setback to Houston and a 28–20 decision over the Chiefs. Denver quarterbacks John Hufnagel and Steve Ramsey were overrun by 10 Raider sacks. Two missed extra points made the difference against Houston, but Al Davis was incensed with the officiating when an illegal pick was not called on the winning Oiler touchdown pass from Dan Pastorini to Mack Alston. "We have to get rid of the incompetent officials in this league and we will," Davis said. Before Pete Rozelle started cleaning out the officials, he fined Al Davis for mouthing off. Warming up for the playoffs against Kansas City, Stabler completed 11 of 12 passes for 131 yards in the first half, and reserve running back Jess Phillips gained 84 yards for Oakland.

Cincinnati, the wild card team, met the Raiders in Oakland to start the playoffs. The Raiders had a big lead but nearly gave it away in the fourth quarter. Touchdowns by Banaszak, Bob Moore, Mike Siani, and Dave Casper, coupled with a Blanda field goal, propelled the

Silver and Black to a 31–14 lead. But Bengals safety Ken Riley intercepted Stabler, which started a Cincinnati comeback. When the dust had settled, the Raiders escaped with a 31–28 victory.

The championship game was in Pittsburgh. And it was another Oakland disappointment, as the Steelers won 16–10 on a brutally cold day at Three Rivers Stadium. A Stabler-to-Siani pass resulted in the only Raider touchdown of the contest. It was certainly not an artistic performance by either side: The Steelers fumbled five times and Bradshaw was intercepted three times. But Stabler was picked off twice and four Oakland fumbles were all converted by the Steelers into points. The Raiders did try for another miracle finish: A Blanda field goal made the score 16–10 with 12 seconds left in the game. Oakland then recovered an onside kick. Attempting a desperation pass on the last play of the game, Stabler found Branch at the Steeler 15 but Cliff could get no further.

In 1976, Madden would be starting his eighth year as head coach. He had compiled a better career winning percentage than Chuck Noll, Don Shula, or Tom Landry but still hadn't won the big one. Al Davis had also watched the team that he had built and continually reinforced always come up short. Could divine intervention be a factor? "I am thinking that God knocked the ball out of Banaszak's hand on that fumble in Pittsburgh," said Davis in an interview. "He certainly had a hand in that catch of Franco Harris that beat us," added Al.

Were the Raiders jinxed? In retrospect, the Miami and Pittsburgh teams that eclipsed the Raiders in the first part of the 1970s were probably two of the three or four greatest teams of all time. The 1973 to 1975 Raiders probably were good enough to win Super Bowls in any other year or era. A break or two and maybe the Raiders of the mid-seventies could have gone to three or four Super Bowls. It makes for good talk, but there was really nothing else to do but look ahead to 1976.

With their first pick in the draft gone in the Ted Hendricks signing, the Raiders selected defense tackle Charles Philyaw in the second round. The massive Philyaw was an Al Davis favorite but never fulfilled his promise as a dominant lineman.

With Blanda retiring at age 49 (or being made to retire, as would later become common with Raider coaches), the Raiders drafted kicker Fred Steinfort of Boston College. When he got hurt, veteran Detroit Lions kicker Errol Mann joined the club. New England running back Carl Garrett was added to support Clarence Davis in the backfield and bolster the special teams.

Let us not forget "the Tooz"! John Matuszak played his college football at the University of Tampa and the defensive tackle was the first draft choice of the entire NFL in 1973 with Houston. He feuded with Houston coach Sid Gillman and was traded to Kansas City. Then he was dealt to George Allen in Washington. The Tooz found a home in Oakland where he played inspirational football through the 1981 season. After a back injury ended his career, Matuszak appeared in some movies. But life in the fast lane contributed to his unexpected death in 1989 at the age of 38. It was a crushing blow to all who knew this colorful giant. Delivering the eulogy at a church in the Bay Area was his former boss, Al Davis. "John Matuszak was one of those great players who wore the Silver and Black with poise, pride and charismatic class," said Al.

The 1976 Raiders compiled a 13–1 record. Except for a 48–17 loss in New England when the Patriots pulled away in the fourth quarter, this Oakland team was nearly perfect.

The schedule makers granted the Raiders a rare opening day game at home. Against the Steelers, of course. Stabler rallied the boys to two fourth-quarter touchdowns and a 31–28 victory. A blocked Steeler punt started the comeback, which was completed with a 10-yard Stabler pass to Casper. This was the game that led to the "criminal element" charges and the subsequent trial. The rushing attack and a Stabler-to-Siani touchdown made the difference in a 24–21 decision at Kansas City. In a 14–13 win at Houston, reserve quarterback Mike Rae, another Canadian import, replaced an injured Stabler. Rae threw two touchdown passes, including the winner to Branch.

After the New England loss, the Raiders won the last 10 games. The passing game was lethal: Stabler completed more than 68% of his passes and Branch, Biletnikoff, and Casper were catching everything in sight. Clarence Davis and van Eeghen were leading a vicious ground game and Banaszak was frequently brought in for the tough yard or two. The offensive line was opening holes for the runners and giving Stabler the time needed to pass. The defense was outstanding. The Chargers were 27–17 losers when Stabler connected for three touchdown passes. The Raiders then beat the Broncos twice and also downed Green Bay. In Denver, Branch and Banaszak reached the end zone in a 17–10 game. The Raiders missed all three extra points following Stabler touchdown passes but beat the Packers 18–14. The defense sacked quarterback Steve Ramsey 10 times, and two late touchdowns helped stop the Broncos at home by a 19–6 count.

The closest game of the streak was a 28–27 win at Chicago. Branch burned the Bears defense for two important long pass plays. Casper and Biletnikoff were the stars in a 21–10 decision over Kansas City. In the Eagles' 26–7 loss to the Raiders, Philadelphia quarterback Roman Gabriel spent most of a Sunday afternoon on the Veterans Stadium turf. A 7–0 deficit was overcome by a potent ground attack led by van Eeghen. The Philadelphia victory clinched the division title. They destroyed the new Tampa Bay Buccaneers 49–16, with Stabler and Rae both accumulating touchdown passes.

In week 13 on a Monday night, the Raiders met Cincinnati in the Coliseum. The Raiders had wrapped up their division while the Bengals were in a dogfight with Pittsburgh for the AFC Central. There was talk out of Pittsburgh that the Raiders would let Cincinnati win so that Oakland could avoid facing the dreaded Steelers in the playoffs.

The talk was ridiculous. The Stabler-to-Branch connection enjoyed a big night in a 35–20 Raider win. Casper and Biletnikoff also got into the end zone and the defense intercepted three Ken Anderson passes. In the last week of the regular season, Mike Rae threw three touchdowns and van Eeghen gained 95 yards for a 1,012 season total as Oakland shut out San Diego 24–0. Pittsburgh won the AFC Central Division and Cincinnati missed the playoffs. For the 10-year period of 1967 to 1976, the Raiders compiled a spectacular 108–25–7 record for an .812 winning percentage. But they still had not won a World Championship.

The upstart New England Patriots, who improved from 3–11 in 1975 to an 11–3 record under coach Chuck Fairbanks, came into the Coliseum as the AFC wild card representative. This was the game where the Raiders had to rally from a 21–10 deficit to edge the Pats 24–21. Stabler moved the Raiders downfield with two key passes to Biletnikoff, and van Eeghen ran one yard to reduce the score to 21–17 Patriots. The Raiders got the ball back and Stabler started waving his magic wand again. With 57 seconds to play, the Raiders were third down and 18 on the New England 27 when Stabler threw an incomplete pass. However, a roughing-the-passer penalty against New England defensive end Ray "Sugar Bear" Hamilton enabled the Raiders to keep the decisive drive alive. When Stabler scooted into the end zone with 10 seconds left, the Raiders had their win.

Immediately after the game, New England (and former Raider) assistant coach Charlie Sumner charged the officials dressing room, ready to fight anybody and everybody. Hamilton swore he tipped the pass, but Raider offensive tackle John Vella said it was the proper call. The Patriots could keep arguing; for the Raiders it was time to move on.

The Raiders knew that the road to the Super Bowl went through Pittsburgh, and the Steelers clubbed the Colts 40–14 in their first round game in Baltimore. Pittsburgh came into the Coliseum with both Franco Harris and Rocky Blier injured and out of the contest. It probably wouldn't have made any difference if Jim Brown and Gale Sayers had played in the Steelers backfield on that Sunday afternoon. The Raiders were ready. Surprisingly, the AFC Championship game lacked the ferocious hitting of the first Oakland-Pittsburgh meeting. Playing a conservative game offensively and shutting down Terry Bradshaw, Lynn Swann, John Stallworth, and the runners, Oakland was not going to be denied by Pittsburgh again. Following an interception by linebacker Willie Hall, a 31-yard pass from Stabler to Biletnikoff gave the Raiders a 10–7 halftime lead. Former Steeler Warren Bankston and Pete Banaszak both caught short TD passes in the second half. Final score: Oakland 24, Steelers 7.

Finally. Finally, the burden was off Madden's massive shoulders. Super Bowl XI pitted the Oakland Raiders against the Minnesota Vikings at the Rose Bowl. Minnesota was 11–2–1 during the regular season and had easily dispatched Washington and Los Angeles in the playoffs. This was the Vikings' fourth Super Bowl appearance in eight years and the third in the past four seasons. Fran Tarkenton was the quarterback in the last two and he and his teammates had played poorly. Super Bowl XI was to be no different.

Early in the game, the Vikings blocked a Ray Guy punt deep in Raider territory. Two plays later, halfback Brent McClanahan fumbled the ball and Willie Hall recovered at the Raiders two-yard line. Stabler then moved the offense crisply down the field. Casper and Biletnikoff caught short passes from Stabler and Pete Banaszak plunged over from the one. Errol Mann's extra point try was blocked, but he later atoned with a 40-yard field goal. Minnesota trimmed the Raider lead to 19–7 in the third quarter but another Banaszak run pushed the count to 26–7. Willie Brown then intercepted Tarkenton and ran 75 yards for a score to put the icing on the cake. A late Minnesota touchdown didn't matter. The final score was Raiders 32, Vikings 14. Clarence Davis gained 141 yards and Stabler was brilliant. The defense shut down the Vikings. Art Shell and Gene Upshaw neutralized the Viking Purple People Eaters. Biletnikoff, who caught four clutch passes, was selected as the Most Valuable Player.

When the Raiders won Super Bowls following the 1980 and 1983 seasons, there was much anticipation about a possible confrontation between Commissioner Pete Rozelle and Al Davis. However, after Rozelle gave the Super Bowl XI trophy to Davis, he was met by George Atkinson and Jack Tatum, who were in the midst of the "criminal element" incident. They briskly "escorted" the commissioner out of the locker room. Fortunately, or maybe unfortunately, the incident was out of view of the NBC cameras.

Fourteen years after he came to Oakland and started building the best organization in professional sports, Al Davis could rightfully proclaim that the mission was accomplished. With about five minutes to play, well-wishers were hovering near the Raiders' luxury box, but Al never moved from his chair and stared intently onto the field. He later reflected on the long overdue triumph, indicating a lingering discomfort with the merged NFL. "I still have the NFL/AFL feeling. I grew up with it. I remember the obstacles put in our way."

Even though John Madden was carried off the field

on the shoulders of his players, the moment also belonged to Al Davis. *Los Angeles Times* columnist Jim Murray summed it up in one sentence. "Without Al Davis, Oakland would be Tampa Bay."

Chapter 9

1977–1981:
THE END OF AN ERA

"If we move to L.A., Al promised to buy me a home in Beverly Hills."
                                    —*Tom Flores, 1979*

*T*he Super Bowl victory over the Vikings meant that the stigma of losing in the clutch had finally been removed from the Raider organization. All of the frustration was a thing of the past. But could they match Green Bay, Pittsburgh, and Miami and win back-to-back championships?

The ingredients were certainly there in the form of the holdovers from Super Bowl XI. And there were some impressive newcomers. From the college draft came defensive backs Mike Davis of Colorado and Lester Hayes of Texas A&M. Hayes would see limited action in 1977, Davis none; their best days would be reserved for the 1980s. But they would certainly keep Tatum, Colzie, Atkinson, Willie Brown, and Skip Thomas on their collective toes.

Guard Mickey Marvin came from Tennessee. He would eventually find a home at right guard. Marvin played 11 years with the Raiders and realized what must have been every man's dream in Oakland: He married a Raiderette. Marvin spent almost all of his final season on

injured reserve, but was activated for the meaningless
1987 finale against the Chicago Bears. After his retirement, Marvin became a member of the Raiders scouting
department.

Based on a recommendation from USC coach John
Robinson, linebacker Rod Martin was drafted by the
Raiders in the tenth round in 1977. Wise move. Martin
became a starter during 1978 and starred in Super Bowl
XV with three interceptions of Philadelphia quarterback
Ron Jaworski. Martin gave the Raiders 12 good seasons
as both an outside and inside linebacker. Randy
McClanahan was another rookie linebacker on the 1977
team. Like Martin, he would be a starter in 1980. Still
another linebacker, Jeff Barnes of the University of
California, started his pro career in 1977. Barnes played
11 years for the Silver and Black, mostly on special teams.
Jeff now owns a restaurant in his hometown of Hayward,
California.

To add to the mix, the Raiders attempted to bolster
their defensive line by two veteran acquisitions: tackle
Mike McCoy and end Pat Toomay. The price for McCoy
was steep, the No. 1 choice in 1978 and No. 4 in 1979.
This was not one of Al Davis's better deals. The former
Notre Dame All-American was a big bust. A 300-pound
bust.

1977 opened the same way that 1976 closed: The
Raiders beat the Chargers 24–0 as San Diego quarterback James Harris was limited to 77 passing yards. Lester
Hayes blocked a punt in his first professional game. The
defense was the story the following Sunday as Oakland
topped Pittsburgh 16–7. Franco Harris and Rocky Blier
were healthy but not a factor in the game. Toomay paid
immediate dividends by registering three sacks of Terry
Bradshaw.

Road wins at Kansas City and Cleveland followed.
The Raiders were trailing the Chiefs 21–10 when they
exploded in the second half. A 28-yard touchdown run

by Clarence Davis cinched the KC affair. The Browns tried to intimidate the Raiders with roughhouse style play, but it backfired by a 26–10 count. Errol Mann hit four field goals for the 4–0 Raiders.

On October 16, it was the undefeated Raiders against the undefeated Broncos at the Coliseum. Denver surprised Oakland 30–7, with rejuvenated quarterback Craig Morton picking the Raiders apart. Stabler had seven passes intercepted. A successful Bronco fake field attempt broke the game open. The loss ended the Raiders 17-game winning streak, one short of the NFL record.

The Raiders overcame four touchdown passes by Jets quarterback Richard Todd in a 28–27 win at New York. Stabler fired fourth-quarter touchdowns to Mike Siani and Fred Biletnikoff, and van Eeghen carried the ball 36 times for 143 yards. The Raiders next met the Broncos on a Monday night in Denver. This time the ground game was the difference as Denver tasted their first 1977 defeat in a 24–14 game. Toomay sacked Morton four times. "It was a hell of a victory," said Madden. The Raiders then bashed Seattle 44–7 in their inaugural meeting before edging Houston, 34–29. Oakland outgained the Seahawks, 397–177, in overall yards. In the Houston game, the Raiders came from behind as Willie Brown and Jack Tatum had important interceptions in the fourth quarter. Stabler was 23 of 31 for 264 yards and drilled the Oilers with six consecutive successful third-down passes.

Gene Klein's Chargers won their first game against Oakland since 1968 with a 12–7 decision. Led by obscure quarterback Cliff Olander, the Chargers outgained Oakland 212 to 10 in the second half and kicker Rolf Benirschke, who had been released by the Raiders, booted two field goals in the second half. Benirschke would later attain fame as both the host of the "Wheel of Fortune" TV show and as a boyfriend of letter-turner Vanna White.

An easy 34–13 Monday night win over Buffalo preceded a 20–14 loss to the Rams in Los Angeles. Stabler, who injured his knee against San Diego, returned to hurl three touchdown passes against the Bills and the rushers amassed 307 yards on the ground. A Pat Haden-to-Harold Jackson pass won the game for the Rams as the Raiders self-destructed with four interceptions, two fumbles, and a blocked field goal. The Raider loss gave Denver the AFC Western Division title.

Victories over Minnesota and Kansas City brought the final record to 11–3, one game behind Denver but good enough for a wild card berth. Three recovered Viking fumbles helped build an early 24–0 lead and Stabler rediscovered his sharpness with three scoring passes. The win against the Chiefs was the 150th for Oakland since 1960, the most of any NFL team in that span. Tim Collier of Kansas City had a 100-yard interception return and kicker Jan Stenerud ended the sloppy 21–20 game by shanking a field goal attempt.

The wild card Raiders traveled to Baltimore to play the AFC East Champion Colts in a first round playoff match. It would be the last time that Baltimore hosted a post-season game. Nobody among the 60,763 at Memorial Stadium that day could have dreamed that the next time these two teams would meet, it would be the Los Angeles Raiders versus the Indianapolis Colts.

The game was a classic, featuring great performances by both Stabler and Baltimore's Bert Jones. The lead changed hands all day. Oakland scored first on a 30-yard run by Clarence Davis. A Bruce Laird 61-yard interception and a Tony Linhart field goal put the Colts ahead at halftime, but Stabler and Casper combined for an eight-yard touchdown to tie the score. The Colts returned the ensuing kickoff into the Raider end zone. Stabler and Casper answered back with another TD. A Pete Banaszak touchdown was sandwiched around two short yardage scores by Ronnie Lee for the Colts. It was time for a typical last-minute drive for the Snake. In a play that has become known in Raider folklore as "ghost to the post," Stabler hit Casper for 42 yards. Madden played it safe and, with 26 seconds remaining in the fourth quarter, Errol Mann kicked a 22-yard field goal to knot the score at 31–31.

Both teams could do little during the overtime. With the fifth period nearly over, Stabler started moving the Raiders again. A 19-yard pass to Cliff Branch moved Oakland deep into Baltimore territory. Stabler found Casper open in the end zone on the second play of the sixth period. Final score: Raiders 37, Colts 31.

The Broncos beat up the Steelers the next day, so the following Sunday it would be archrivals Oakland at Denver for the right to go to Super Bowl XII.

The Broncos won 20–17, but the game will always be remembered for one name and one play. Or one nonplay. Rob Lytle. It was his fumble and the subsequent recovery by the Raiders' Mike McCoy that was disallowed because the officials didn't see it. On the next play Jon Keyworth scored a touchdown for the Broncos that made the difference in the game.

The Lytle "fumble" marred what should have gone down as a great game. After Errol Mann opened the scoring with a 20-yard field goal, Morton connected with Haven Moses for a 74-yard bomb to give Denver the half-time advantage. "What's going on here? That's a fumble," yelled Al Davis from the pressbox after watching the Lytle play. Keyworth's touchdown gave Denver a 14–3 lead. A seven-yard Stabler-to-Casper pass cut the Denver edge to 14–10, but an interception by the Broncos led to another Moses touchdown. A final Casper score made it a 20–17 game.

After the game, the officials issued a mimeographed sheet defending the non-call on Lytle. Al Davis was livid: "What I don't like is how they come up with excuses. The Big Lie, just like Vietnam." Added Jack Tatum, "The officials are prejudiced against Oakland. Tell the commissioner to fire some of those refs." The fines that were levied against Tatum and Davis were never disclosed.

After a remarkable run of six years in the playoffs, which featured a high scoring offense and a tough defense, the 1978 team slipped badly. Injuries in the offensive line and sub-par seasons by Upshaw and Shell forced Stabler to run for his life. The Snake slipped to 16 touchdowns and a career-worst 30 interceptions. The usually productive Branch caught only one touchdown pass during the entire season. Six times in the expanded 16-game schedule, the offense produced less than 17 points. The secondary, which had been a strong point for so many years, started springing large leaks and the pass rush was inconsistent. The place kicking of Errol Mann and rookie Jim Breech became an adventure. Despite all of the problems, the Raiders finished 9–7, only one game behind Denver. What doomed the Silver and Black was a 3–5 record within the AFC West. Two of the three wins were against last-place Kansas City. "The Raiders lacked a killer instinct in 1978," was the assessment of columnist Ron Bergman of the *Oakland Tribune*.

Because of the Mike McCoy trade, the Raiders had no Number 1 draft pick in 1978. The only player from the rookies who would eventually contribute was running back Arthur Whittington, who was to become a starter in 1979.

Another expensive acquisition was cornerback Monte Jackson from the Rams. The price was the top pick in the 1979 draft. Jackson, nicknamed "Matzo Ball" by his teammates, started many games in his three years with the Raiders but left his best days behind in Los Angeles.

After the first week of the season, in a little-noticed move, the Raiders signed quarterback Jim Plunkett, who had been released by the San Francisco 49ers. Plunkett, who won the Heisman Trophy at Stanford in 1970 and was the NFL Rookie of the Year with the Patriots, played with mostly bad teams in New England before being traded to San Francisco in 1976. He had trouble with the offense there and was released in 1978. He quietly became the third-string quarterback in 1978 and sat on the bench the entire season.

Most preseason games are humdrum affairs that are not worthy of serious discussion. But the Raiders' second exhibition game of 1978 would never be forgotten. The New England Patriots met the Raiders on a Saturday night in Oakland. Early in the contest, safety Jack Tatum was defending against Patriots wide receiver Darryl Stingley when an attempted pass was thrown too high. Tatum hit Stingley low with his shoulder. The result left Stingley permanently paralyzed. "It's distressing," said Tatum after the game. He added, "You hate to see anybody get hurt. It's unfortunate. But I was just doing my job." Patriot coach Chuck Fairbanks also dismissed any condemnation of Tatum. "There was nothing illegal or flagrant of a type to be criticized in any way and I don't think anything like that could be intimated," said Fairbanks.

Stingley was hospitalized in nearby Castro Valley. John Madden was among the visitors. Tatum was to receive criticism later for not seeing Stingley after the injury. Stingley's career was over, and combined with the "criminal element" incident of 1976, Tatum's reputation was soiled beyond repair. Naming his first book *They Call Me Assassin* has not helped Tatum's image either.

The Stingley injury may have been an ominous sign that bad days were ahead, because the regular season began with a 14–6 loss in the 90 degree heat of Denver. When a Stabler pass slipped through Biletnikoff's fingers, Bronco defensive back Bernard Jackson returned it for a touchdown. There was also a crucial pass interference call on Monte Jackson. Al Davis blasted the

official who assessed the penalty. "He had no right to
make that call. He was talked into it," said Davis. The
opening loss would be a microcosm of the entire season.

Game Two against improved San Diego will also be remembered for one play. Unlike the Rob Lytle fumble,
this bizarre play won the game for Oakland. With 10 seconds to go, Stabler was at the San Diego 15-yard line trailing, 20–14. The Raiders had no more time-outs. With his
receivers covered, Stabler was hit by linebacker Woody
Lowe as he attempted to pass. The Snake then fumbled
the ball forward. It was batted around at the three by
Banaszak and then rolled into the end zone, where
Casper fell on it for a touchdown. The "holy roller" play
gave Oakland a 21–20 victory. "We were damned lucky,"
said a grateful Stabler. "There shalt be no more holy
rollers again," declared the NFL. After the season, the
rules concerning fumble recoveries were changed to dis-
allow the play in the future.

The Raiders next beat Green Bay before losing at
home to the Patriots. A total of 348 yards rushing was
amassed against the Packers, and not one pass was fired
by Stabler in the final three touchdown drives of the 28–3
win. The New England game was a forgettable performance. The Raiders blew a 14–0 first-quarter lead and
were outgained 381 to 140 yards by the Pats over the last
three periods. The winning Patriots awarded the game
ball to the injured Darryl Stingley. At Chicago, Stabler returned to form with a 25 for 43 performance for 278
yards and *no* interceptions. The Bears and Raiders were
tied and went into overtime. Safety Neal Colzie intercepted a Bob Avellini pass to give the Raiders possession
at the Chicago three. Whittington then scored the winning touchdown.

Wins over Houston and Kansas City followed. The
Oilers were ahead 17–7 and were about to score again
when defensive back Charles Phillips picked up an Earl
Campbell fumble and ran 96 yards into the end zone. A

three-yard Stabler-to-Casper touchdown pass then won the game. Chiefs Coach Marv Levy tried a wing T formation to get his offense going, but it was the Raiders who regularly moved the ball. Van Eeghen scored twice and Stabler was 15 of 20 for 222 yards as the Raiders had an easy 28–6 victory over the Chiefs.

Call him "Zorn the thorn." Quarterback Jim Zorn became a frequent Raider nemesis in 1978 and 1979. In Seattle, he led his Seahawks to a 27–7 win. Stabler had three passes picked off. "This was one of the Raiders all-time low points, maybe the all-timer," wrote Ira Miller, who covered the game for the *San Francisco Chronicle*. Another low point had to be the San Diego rematch in Oakland. In this debacle, the Raiders squandered a 20–7 second-quarter lead. The Chargers scored on all four of their second half possessions as the Raiders played conservatively but couldn't run the ball. While the Chargers were avenging the "holy roller" defeat, Al Davis was quietly becoming critical of Madden's play calling. The coach became annoyed with his boss. Both men sensed that there would be a new man coaching the Raiders in 1979.

The Raiders fought back from the doldrums with victories over Kansas City, Cincinnati, and Detroit. Madden's play calling looked good when van Eeghen gained a key fourth down yard that led to a clinching touchdown in a 20–10 win at Kansas City. The opportunistic defense caused seven Cincinnati turnovers. Four led to Raider touchdowns in a Monday night 34–21 victory. Punter Ray Guy and van Eeghen were the stars of a 29–17 decision over Detroit on a muddy field at the Coliseum. The rejuvenated 8–4 Raiders were again looking like a sure playoff team.

Then came a frustrating 17–16 loss to Seattle. The difference was a botched extra point, the fifth week in a row that a conversion had been missed. The winning last second field goal by Efren Herrera of the Seahawks left the Raiders at 8–5 but still in first place. Nobody was overly worried.

A Sunday night game against Denver was characterized by another good start but a flat ending. The Raiders made the initial 12 first downs of the game but could only lead 3–0. The Denver defense and special teams led by linebacker Tom Jackson and defensive end Lyle Alzado dominated the second half. "We own Oakland," said the talkative Jackson, who is now a mild-mannered commentator for ESPN. Stabler ran for his life against Denver and was sacked twice by the colorful Alzado, who was not wearing an earring in those days.

The ineptness of 1978 was completed in the Orange Bowl against Miami. The Raiders took a 6–3 lead when Stabler hit Biletnikoff with a 16-yard pass, but a blocked kick led to one Miami score and an interception gave the Dolphins another. The 23–6 defeat knocked the 8–7 Raiders out of the playoffs. A consolation 27–20 win over the Vikings brought the final 1978 mark to 9–7, the poorest Raider record since 1964.

By season's end, there were rumors that Madden was headed for the New York Giants. "I will only coach for the Oakland Raiders," was Madden's statement to the media after the season. He was right, sort of. In his bestseller, *Hey Wait a Minute, I Wrote a Book,* Madden paints a rosy picture of his relationship with Davis and says he was thinking of quitting anyway. There were always some disagreements over personnel. For example, Madden was not consulted by Davis when either Bubba Smith or Monte Jackson was acquired. And Madden had no use for the underachieving Charles Philyaw. But what Madden didn't tell his readers is how the Davis–Madden relationship deteriorated rapidly following the first Seattle and second San Diego games. During the remainder of the 1978 season, the two strong-willed men rarely spoke. Assistant coach Flores was offered the offensive cooidinator position in Detroit but Davis hinted that Tom should stick around in Oakland.

Related to the coaching situation was a rare dose of public criticism by Davis. This time the target was Stabler. "It's not just Stabler, the whole club didn't play well. But you've got to point to someone. So blame Stabler. He makes the most money. He gets paid to take the pressure."

The Bay Area media was stunned by the blast at Stabler. With reserves Mike Rae and Jim Plunkett not considered starting candidates, there was nobody else on the horizon to play quarterback.

Stabler was incensed by the remarks. When asked later if he buried the hatchet with the boss, the Snake said something like "Sure, right between the shoulder blades." It would be 10 years before the two men patched their differences.

The criticism was also indirectly aimed at Madden. The Madden-Stabler relationship as coach-quarterback was as close as any in the game. Davis was sending smoke signals to big John. And the message was clear: "new coach."

Al Davis had decided to trade in his 1978 Madden for a late model Flores. But how to change coaches without catching both fan and media criticism was a problem. With his sideline gyrations and blond hair flapping in the breeze while he fought for his players and against the officials, Madden symbolized the fight and spirit of the Raiders and was very popular. Until 1978, the Raider players always responded positively to his leadership, and second-guessing by the boss was minimal. Those days were now over.

On January 4, 1979, Al Davis called only the third press conference since he returned to the Raiders in 1966. The announcement: John Madden, at the age of 42, has "retired" as the Raider coach, blaming an ulcer for his decision to step down. Madden was kept on the payroll as they concocted the position of director of special projects. After lounging around the house for a few months while working on all of the special projects, Madden was auditioned for a color commentator position at CBS. You know the rest of the story. Bam, boom, wham!

Believe it or not, names like outsiders Bud Carson, Dan Reeves, and Ray Perkins were mentioned for the job. But Al stayed within the Raider organization and chose quarterback coach Tom Flores as his next coach. "Tom did a good job as an assistant. He's wanted this type of thing for a long time," was the reaction of Madden. Columnist Glenn Dickey of the *San Francisco Chronicle* figured that Al wanted Flores all along and used the interviews with outsiders to mislead the press. "Davis is a natural con man," said Dickey. "Had he been born a century earlier, he would have sold snake oil to the early settlers in the West."

In addition to Madden, the Raiders were phasing out many other familiar faces. Morris Bradshaw became a starting wide receiver at the expense of Biletnikoff. Freddie B was released in training camp in 1979 and played in Canada for a year before starting a coaching career north of the border. In 1989, he returned to the Raiders as receivers coach. Pete Banaszak hung up his cleats and so did Willie Brown, who became defensive backfield coach.

Another surprise casualty was assistant coach Tom Dahms, who had been with the Raiders since he was hired by Al Davis in 1963. He was replaced by Sam Boghosian who would serve the Raiders as offensive coordinator through 1987 when he would depart with Flores.

Again without a first-round pick, the Raiders did receive some draft day help in 1979. Offensive tackle Bruce Davis of UCLA would eventually replace Art Shell in the starting lineup for most of the next nine seasons. He was traded to Houston for a second-round draft pick in 1987 but re-signed by the Raiders in 1990. Defensive end

Willie Jones of Florida State would make valuable contributions for the 1980 World Championship team. Wide receiver Ira Matthews of Wisconsin became a sensation as a kick returner. Another solid special-teams player would be Derrick Jensen of Texas Arlington. Rookie wide receiver Rich Martini of California-Davis replaced Biletnikoff and an injured Bradshaw as a starting wide receiver. From the University of Oklahoma came Reggie Kinlaw, who would later play nose tackle when the Raiders switched to a three-man defensive line.

After the first month of the 1979 season, the Raiders signed running back Todd Christensen of Brigham Young University, who had been the No. 2 draft choice of Dallas in 1978. He was traded to the Giants in 1979 and then waived. Christensen played on special teams while being converted to tight end. It was another master stroke by the Raiders as Christensen became the leading receiver in the NFL during the mid-eighties.

"Up and down" and "great at home; miserable on the road" would be the most fitting descriptions for the 1979 Raiders. When it was over, two more losses to the upstart Seattle Seahawks would cost them a playoff berth for the second straight season. Stabler threw for a team record 3,615 yards in what would be his swan song in Silver and Black. Van Eeghen slipped to 818 yards after three 1,000-yard seasons, and neither Whittington nor reserve Booker Russell proved to be the breakaway threat the Raiders needed. The defense was in a transition period and lacked a dominant pass rusher.

Amid rumors of a move, the Raiders opened the season with a 24–17 upset of the Rams in the Los Angeles Memorial Coliseum. The special teams won that one. After failing to block a punt during the entire 1978 campaign, they blocked a pair in the second quarter. The defense chipped in with three interceptions of Rams quarterback Pat Haden. Traveling down to San Diego for game No. 2, Dan Fouts and his receivers manhandled the

Raiders 30–10. Stabler passed for 343 yards, but the Raiders were completely dominated at the line of scrimmage by the fired-up Chargers.

Lackluster performances followed in losses at Seattle and Kansas City. Jim Zorn bruised the Raiders with three touchdown passes; two were caught by receiver Steve Largent, who would keep haunting the Raiders through the 1980s. Numerous dropped passes and continuous poor field position did not help Oakland. The Chiefs rushed for 222 yards in a 35–7 rout. Stabler was sacked six times and passed for only 91 yards. "We just played a poor game," said Tom Flores, who may have been second-guessing his decision to accept the head coaching job.

The home season finally started, and the Raiders responded to the Coliseum fans by beating Denver, Miami, and Atlanta. In an attempt to better protect Stabler, the Raiders employed a double tight end offense against the Broncos. It worked in a 27–3 victory. The defense put the pressure on Denver quarterbacks Craig Morton and Norris Weese, and Monte Johnson recovered a fumble in the end zone for a touchdown. The Dolphins were also limited to a field goal, as a strong pass rush on Bob Griese and superb punting by Ray Guy had Miami backpedaling all night. Ted Hendricks sealed the victory with a 23-yard touchdown interception. The Falcons contributed six turnovers to the 50–19 rout; one of them was a touchdown for Lester Hayes. Van Eeghen scored three times.

Despite 360 yards through the air by Stabler, the Raiders lost 28–19 at Shea Stadium to the Jets. The Snake also threw five interceptions, and the Raiders self-destructed with four clipping penalties on kickoff returns. Four days later, Howard Cosell and his mates were present on a Thursday night when the Raiders exploded past San Diego 45–22. The game was highlighted by an Ira Matthews 104-yard kickoff return and another Lester Hayes touchdown interception. The Raiders gave the game ball to Carole Davis, who had suffered a massive heart attack a few days earlier.

In a sloppy game that had 11 turnovers, the Raiders beat San Francisco 23–10. Cliff Branch scored twice. "We were walking around like we were in Central Park, looking around, checking it out," said Art Shell, who awakened his lethargic teammates with a halftime pep talk. The Raiders couldn't stop Earl Campbell the following week; Campbell rushed for 107 yards in a 31–17 loss at Houston. Then the Silver and Black were upset by Kansas City 24–21. Kicker Jim Breech helped lose this one by missing an 18-yard field goal with five seconds to play that would have forced overtime. He would also lose his job after the season. Similar to their first meeting with Oakland, the Chiefs compiled 241 yards rushing in a potent ground game to offset Stabler's three touchdown tosses. Raider wide receivers also dropped a few passes. This was not a game to write home about.

In a 14–10 win at Denver, Number 6 draft choice Booker Russell gained 72 of his 100 yards on one play. It was followed by a memorable Monday night game at New Orleans. After trailing 35–14 early in the third quarter, Stabler passed the Raiders to a 42–35 comeback win. Cliff Branch caught a 66-yard touchdown pass to tie the game, and then safety Mike Davis recovered a Chuck Muncie fumble to set up the winning score. The Raiders concluded the decade with a gaudy 13–1–1 record for "Monday Night Football."

Breech atoned for his fluff at Kansas City with a 45-yard field goal in a 19–14 victory over Cleveland. Stabler completed 23 of 34 passes for 196 yards and was never sacked. And miracle of miracles, there were no holding penalties against the offensive line. The win gave the Raiders a 9–6 record. If they could beat Seattle in the finale, and if Denver would lose to San Diego on Monday night, the Raiders would make the playoffs. The Chargers were cooperative and routed the Broncos. But it didn't matter. Jim Zorn burned the Raiders again, completing 23 of 34 passes in a 29–24 Seahawks victory. The disappointed Flores finished 9–7 as a rookie head coach.

After two also-ran years, some major changes were due. In March, Davis took time out from preparing for the trial against the NFL and traded Stabler to Houston for their quarterback, Dan Pastorini. The Oilers had lost to Pittsburgh in two straight AFC Championship games and coach Bum Phillips had lost confidence in Pastorini. It looked like the blockbuster trade of the year, but it would ultimately prove to be insignificant for Oakland.

Another major trade sent linebacker Phil Villapiano to Buffalo for wide receiver Bob Chandler. With the "retirement" of Biletnikoff, the Raiders lacked a reliable "possession" type receiver, so it was hoped that the Chandler would solve that problem. Two trades with Houston relieved the Raiders of Jack Tatum and brought seldom-used halfback Kenny King to Oakland.

The defensive line was bolstered by the acquisition of veterans Cedrick Hardman and Joe Campbell. Two other seasoned players, Dave Pear and Dave Browning, would also be counted on in 1980. Veteran linebacker Bob Nelson was added to the squad. Ditto defensive backs Odis McKinney from the Giants and Dwayne O'steen from the Rams, who eventually replaced Monte Jackson as a starting cornerback. A master stroke was the acquisition of Burgess Owens of the Jets, who replaced Tatum at free safety. Another positive move was the release of Jim Breech and the signing of kicker Chris Bahr.

The star of the college crop was Penn State linebacker Matt Millen, who immediately became a starter on the inside. Not much was immediately expected from quarterback Marc Wilson from Brigham Young, the No. 1 choice. Hopefully, he would watch and learn from Pastorini and Plunkett and perhaps be the quarterback of the future (it's not *that* funny).

The many newcomers did not impress most football experts. A last-place finish was widely forecast for the Silver and Black, who were fourth in 1979. Many also saw the battle between Al Davis and the NFL over the move to Los Angeles as a disruptive influence on the players.

And when the Raiders started with a 2–3 record, the experts were looking good. The Pastorini-to-Chandler combination clicked in a 27–14 opening victory at Kansas City. Against San Diego, Pastorini was hurt in the fourth quarter. Plunkett entered the game and threw a game-tying touchdown pass to Raymond Chester. He then returned to the sidelines as the Raiders lost 30–24 in overtime. The Raiders combined 230 rushing yards and three sacks of Washington quarterback Joe Theismann by John Matuszak for a 24–21 win over the Redskins. A lackluster 24–7 loss at Buffalo was followed by a 31–17 defeat to Kansas City. In the fourth quarter against the Chiefs, Pastorini suffered a broken leg. The Oakland fans were roundly criticized for booing as the injured Pastorini was carried off the field. Plunkett took over. Perhaps the fans knew something.

In his Raider career, Jim Plunkett had seen little action. He appeared in a few games in 1979 when a contest had already been decided. He threw the touchdown to Chester in the San Diego loss and then returned to the bench. Plunkett seemed to have trouble in New England and San Francisco handling the pressure of being the starting quarterback. Perhaps he was a good backup quarterback, nothing more. With the injury to Pastorini, the fickle football gods were giving him one more chance to excel. For the 1980 Oakland Raiders, there was no other alternative. Rookie Wilson wasn't ready. Mike Rae, David Humm, and Larry Lawrence had come and gone. For better or worse, Jim Plunkett was the quarterback.

The first-place Chargers came to town. If the Raiders entertained any title hopes, they had to win this game. The gods must have bet Oakland. Plunkett was sharp and everybody played well. Defensive end Willie Jones was credited with three sacks of Dan Fouts. Kenny King scored on an 89-yard run. Plunkett had passed his first test. Late in the game Marc Wilson connected with Bob Chandler for his first career touchdown pass. Final score: Raiders 38, Chargers 24.

Next stop. Pittsburgh on a Monday night. It was another great cumulative effort as the Raiders prevailed 45–34. Plunkett passed for touchdowns to Chandler, Cliff Branch, and Morris Bradshaw. Rod Martin returned an interception for a score and Terry Bradshaw was sacked five times.

The Raider scoring machine continued in a 33–14 decision over Seattle. Plunkett found Chandler for three touchdowns. Lester Hayes had two interceptions and the defense registered six more sacks.

Hayes continued his All-Pro season with another interception against Miami. Chester and Chandler scored the touchdowns in a 16–10 win. Next the Raiders overcame three fumbles, two interceptions, and 92 yards in penalties to beat the Bengals 28–17. Arthur Whittington had a 90-yard kickoff return. A fourth-quarter safety was the margin of victory in a 19–17 cliffhanger in Seattle.

The Raiders next took their six-game winning streak into Philadelphia. A missed blitz by Millen against quarterback Ron Jaworski led to the only touchdown of the game in a 10–7 loss. Up next was a tense 9–3 Monday night win over Denver. Plunkett scored the only touchdown. Kicker Chris Bahr missed an extra point and three field goals but the defense held firm. The Raiders then lost 19–13 to Dallas, so victories in the final two games were imperative if they hoped to make the playoffs.

In a 24–19 victory at Denver, Chandler crossed the goal line twice. A clutch Burgess Owens interception clinched the win. The playoffs were attained with a 33–17 over the Giants in week 16. Branch, Chandler, and Chester scored touchdowns for the offense but the coup de grace was administered by the special teams when Derrick Jensen scooped up an attempted onside kick and raced into the end zone.

The Raiders and the Houston Oilers were the wild card teams. Houston came into town with some old friends: Ken Stabler, Jack Tatum, and Dave Casper, who was traded to the Oilers during the season.

Stabler was treated rudely by the Raider defense and was sacked seven times. Halfback Earl Campbell was shut down. A Plunkett-to-King pass set up a touchdown to reserve tight end Todd Christensen. Whittington scored another touchdown, as did cornerback Lester Hayes. The Raiders ripped the Oilers 27–7.

AFC Central Champion Cleveland was the next opponent. The wind chill factor along Lake Erie was minus 16 degrees. It was a brutal day and a bruising game. Oh yes, there was another Lester Hayes interception. Mark van Eeghen's fourth-quarter touchdown put the Raiders ahead by 14–12. With time running out, Cleveland quarterback Brian Sipe started driving the Browns toward the Oakland goal. Rather than try a field goal, Sipe looked for tight end Ozzie Newsome in the end zone. Mike Davis stepped in front of Newsome and intercepted the pass, and the Raiders were headed to San Diego for a showdown against the Chargers.

Unlike the Cleveland game, the AFC Championship game was a wide open, high-scoring affair. The Raiders opened the scoring when a deflected Plunkett pass was grabbed by an alert Chester, who ran 65 yards into the end zone. Kenny King and van Eeghen also scored. After a fourth-quarter Chris Bahr field goal made it 34–28 and San Diego had to punt, van Eeghen and King controlled the ball on the ground for the final seven minutes. Wild card Oakland had won three playoff games, two on the road. No team had ever accomplished that before.

The last stop for this miracle team was Super Bowl XV in New Orleans against Philadelphia. The Raiders dominated this game from the coin toss. Branch scored the first touchdown following a Rod Martin interception, as the defense stymied Jaworski and his receivers. In the second quarter, Plunkett hit King with a pass along the sidelines, and Kenny scampered 80 yards for a record Super Bowl score. The Raiders increased their 14–3 halftime lead with a 29-yard touchdown pass to Branch. Martin had two more interceptions and van Eeghen, in his last big game as a Raider, gained 80 yards on 19 carries. Plunkett, capping a Frank Merriwell season, was named Most Valuable Player, based on 21 completions in 33 attempts for 261 yards.

With the game over, the real drama of the day was yet to come. Commissioner Pete Rozelle would have to present the Super Bowl trophy to his archenemy, Al Davis, in the Raider dressing room. Although the players and Al had a code word arranged to throw Rozelle out, it was not used. His fight with Rozelle would wait for another day. Al graciously accepted the trophy. If we could only read their minds.

Another touching moment in the Raider locker room occurred when NBC announcer Bryant Gumbel attempted to interview Lester Hayes. Only then did America become aware of Hayes' severe stuttering problem. The Raiders would arrange for therapy, and after several years Hayes' speech impediment was overcome.

The trade of Tatum to Houston gave the Raiders two first round picks for 1981. They were used to select defensive back Ted Watts of Texas Tech and guard Curt Marsh of the University of Washington. But the biggest catch was the second-round pick, defensive end Howie Long of Villanova. The native of Somerville, Massachusetts, was first noticed by the Raiders in the 1980 Blue-Gray college All-Star game. Long became a starter in the later part of the 1981 season and became a mainstay on the defensive line. By the end of the 1989 season, Long was the only "Oakland" Raider still with the club.

There was some other interesting young talent. Like Long, fullback Frank Hawkins of Nevada-Reno was not a well-known college player. Hawkins eventually became the starting fullback in 1983 and would provide strong blocking for Marcus Allen and the quarterbacks. Hawkins could also run the ball. Malcolm Barnwell of Virginia Union was a starting wide receiver for much of the 1982 and 1983 seasons. After losing his job to Dokie Williams, Barnwell was traded to Washington in 1985. From Yale came safety Kenny Hill, who was a valuable reserve and special teams player. He was sent to the Giants following Super Bowl XVIII.

With the specter of Los Angeles continuing to hover over the Raiders, the attendance at the Oakland Coliseum started falling. Only two games were sold out in 1981. And the team didn't play with the same intensity or efficiency as in years past. This was the last year for Upshaw and Shell. Van Eeghen saw limited action and was waived by the Raiders in 1982. He was claimed by New England.

There were injuries galore, including a ruptured spleen for Bob Chandler, which led to the end of his career. Either Plunkett or Wilson was the starting quarterback, depending upon which one was physically able to play. Following his league-leading 13 interceptions in 1980, the NFL outlawed stick-um, the substance that Lester Hayes poured on his hands. There seemed to be bad karma to the Raiders in 1981, which was their last season in Oakland.

After losing twice to the Raiders in 1979 and 1980, Denver and new head coach Dan Reeves got their revenge in a 9–7 opening day victory. The Broncos defense put extreme pressure on Plunkett. The Raiders looked like a Super Bowl club the following Monday night in a 36–10 blowout of the Vikings at Minnesota. There were eight sacks of Minnesota quarterback Tommy Kramer; one became a touchdown for Cedrick Hardman. Plun-

kett threw a touchdown to Todd Christensen, who was
seeing more action on offense. After the regulars were
removed, Wilson threw a long touchdown pass to
Barnwell. The home opener was a 20–10 win over Seattle. Bradshaw caught a touchdown pass and reserve running back Derrick Jensen also scored. The future sure
looked bright!

What happened next? After scoring in 217 straight
games, the Silver and Black was shut out three straight
times against three relatively bad teams: Detroit, Denver,
and Kansas City.

They did score on the following Sunday. But it took a
blocked field goal on the final play of the game to save an
18–16 victory over Tampa Bay. Chris Bahr kicked three
field goals, including a 51-yarder. The Coliseum crowd
of 44,811 was the smallest since 1969. In the fourth quarter against the Chiefs, the Raiders were trailing 21–17
when they got down to the Kansas City five-yard line. On
the last play of the game, Marc Wilson was blindsided by
the Chiefs and fumbled, and Kansas City returned the
ball for a touchdown.

More inconsistent football followed. Although Art
Shell was injured against New England, the Raiders rallied to beat the Patriots. Howie Long and Matt Millen led
the pass rush and Willie Jones recovered a fumble. A loss
to Houston was followed by an impressive 33–17 win at
Miami. Wilson gave a fine performance by throwing TD
passes to Christensen, Derrick Ramsey, and Chandler,
who returned from the injured list. Miami quarterback
David Woodley was sacked six times.

The first-place Chargers then came to town. Wilson
was sharp early as the score was 21–21. Then the Fouts-
to-Kellen Winslow combination blew the Raiders away
55–21. Eddie Erdelatz was the coach when the Raiders
last gave up 55 points. Maybe the Oakland team had
come full circle.

At Seattle, the Raiders came from behind in a 32–31

thriller. With the score 24–3 Seattle, Marc Wilson fired touchdowns to Ramsey and Chandler, and Whittington also scored.

The last ABC "Monday Night" game to be played in Oakland would indicate the fortune-telling talents of Howard Cosell. The Coliseum was empty at the beginning of the contest as the fans formally protested the move to Los Angeles by purposely not entering the stadium. Early in the game Pittsburgh quarterback Terry Bradshaw was injured. Coach Chuck Noll turned his offense over to rookie signal caller Mark Malone. So while a national television audience was expecting Plunkett against Bradshaw, they were "treated" to Malone versus Wilson.

It was an exciting night. Kenny King raced 63 yards for one score and Wilson found Derrick Ramsey for another as the Raiders rallied for a 30–27 win. The 7–7 Raiders were still mathematically alive for a wild card berth. But barely. Showing his true football expertise, sportscaster Howard Cosell said "I know one thing, we've seen two great quarterbacks of the future here tonight."

When the Jets beat the Browns on the following Saturday in a game remembered for being broadcast by NBC without a color commentator, the Raiders were eliminated. On Sunday, December 13, 1981, the Raiders played their final home game at Oakland Coliseum. They stunk up the joint. Chicago quarterback Vince Evans led the Bears to a 23–6 victory. It wasn't just the weather that made this a dark day in Oakland.

The final game of the season was a Monday night affair in San Diego, and the Chargers needed the game to win the division. The Raiders broke into the lead but, hampered by injuries, both Plunkett and Wilson were ineffective, and the Chargers prevailed 23–10. It was only the second Monday night loss ever for the Raiders.

Even though they were still the Oakland Raiders, there was a foreboding feeling around the East Bay that they were all but gone. Gone south. Al Davis was saying even back then that "the greatness of the Raiders in is our future." The first trial had ended in a hung jury and the second trial would start in the spring. Al Davis doesn't like to lose and he certainly doesn't like to tie. It was only a matter of time before the divorce of the Raiders and Oakland would be final.

Although the overall record for the final five years in Oakland didn't match previous performances, there was one Super Bowl winner led by a Cinderella quarterback and an "almost" in another season. In their chortling over the San Francisco 49ers' achievements of the 1980s, the Bay Area media occasionally resorts to revisionist history and conveniently forgets that Oakland won two Super Bowls before San Francisco ever got started.

The Raiders may have been mediocre in some of the Oakland years, but they were never dull. The loyal Oakland fans would soon miss out on another successful Al Davis rebuilding program. The next Raider championship club would be playing somewhere else.

Chapter 10

THE DECLINE OF A GREAT ORGANIZATION

"The Raiders remain a mom and pop operation. They don't have a public relations specialist. The word promotion *is missing from their vocabulary."*

—*Alan Malamud,* Los Angeles Times

Yes. The Los Angeles Raiders *are* a mom and pop operation. And Al Davis is the mama and the papa. Procedurally, the Raiders probably are doing business very similarly to 1966 or 1976.

It was not too long ago that just about every player in the National Football League wanted to be traded to the Raiders. And why not? Al Davis usually had the highest payroll in the NFL, and compared to most other teams, the coaching staff and front office usually treated the players like adults. There was rarely a contract holdout. In fact, Davis would routinely reward good performances by giving raises and contract extensions without a player even requesting it. Many of the retired players who played elsewhere confirm that, compared to other clubs, Al Davis did everything first class. Once in a while there might be a problem, such as with Stabler after the 1978 season. But it was usually one big happy family.

So there must be something very good about the way
Al Davis runs his store. Because even though he has been
hated and despised by fellow football owners and a large
segment of the media, almost every player who has
passed through the hallowed halls of Al Davis University
has usually been very pleased. Following is a sample of recent quotes from former Raiders:

"The Raiders were the first team to let me be the type of
player I really wanted to be. My only regret is that I
played in Los Angeles so late in my career. Al Davis was
very loyal and encouraging to all his players when I was
there."—Lyle Alzado.

"When it comes to being a gentleman, when it comes to
treating their players like men, when it comes to being
champions—no other team comes close . . . Everything
stems from Al Davis, everything. He's the kind of guy you
want on your side."—John Matuszak, 1988.

"And he [Davis] never put you on the field without giving
you all the tools necessary to perform. . . . I always tell
people I was extremely fortunate to play for three of the
greatest coaches ever: Weeb Ewbank, Hank Stram, and
Al Davis."—Cotton Davidson.

"No matter who the coach is for the Raiders on the
sidelines, it has always been Al Davis's show. He is always
for the players, so it was really easy to play for him and
want to win for him."—Rod Sherman.

"I still feel very close to Al Davis. . . . It's always been like
a father-son relationship."—Ray Guy.

"I just think the world of Al . . . If you take care of business for Al, he'll try to take care of you and will bring you
back if at all possible."—David Humm.

"Al Davis was my first head coach with the Raiders, so I
know that all he cares about is winning and how dedicated he is to his players."—Ben Davidson.

"My allegiance is with the Raiders. It's a great organization . . . I'm still a Raider."—George Atkinson.

"Looking back now, if I had just kept my mouth shut that

one year, Al would never have traded me. I came to appreciate the Raiders more after I left."—Mike Siani.

"It was a great organization to be associated with . . . but being with the Raiders was different. Everyone—starting with Al Davis on down—was very goal-oriented, and that made things exciting all the time."—George Buehler.

"I love the man [Davis]. He's true to his word. I'd die for the man. I love him to death."—Mickey Marvin.

"I thank my lucky stars that I was in the right place at the right time, going to the Raiders. In those days especially, we were winners."—Pete Banaszak.

"But when it gets right down to it, the big difference between winning and losing in anything are the organizations. . . . but Al Davis has proven the Raider organization just wins."—Dave Casper.

"I really wanted to come here and coach. I had always wanted to be here in some capacity. So I talked to Al, and a few days later, I had the job. I was happy as I could be."—Fred Biletnikoff.

"There were a number of games in those days that were going to be played in the South that I refused to play in. And he [Davis] canceled them. That told me what type of individual I was dealing with."—Art Powell.

"If I could have picked any one team to play with, where the personality matched mine, it definitely would have been the Raiders. I knew they never quit and would fight till the end."—Daryle Lamonica.

"All of my good years in the National Football League came when I was playing for teams that Al Davis put together and John Madden molded, and I thank them for giving me the opportunity."—Ken Stabler.

In recent years, there has been another side to the story. When a team doesn't win, something has to be wrong. And four consecutive non-winning seasons indicates that the problem is more than an aberration.

Maybe "mom and pop" has spent too much time away from the store in the last few years. Even though Howie

Long says that "Mr. Davis can be six rooms away and knows what's going on in here," nobody can be everywhere at once, not even Al Davis. The man who once pledged to make the Oakland Raiders the best organization in professional sports is reluctant to delegate authority to many in the organization and recently has encountered rare hostility from some of his own players.

Both the efficiency and the function of the people in the Raider front office who are supposed to assist Al Davis, and their recent contributions to winning football games, have to be questioned. Al Davis says he learned how to set up a football organization from Sid Gillman. But Gillman never operated as a lone ranger. Al LoCasale allegedly handles the "administration," and the title on the door of the office of Ron Wolf said that he was in charge of "personnel operations." But those titles are misnomers. "Little Al," as some have called LoCasale, seems to split his time between being a quasi media point man in an organization that largely ignores public relations and a mouthpiece for Davis. LoCasale was once director of player personnel for both the Chargers and Bengals. Ron Wolf was the alleged head of personnel operations. If this were a position of authority, Davis should have sent Wolf into the woods after the poor drafts of 1985–87. Tampa Bay was unimpressed with Wolf when he was hired by Bucs coach and general manager John McKay in 1976–1977 and was sent back to Davis. Perhaps John McKay was venting his old USC hostilities toward "Big Al." Of course, Wolf and LoCasale have no real authority. In July 1990, Wolf moved to the New York Jets as director of player personnel. There is only one real boss with the Raiders. Guess who? And perhaps that's as it should be.

Until 1989, there was an overabundance of senior administrators on the staff. Mike Ornstein and Irv Kaze were basically serving as "troubleshooters," but only in areas off the football field. Kaze was the team spokesman when the Raiders were feuding with the Los Angeles Coliseum Commission in 1986 and 1987, but the decision to suspend construction of the luxury boxes was made by Davis. Ornstein's main claim to fame in three years with the Raiders was a fistfight with John Herrera, another senior administrator. Herrera was in charge of the Irwindale deal and he obediently did the legwork with Davis really calling the shots. Good work, John.

The bigger problem is that many in the Raider front office are generally in fear of Davis, and few ever challenge his decisions or authority. And of course nothing gets done without the OK of the Genius. Davis has always said that employees perform better when intimidated. Perhaps fear and scare tactics work on the playing field, but it may not cut it anymore in the front offices of the 1990s. It may have also contributed to the rocky relationship between Davis and former head coach Mike Shanahan. Even at a slimmed-down 280 pounds, Art Shell is not easily intimidated by anyone, including Al Davis. Based on the track record of recent years, a Raider front office overhaul may be necessary, and Davis should update the scouting system. It is just not delivering the goods anymore.

Kaze and Ornstein both cut their teeth in the public relations and promotions field and therein lies another problem with the Raiders: their complete deficiency in the area of how to win fans and influence media.

It is amazing how the rise to power of Al Davis with both the Raiders and within the National Football League has been matched by a subsequent decrease in a public relations effort. When Al Davis first came to Oakland in 1963, the young coach and general manager was somewhat shy and reticent but would occasionally make public appearances on behalf of his team and the American Football League. As a coach, Davis always kept the beat writers informed. Win or lose, Davis was usually glib and refreshing with his post-game comments. Al's play-

ers were always accessible. The American Football
League and the Oakland Raiders had to be "sold" to the
people of the East Bay. A colorful, exciting, and improving team always makes the sales pitch easier, of course.
Obviously, it was a successful endeavor.

When Davis returned to Oakland in 1966, he pulled
back from personal appearances and let the performance of his young team and the opening of a new
stadium sell the tickets. And it worked. The Raiders sold
out every game for 11 seasons. Mostly of their own voli-
tion, the players were involved in the community. The
team was loved. Al was still considered a hero.

After he pulled up stakes for Los Angeles, Davis relied on the famed Raider mystique to sell the tickets. At
first it was successful, although the first wave of season
ticket applicants were greeted by a computer snafu that
misassigned seats. In their second year in Los Angeles,
the Raiders won the Super Bowl. The euphoria of a
championship club carried over into 1984, when the average attendance in Los Angeles Coliseum was 70,000,
although the turnstile count would dip into the 40,000
range when a bad team came to town. But the groundwork should have been laid to reach out to the community and also store chestnuts for the lean years. Because
when the team slipped on the field the crowds declined.
Davis started blaming the shabbiness of Los Angeles Coliseum for the declining attendance. He also faulted the
Los Angeles Times for favoring the Rams in their coverage.
Irwindale would solve the stadium problem. What about
the lack of public relations?

Like a minor league baseball team, the Raiders started
giving away license plate frames, posters, and other
goodies, but the crowds didn't improve in Los Angeles.
The rancor between the Raiders and the *Los Angeles Times*
continued. Davis treated beat writer Mark Heisler as if he
were the second coming of Pete Rozelle. Paraphrasing

one of Davis's favorite words, it is not "self-serving" to mistreat the largest newspaper in Southern California.

The Raider organization did participate in charity events such as golf tournaments and basketball games. Players would visit hospitals. But nobody seemed to know. Where was the public relations expertise of Kaze and Ornstein when it was needed, Al?

When the Raiders announced their return to Oakland, the habitual reclusiveness and aloofness of Al Davis came crashing down like a house of cards. Davis and Al LoCasale were in Orlando at the NFL meetings, so Oakland mayor Lionel Wilson and Alameda County supervisor Don Perata announced the move to the public and then were basically defenseless trying to fend off the furor that was to follow until they were buried under it. Where was the Raiders organization? Shouldn't either Davis or LoCasale have been at Oakland City Hall when the return was announced? How about LoCasale or John Herrera at the public hearings? Or coach Art Shell, still loved in the Oakland community. Why not publicize the charity work that the ex-Raiders still perform in Oakland and environs? Say something warm like: "Hey, it's great to be back." Or "We made a mistake leaving and now we're going to make it up to you loyal fans." Perhaps consider starting an earthquake fund in the name of Raider players and executives who have passed on? What Al Davis is really telling Oakland is "I've become too much of a big shot to talk to you people. Expressing happiness or apologizing shows weakness. We must intimidate, just like on the football field." In Oakland, selling pro football in 1990 may not be all that much different than in 1960. Initially, the Raiders failed.

The "one big happy family" concept of the Raider organization also may be a thing of the past. Sometime in the good year 1984, Davis had a falling out with Marcus Allen, who is arguably his best player, perhaps ever. But

Marcus was the good soldier and pleased the boss by being present with many others when Tom Flores retired in 1988. But there were still problems. In the option year of his present agreement, Marcus did not report to the 1989 training camp. The Raiders never attempted to negotiate with Allen, leaving him twisting in the wind. He joined the team for the regular season and his running helped beat San Diego in the opener. Late in the season when a victory in Seattle was imperative, Davis allegedly told Art Shell that there were to be no air Allen calls. No more cheap touchdowns for Marcus. "We'll teach that little squirt a lesson" was the thinking. So what happened was not unexpected. The failure of Bo Jackson to score on a play tailor-made for Allen cost the Raiders the game and the playoffs.

Pettiness doesn't contribute to the greatness of the Raiders, Al.

By contrast, the contract of Davis's favorite Howie Long was extended for seven years at about a million per year in 1988. The decline in the performances of Long seems to neatly coincide with the current misfortunes of the Raiders on the playing field; both began in 1986 and did not appear to be over at the end of 1989. After being a dominant player in his first five seasons, Long has become basically just another good defensive lineman.

In Oakland, the Raiders used to fight and claw and the players would play hurt, just to win. When Daryle Lamonica says, "They became more country club types [in Los Angeles] rather than the tough guys I was accustomed to playing with," or when Jim Otto claims that "some of the players who normally would have played in Oakland don't do that in Los Angeles because they're afraid it might hurt their movie careers," they seem to be talking about Howie Baby and his bruised calf muscle of 1988 or his sore ankle of 1989. And *he* gets a long-term contract.

When Marcus Allen broke his hand and had other assorted ailments in 1988, he only missed one week. Remember the game in New Orleans that season when the untouched Bo Jackson took himself out after two rushes because he hurt his hamstring? Marcus Allen played the entire New Orleans game with blood oozing out of his bandages. And still gained 102 yards.

Just reward, baby!

Matt Millen was a 1988 holdout who didn't sign a contract until a week before the season. Although Millen seemed to lose some quickness, he still could stop running plays through the middle of the Raider defense. Although originally an alternate selection, Millen played in his first Pro Bowl following the 1988 season. In 1989, Millen was waived and signed with the 49ers, and you know the rest. The Raiders tried impostors such as Ricky Hunley, Thomas Benson, and a misplaced Jerry Robinson to play interior linebacker but still couldn't contain the inside run.

Then there is the strange case of Bill Lewis. In the first 25 years of the Raiders, the total number of dissatisfied players toiling for Al Davis could be counted on the fingers of one hand. Let's see. There was Stabler, Rod Sherman and Dan Pastorini. Then came a relative avalanche. But the most blatant discontented Raider of them all was offensive lineman Bill Lewis. Lewis was drafted in 1986 from the University of Nebraska and saw some action at tackle and guard. After Jim Lachey was traded in 1988, the Raiders installed Lewis at center, moving Don Mosebar to right tackle. Lewis did not perform well at his new position and was frequently overpowered by the stronger nose tackles in the NFL. So while Lewis was expecting a raise for 1989, the Raiders were instead unhappy with his performance. Subsequently, Lewis's agent attempted to sue the Raiders to get a favorable contract. Lewis eventually signed a one-year deal, suited up, but saw absolutely no action during 1989. He was instructed by his agent not to talk to the media. After the season-ending loss to the Giants, Lewis did not accompany the team back to Los Angeles. When the Raiders exposed Lewis as a Plan B free agent in February 1990, he was grabbed by the Phoenix Cardinals.

The Bill Lewis saga is sad. With Rory Graves and John Gesek spending 1989 trying to outdo one another in accumulating penalties and missing blocks, the Raiders could have neatly plugged Lewis into the left side of the offensive line and perhaps won a few more games.

There are many who view these recent problems as solid evidence that Al Davis has lost his Midas touch. The hiring and firing of Shanahan was probably the worst misjudgment of all.

Lamonica and Otto have mentioned how the Raiders have become soft in Los Angeles. When Ted Hendricks retired after Super Bowl XVIII, only Matt Millen and Vann McElroy remained on defense to continue the tradition of Raider toughness. Lester Hayes and Mike Haynes were great defenders, but neither could hit receivers with the ferocity of Jack Tatum, George Atkinson, or Skip Thomas. Linebackers like Brad Van Pelt and Reggie McKenzie were mere pussycats when compared to Villapiano, Hendricks, and Dan Conners. When Matuszak and Alzado retired, they took much of the up-front intimidation with them. It happened over a period of seven seasons, but the growl of the Raider defense is a thing of the past.

The saga of Vann McElroy may be more indicative of the decline of the Raiders than any other evidence available. McElroy is a hard-hitting free safety who has been nagged by minor injuries in recent years. During the strike in 1987, Eddie Anderson was signed as a replacement player and was kept on when the work stoppage ended. Originally a special teams player, Anderson began to see more action in the secondary. When McElroy couldn't play, Anderson started at free safety. Although Anderson may be faster than McElroy and a hard hitter, Eddie lacks the savvy and smarts of the veteran McElroy. Who would you play, Coach?

The absence of leadership when the Raiders are on offense is another ongoing problem that is contributing to 8–8 seasons. Although Lamonica may have been somewhat aloof, he was a respected leader. So were Stabler and Plunkett. Much of the respect was gained off the field.

Marc Wilson could never muster the respect of his fellow players and apparently neither can Jay Schroeder. Rusty Hilger appeared to be a fiery commander but was not a proficient quarterback. Steve Beuerlein offers the best hope of filling the leadership vacuum.

Perhaps higher salaries have changed the ways of current athletes. The days of Halas or Lombardi berating or insulting players may be over. But the San Francisco 49ers are winning with the players of today. So are baseball's Oakland Athletics. And basketball's Detroit Pistons have proven that toughness, fear, and intimidation still win championships.

Art Shell was hired to help return a floundering club to Raider football. Hopefully he can transfer his quiet but effective leadership qualities to his charges. It's a good start.

Two burning questions remain: 1) Has Al Davis lost his touch? and 2) How many consecutive non-playoff seasons will the Raiders endure before Davis is no longer the Genius?

Chapter 11

THE MOVE TO L.A.: PLAYING THE PART OF A ROGUE ELEPHANT

*I*n retrospect, the entire saga of the Raiders' move from Oakland to Los Angeles still seems incredible. Six years after Al hinted that the Oakland Coliseum was inadequate, he began an apparent infatuation with Los Angeles. It would be another six years from the time when Al Davis was first approached by Los Angeles interests until the Supreme Court rejected the last appeal by the NFL to overturn the lower court decisions that allowed the move. And yet it all seemed to happen so fast. A nightmare for the City of Oakland and the National Football League to be sure. After Al Davis announced he was moving to L.A., the Raiders were forced to stay in Oakland for two seasons and then, amazingly, won a Super Bowl as a lame duck team. Certainly the spectacle of one owner suing an entire league over the right to move was one of the most embarrassing chapters in NFL history. It caused the accelerated aging of a commissioner that may eventually have led to his retirement. And to complete the bizarre tale, eight years after he moved to Los Angeles, Al Davis announced a desire to return to Oakland for the same reason he transferred from Oakland to Los Angeles, failure to get luxury box seats

173

and other stadium improvements and an acrimonious relationship with his landlords. Do you follow?

There are two men who were largely responsible for ultimately securing the Raiders for Los Angeles. One was Bill Robertson, who was a member of the Los Angeles Memorial Coliseum Commission from 1978 until 1987. The other was syndicated sports columnist Melvin Durslag, whose home newspaper in those days was the *Los Angeles Herald-Examiner*. Durslag relentlessly led the campaign by the *Herald-Examiner* to put a new team in Los Angeles Coliseum to replace the Rams, who were moving to Anaheim. Yes, Virginia, politicians *do* read the newspapers and can be coerced into what are considered to be positive political actions. Anything to get reelected. Durslag also played matchmaker for restless NFL owners and influential Los Angeles politicians. Robertson, a former union leader, was able to patiently navigate through the murky political waters of Los Angeles and negotiate a memorandum of understanding with the elusive and sometimes difficult Al Davis.

In April 1978, after months of secret negotiations, Carroll Rosenbloom, the owner of the Los Angeles Rams and a close friend of Al Davis, announced that he was considering a move from Los Angeles Coliseum to suburban Anaheim, located about 30 miles down the Santa Ana Freeway. Citing declining attendance in 1976 and 1977 for his contending team, Rosenbloom hinted that the Los Angeles Memorial Coliseum Commission had not answered his call for stadium improvements. In early July 1978, Los Angeles County supervisor Kenneth Hahn, who played a major role in bringing the Dodgers to Los Angeles in 1958, wrote a letter to all NFL teams inviting them to transfer to Los Angeles. On July 26, 1978, Rosenbloom formally announced that the Rams would move to Anaheim for the 1980 season. Even though a replacement in the Coliseum would encroach on his 75-mile "territorial rights," Rosenbloom said that he would not stand in the way of Los Angeles acquiring another team. Strangely, the Rams' new Anaheim home was within the 75-mile territorial limit of the San Diego Chargers. What would be significant later for the Raiders is that Rosenbloom never asked for league approval, he just moved to Anaheim and silently defied anybody to stop him.

While Rosenbloom was publicly playing the role of a neglected tenant of an inefficient landlord, Durslag revealed the real reason for the Rams' move to Orange County. Anaheim was giving Rosenbloom lucrative development rights to 95 acres of land located adjacent to the ball park. Disneyland, which annually attracts millions of tourists, is located only a long touchdown pass down the road from Anaheim Stadium, so the development potential of the 95 acres was considered enormous.

Two interesting columns appeared immediately in the newspapers. Under the title of "The L.A. Raiders? Not Likely," *Los Angeles Times* writer Bob Oates predictably blamed the politicians."L.A. officials never did find out exactly what it would take to hold the Rams in the Coliseum: that neither Mayor Bradley nor anyone else intervened to keep them, . . . that the Dodgers would have accepted the football team if assured their tax bill wouldn't go up, and that the Rams preferred Dodger Stadium to Anaheim . . . The three-headed Coliseum Commission (city, county, state) is the real culprit."

Oates then speculated on a possible replacement for the Rams and his tarot cards came up saying "Oakland." "Today's legal climate is baffling to many businessmen and getting more so all the time. For this reason it is possible that the Oakland Raiders would, for instance, play the part of a rogue elephant and simply announce a move to the Coliseum. . . . Conceivably, Oakland could get away with a rogue transfer. The NFL wouldn't vote the Raiders into the Coliseum but the Raiders just might come, defying the league and gambling that the courts would support what in other businesses would be ruled a legitimate move, if indeed, it got before the courts at all." Oates would have the correct scenario but concluded that Davis would probably only use Los Angeles to extract a better deal from Oakland.

In a column in the *Herald-Examiner* called "Can Raiders and Vikes Be Tempted?" Alan Malamud discussed what a move to Los Angeles might mean to Al Davis. "Potentially a move south (by the Raiders) could mean more than a million at the gate annually and a couple of hundred thousand extra from radio and exhibition game television. Besides, Raider chief executive Al Davis has liked L.A. since his days in the late fifties as a USC coach."

They were not exactly asleep at the wheel up in Oakland. Ron Bergman of the *Oakland Tribune* seemed to sense the bad vibes. "The ominous aspect to me is that the Raiders have yet to deny that they are considering moving to L.A. For all anyone knows, Davis might have already decided to try to move south where the Raiders can boost the take by at least $2,500,000 a year because of about 20,000 more available seats and higher radio-TV revenues." But Bergman gave Oakland fans some hope. "While the Raiders haven't made any overt threats to move, they have pointed out, off the record, that their departure would leave a large void in East Bay life. They're right there."

Because Rosenbloom relocated within 75 miles of Los Angeles Coliseum, NFL commissioner Pete Rozelle called the Rams' transfer to Anaheim a "suburban" move, similar to the New York Giants' recent shift from Yankee Stadium to the New Jersey Meadowlands, the Dallas Cowboys' transfer to Irving, Texas, the Boston Patriots' journey down the road to Foxboro, Massachusetts, and the Detroit Lions' saunter to Pontiac, Michigan. Commissioner Pete Rozelle, an L.A. native and former general manager of the Rams, did not necessarily share the opinion that obtaining another team in Los Angeles was a matter of extreme urgency. Within a week after the Rams' move, Durslag started hammering away at Rozelle and the NFL, using two themes that were to continue unabated in the *Herald-Examiner* for the next six years: 1) although Los Angeles and Orange counties were adjoining geographically, they were really two separate entities, and 2) the comparable distances between Oakland–San Francisco and Los Angeles–Anaheim. "Orange County has its own baseball team, its own pro soccer team, its own World Team tennis, its own outdoor stadium, its own indoor stadium. It's even more detached from Los Angeles than Oakland is from San Francisco and thereby in no legal position to isolate the 8,000,000 people in Los Angeles County from pro football."

But the immediate hot prospect for Los Angeles Coliseum was not the Raiders, it was the Minnesota Vikings. Bloomington Stadium, where the Vikings played, had the smallest seating capacity in the NFL. A proposal to build a domed stadium in downtown Minneapolis was going nowhere. Pete Rozelle then told Minnesota legislators that if they failed to build a new stadium for Vikings owner Max Winter, the NFL would be justified in voting for a Vikings move to Los Angeles. In fact, Winter did visit Los Angeles and discussed a possible transfer with Bill Robertson in the fall of 1978. Rozelle's threat and the Winter meeting in Los Angeles produced the desired results; the Vikings got their new stadium and stayed in Minnesota.

Robert Irsay, the unpredictable and irascible owner of the Baltimore Colts, was threatening to move to Los Angeles. He was also threatening to move to Jacksonville, Memphis, Phoenix, and almost every other place in America with a city hall and a park bench. A statement to the Baltimore press by Irsay that he discussed a shift to L.A. with California governor Jerry Brown and Los Angeles mayor Tom Bradley was later proven false. Irsay continued to bicker with the City of Baltimore and State

of Maryland for another five years before finally departing for Indianapolis in March 1984.

Another owner who kept an L.A. threat in his arsenal
was Joe Robbie of Miami, who was having problems with
his lease in the Orange Bowl. Eventually Robbie built his
own stadium in suburban Broward County.

And then there was NFL Rule 4.3, the part of the NFL
constitution that governed franchise shifts. In August
1978, Rule 4.3 required a unanimous 28 votes to move an
established team more than 75 miles from its present location. A unanimous vote was also necessary to move into
the territorial orbit of another team. For approval of a
"suburban" move, 75%, or 21 positive votes, were necessary. It was first believed that the Rams' transfer could be
approved by 21 votes, but when it was learned that
Anaheim was within 75 miles of San Diego, a unanimous
vote was needed. Moving a team from another city into
Los Angeles would require a 28–0 vote. Following the
Rams' departure, Bill Robertson discussed the possibility
of Los Angeles Coliseum getting a new football tenant
with Rozelle. He received a less than enthusiastic answer
from the commissioner. In September, the Los Angeles
Memorial Coliseum Commission filed suit against the
NFL, charging that Rule 4.3 was an illegal restraint of
trade and prevented the Coliseum from acquiring a new
football tenant.

The NFL owners met in Chicago in October 1978 to
discuss the LAMCC lawsuit. They voted 27–0, with one
abstention, to change the approval for any franchise shift
to 21 votes. The abstention came from the Oakland Raiders. Al Davis allegedly told the other owners that "I reserve my rights." Or was it "I preserve my rights"? Rule
4.3 was changed. The owners then voted 27–0, with
Davis purposely absent, to approve the Rams' move to
Anaheim. It was considered unanimous. Both Al Davis's
utterings and his failure to vote would later haunt the
NFL and Rozelle. The Los Angeles Coliseum did not

drop its lawsuit but decided not to actively pursue it either.

Rumors kept arising that the Raiders were talking to Los Angeles. Because his lease was to expire following the 1979 season, many observers assumed that Al Davis was floating rumors about Los Angeles to extract a better deal from Oakland. At his Super Bowl press conference in 1979, Commissioner Rozelle reassured the City of Oakland. "I don't see any L.A. move," he said.

On April 2, 1979, Carroll Rosenbloom drowned off the coast of South Florida near his exclusive summer home. Three days earlier, Rosenbloom was told by Al Davis that the Raiders might be moving to Los Angeles. Surprisingly, Rosenbloom bypassed his children and willed the Rams to his widow and second wife, Georgia. Many students of the Raiders move have said that Rosenbloom's untimely death had a meaningful impact on Al Davis's eventual plans and actions. By not opposing the move, they reasoned, Rosenbloom may have been able to help Al Davis obtain the necessary votes to go to Los Angeles. But the more likely scenario is that the slippery Rosenbloom would have double-crossed Al Davis in his attempt to come to L.A and would have prevented an invasion of his territory. C. R., as his friends called him, was a master at playing league politics but, in a pinch, would probably not have turned away from the other 26 owners to ally himself with Al Davis. Rosenbloom's death did affect some of the court proceedings that were to follow when the Raiders accused Georgia's new husband, Dominic Frontiere, of scalping Super Bowl tickets. But that was a knee-jerk reaction by Raider attorney Joseph Alioto to an NFL smear tactic of injecting the name of Alan Glick, a Las Vegas businessman who co-owned a shopping center with Al Davis, into the proceedings. Glick was once accused of having connections to organized crime, but the charges proved to be false.

The Oakland Raiders opened their 1979 season by

beating Georgia Rosenbloom's Rams 24–17, in Los Angeles Coliseum. Reacting to rumors in the L.A. newspapers, some fans unfurled a banner that said "Welcome Los Angeles Raiders." Needless to say, Georgia Rosenbloom was not pleased. Pete Rozelle kept assuring Georgia that the Raiders were not coming to Los Angeles.

There were some casual discussions between Al Davis and Bill Robertson through much of 1979. The Raiders were having their usual problems negotiating with the Oakland Coliseum Board but few Oakland people seemed very concerned. Davis had been difficult in past negotiations but had always eventually signed on the dotted line. Surely, this time would not be any different.

In the Bay Area press, Al was dropping the usual hints of unhappiness with the Oakland Coliseum. On August 13, 1979, Davis told Ron Bergman of the *Oakland Tribune* that "[linebacker] Ted Hendricks fell down on his way out to the field. The stadium is so freaking cheap." Bergman uncovered another lingering complaint. "The Raiders have always been jealous of the deal given the A's: the preference of dates, the shares of concessions and parking fees. But the A's signed a 20-year lease when it looked like baseball would draw three times as many fans a season as football. It didn't work out that way." (In 1979, the Oakland A's lost 108 games and, under the nearly invisible skeleton administration of owner Charles O. Finley, attracted only 306,000 people.) Bergman seemed to have a good suggestion to settle the poor tenant-landlord relationship. "Why not just give the pink slip, or deed for the stadium, to Al Davis and let him run the place?" Alameda County supervisor Charles Santana suggested that the Coliseum use its profits to pay for Raider improvements.

In late October, Raider executive assistant Al LoCasale admitted that the Raiders had "some discussions with the L.A. Coliseum." On November 2, after Los Angeles had unsuccessfully flirted with the Colts and

Al Davis (C) looks over playbook with Clem Daniels (L) and Tom Flores, a few days after being hired in 1963. (Courtesy: Oakland Tribune)

Al Davis in action at his first Raider training camp in 1963. (Courtesy: Oakland Tribune)

Al huddles with his players at 1964 training camp in Santa Rosa. (Courtesy: Oakland Tribune)

Carole and Al Davis accept award in 1964. (Courtesy: Oakland Tribune)

Coach Davis along the Frank Youell Field sideline with Clancy Osborne, Art Powell, and Tom Flores (September 13, 1964). (Courtesy: Oakland Tribune)

Davis answers the media upon his return to Oakland in 1966. (Courtesy: Oakland Tribune)

The three general partners of the Raiders: Ed McGah, Wayne Valley, and Al Davis (1968). (Courtesy: Oakland Tribune)

Al discusses the Raiders victory in Super Bowl XI (1977). (Courtesy: Norm Fisher)

Ken Stabler at summer training camp in Santa Rosa, 1979.
(Courtesy: Norm Fisher)

Escorted by police through Oakland International Airport as Raiders board plane to San Diego for AFC Championship Game (1981). (Courtesy: Oakland Tribune)

Tom Flores, Joseph Alioto, Gene Upshaw, and Al Davis (L to R) in 1981. (Courtesy: Norm Fisher)

Davis greets rookie Marcus Allen before opening game of 1982 season.
(Courtesy: Oakland Tribune)

Al Davis, at the induction of Gene Upshaw into the Hall of Fame, August 1987. (Courtesy: Jeff Bayer)

Eulogizing John Matuszak at special memorial service. (1989). (Courtesy: Oakland Tribune)

Dolphins, Robertson admitted that "I'm not confident about getting any team next year."

In October 1979, Carole Davis suffered a massive heart attack and was rushed to Peralta Hospital in Oakland. Al Davis basically suspended all football actions, including discussions with Los Angeles, and physically moved into the hospital to be close to his nearly comatose wife. Miraculously, Carole Davis recovered, and by December Al Davis was free to resume his football activities.

During Al Davis's preoccupation with his wife's illness, Ralph Wiley, then with the *Oakland Tribune,* reminded the Raider organization of the tremendous fan support that the Silver and Black would lose if it left Oakland. On the eve of a home game against San Francisco, Wiley wrote, "The 12th man, Oakland's home field advantage of frenzied fans, has helped the Raiders to a faultless 4–0 record at home. . . . Since 1960, this has been it."

As 1979 turned into 1980, negotiations with Bill Robertson became more serious and the Raiders' relationship with Oakland Coliseum became more distant and aloof. Alameda County supervisor Joseph Bort did not seem concerned. "I really hope Al Davis is just rousing us a little, to get a better deal for himself." But fellow supervisor Charles Santana sensed the impending doom for Oakland. "I think the bottom line is that somebody has got to talk to Al. Nothing is going to get settled this way. It's scary. We're to the point where Davis in essence is saying screw it."

Avoiding the larger Bay Area newspapers, Davis gave an extensive interview to the *Hayward Daily Review* on January 4 and warned that the Oakland Coliseum Board "is a greedy organization" and "this thing has gone much further that you would assume." On the same day, Mel Durslag told his readers that the Raider–Los Angeles deal was heating up again.

Preparing for all eventualities, including a court battle, Davis hired former San Francisco mayor Joseph Alioto, considered one of the best antitrust attorneys in America. Alioto quickly put the NFL on notice. "If Rosenbloom did it [move to Anaheim] without asking anybody, there's no reason to think Al would have to ask anyone," he said. On January 7, Al Davis met with Pete Rozelle in New York. No, I would not ask for a vote if the Raiders decided to move to Los Angeles, said Al. Yes, I must enforce the NFL constitution, answered Pete.

Obviously disgusted with the inaction of the Coliseum Board, Oakland mayor Lionel Wilson formed a task force to try to get the East Bay effort off the dime. Jack Maltester, president of the Oakland Coliseum Board, scheduled a meeting with Davis for January 14. In Los Angeles, Durslag was becoming more enthused about landing the Raiders and did his best imitation of Jimmy the Greek. On January 11 he predicted: "It's 11–10, L.A. over Oakland, and pick it." "I'm going to make some decisions of choice soon" was the Davis promise on January 14.

On January 13, Al Davis held a rare press conference in Oakland. After a verbal salvo against the Oakland Coliseum Board, Davis explained his philosophy about the relationship between cities and teams. "The city that gets the team doesn't win you. The city that owns you now, loses you. The city that loses a team makes every effort next time not to lose. That's the situation with Los Angeles." Al may not have had the foresight to envision that years later, Oakland would fall into the very same pattern in its attempt as the city that "makes every effort not to lose."

Observing the turmoil in baseball caused by player free agency, Davis also hinted at the same press conference about why he would eventually choose a move to Los Angeles. "Free agency is coming down the road. I won't be somewhere where I can't compete. I went through that in 1963–65. Love and emotion. That may count for one player in ten. The rest want the money. In baseball, you can see where the players are going. They're going to New York and Dodger Stadium." What Davis failed to say was that the Baltimore Orioles and Pittsburgh Pirates, who played in the 1979 World Series, were both initially ravaged by free agent signings but recovered to win their respective pennants over richer teams such as the New York Yankees, California Angels, and Los Angeles Dodgers.

By mid-January the consensus feeling in the Bay Area was that the Coliseum was entirely to blame for the mess with the Raiders. Dave Newhouse espoused this view in the *Oakland Tribune* of January 14. "Davis gives the impression that he would sign a lease of five years or more. He said he might have signed for that 10 years ago, before things got out of hand with Coliseum Inc. . . . Give him what he wants. If we don't, what chances are there for an expansion team if he moves?"

The saga continued to unfold during the week of January 14–18, 1980. On January 14, Davis met with Oakland officials, who received the impression that he wanted to stay in Oakland. But the next day Al was in L.A. and met for four hours with Bill Robertson, Los Angeles County supervisor Kenneth Hahn, and Los Angeles Olympic Organizing Committee chairman Peter Uebberoth. Los Angeles had just been awarded the 1984 Summer Olympics, and the financial package presented to the Raiders could include money that was earmarked to improve the Coliseum for the games.

Mel Durslag and the *Herald-Examiner* kept escalating the campaign against the NFL and for the Raiders. Under the title, "Why the NFL Is Out of Line Sermonizing to Al Davis," Durslag concluded that "if a guy wanted to move from Los Angeles to Oakland, he would win on a shutout. That's how the Rams won en route to Anaheim, and that's why the whole damn league is suspect." The timing of Durslag's column was perfect. The national media and NFL brass were in town for the Super Bowl, and the article was prominently discussed at Pete Rozelle's annual Friday night pre-game bash.

Durslag's basic argument was that Oakland fans wouldn't be without NFL football if the Raiders moved because the San Francisco 49ers were only 10 miles away. Los Angeles, reasoned Durslag, was further away from Anaheim and therefore was more deserving of the Silver and Black. It must be questioned what Durslag would have written if the Minnesota Vikings, and not the Oakland Raiders, were the team considering a move to Los Angeles. The folks in the Twin Cities would be 300 miles from the Green Bay Packers, the nearest team. Would Durslag, Malamud, et al. shed a tear for the Minnesota fans?

Another flaw in the argument for supporting a Raiders move was that Oakland fans could just start rooting for San Francisco and everybody would live happily ever after. It may work that way in Los Angeles. But Durslag apparently didn't know much about the Oakland fans, who had a closer relationship to the Raiders than any Los Angeles team has with its fans. Or other Bay Area teams either. After the Raiders departed, many Oakland fans didn't just flip the switch and root for the 49ers. It's not that easy to end the deep-rooted passion that Bay Area fans had for the Raiders. From Orange County, the Rams would still be covered on local television, on the radio, and in the newspapers, so all the fans in the Los Angeles area could still closely follow Georgia's club. But when a team totally abandons a metropolitan area for greener pastures, fan involvement is much more difficult, if not impossible. After the Raiders relocated, the Bay Area press coverage was limited to wire service stories, similar to other out-of-town teams. In 1982, Raider games in the Bay Area were broadcast on a weak FM station with no pre- or post-game locker room show. No call-in programs after the game. No daily reports out of training camp in Santa Rosa. Sorry, Mel, there were many people in the Bay Area who felt betrayed when the Raiders moved but couldn't convert their allegiance to the 49ers, despite a Super Bowl XVI triumph, despite Joe Montana and Bill Walsh. Measuring miles on a road map is not the same as gauging the feelings of people who had loyally supported a team for many years.

Durslag, along with Vincent X. Flaherty of the then *Los Angeles Examiner,* was instrumental in enticing Dodger owner Walter O'Malley to the Pacific coast. But neither Durslag, Flaherty, or other Los Angeles journalists were shedding tears for the fans left on the shore when the Rams moved from Cleveland in 1946, when the Dodgers left Brooklyn in 1958, or when the Lakers came from Minneapolis in 1960. Similarly, nobody in San Francisco gave a hoot for the folks in Manhattan, Philadelphia, or Kansas City when the Giants, Warriors, and Athletics came to the Bay Area. That's the way of the sporting world, folks. Local journalists are paid to support the home team and also write what is perceived to be good for both their town and the fans. Reporters also tend to be close to the local politicians, who usually provide most of their news sources. Durslag and company should receive the proper credit for their stance in the "Raiders Move South" story, because their influence over the politicians and public opinion was significant. By supporting the jilted Los Angeles Memorial Coliseum Commission, they directly exposed the pomposity, cronyism, and hypocrisy of the National Football League, which seemed to begin and end with an arrogant commissioner. After all, Al Davis didn't invent greed, he was merely practicing what was learned from other professional sports owners. The NFL was to have other problems in the 1980s, primarily with Congress, with the Players Association, and even with the fans, because of this attitude. But let's leave it right there. If the shoe were on the other foot, which it was to be 10 years later, the press would act totally different, which it did when the Raiders expressed their intentions to return to their roots.

Hindsight is 20-20, of course, but Al Davis should have listened to some of the comments from members of the Rams about the possible move of the Raiders. "I don't think it would be a good move," was the reaction of head coach Ray Malavasi. Added defensive tackle Larry Brooks: "I wonder why the Raiders would want to come to Los Angeles, which is a town not known for accepting teams. This is a tough town. The Dodgers win. The Lakers win. The Rams win. But the minute they lose, they start to boo."

The Rams were playing the Pittsburgh Steelers in Super Bowl XIV at Pasadena, and two days before the game Pete Rozelle reiterated that the Raiders could not move without NFL approval. Meanwhile across town, Al Davis was secretly meeting with Bill Robertson to try to finalize the deal. On the same day, the Los Angeles Coliseum went to court to seek a preliminary injunction that would block the NFL from stopping a possible Raiders move.

On January 20, the day after the Rams lost 31–20 to the Steelers in the Super Bowl, Al Davis met with Oakland mayor Lionel Wilson; Cornell Maier, the chairman of Kaiser Industries, one of the largest employers in Oakland; and George Vukasin, who was then a director on the Coliseum Board. Their offer to Davis included a $4,000,000 loan, which would come from a buyout of the Oakland Athletics' lease, which wouldn't expire until 1988. Denver oilman Marvin Davis (also from Brooklyn but no relation to Al) was attempting to purchase the A's from Charlie Finley and move the baseball team to Denver. After the Marvin Davis bid failed, another batter stepped up to the plate. It was Wayne Valley, Al Davis's old boss with the Raiders. He reportedly offered Finley $10,000,000 for the A's but was probably more interested in making things sticky for Davis as the primary co-tenant in the Coliseum. Valley's offer also was rejected, as Finley did not want to get in the middle of the Raiders-Coliseum battle. The loan offer to the Raiders was kept on the negotiating table. In August 1980, Finley finally sold the A's to Walter A. Haas, the chairman of the board of Levi Strauss.

The feeling around Oakland was that Wilson and Maier would be more productive with Davis than the Coliseum Board. On January 25, the *Oakland Tribune* reported that "since Wilson and Maier have entered into the picture, there has been an about-face." But talk is cheap. Al Davis now wanted a written offer from Oakland.

There were also some unexpected storm clouds down south. On January 24, Jack Disney of the *Herald-Examiner* disclosed that the Los Angeles politicians were worried about the cost to the taxpayers of the Raider deal. "We can't go any higher," was the warning to Bill Robertson.

The Los Angeles proposal was a $17 million financial package that included $5 million from L.A. County, a $7 million loan underwritten by the city, and a $5 million advance on the rental of L.A. Coliseum, the latter courtesy of the Los Angeles Olympic Organizing Committee. Part of the plan had the Raiders building 99 luxury box seats with the loan money and then leasing the seats back to the Coliseum. The luxury boxes would rent for $30,000 per year.

Bill Robertson didn't have to worry about a competitive bid from the Bay Area, because Oakland proceeded to shoot itself in the foot. When Pete Rozelle learned of the generous offer that Wilson and Maier were discussing with Davis, he called Bill Moorish of the Coliseum Board and said something like, "Don't give him so much, we won't let him move anyway." Wayne Valley may have been lurking behind the scenes. Coliseum Board president Jack Maltester was a paid lobbyist for Wayne Valley, who certainly did not want to see Al Davis garnished with a rich lease.

The Alameda County Board of Supervisors then voted 3–2 to repudiate the offer made by Wilson and Maier, with Supervisor Joe Bort casting the decisive negative vote. That afternoon, Wilson and Maier apologized to Al Davis at the Raider offices for their rescission of the offer and their removal from the negotiations. So Rozelle and perhaps Valley thought they had gotten even with Al Davis.

A lesser proposal worth about $8,500,000 was prepared by the Oakland Coliseum Board, but it was too little, too late. When it was finally presented to the Raiders on February 14, Al LoCasale initially threw it away but then snuck a peek. In a letter to the Coliseum Board on February 15, the Raiders said the proposal "was not in the acceptable range." On the same day, Al Davis met with officials of USC and UCLA to discuss their possible joint tenancy with the Raiders in Los Angeles Memorial Coliseum.

All hope was now lost in Oakland and the media started to turn against Davis. After a series of attacks in his *Oakland Tribune* column, Dave Newhouse was chastised by a Raider official over the telephone. Newhouse set the record straight in a February 20 column. "As far as [Newhouse] being anti-Davis, that's not true. The man has a strong humanitarian side, especially in times of death. He has picked up a number of funeral bills. But I don't want the next one to be this town's."

Meanwhile the Raiders were rapidly hurtling toward an inevitable confrontation with the National Football League. On February 5, Joe Alioto told Harry Pregerson, the judge handling the LAMCC suit, what the Raiders intended to do. "It all boils down to this," said Alioto. "We are prepared to conclude a written contract [with Los Angeles] this week and start construction next week."

Georgia Frontiere's Los Angeles Rams entered Pregerson's courtroom on February 12 and filed a brief asking the judge not to lift the three-quarters vote rule for franchise shifts. Bill Robertson was furious. "The Rams management is breaking a solemn commitment that Carroll Rosenbloom made to the people of this community when he promised that the Rams would never do anything to interfere with a move by another NFL team to Los Angeles. Asking the other NFL owners, including the Rams, to approve the Raiders' move is like asking the Raiders to take the gas pipe. Al Davis would have asked for permission long ago if he did not know that NFL commissioner Pete Rozelle had stacked the votes against him. We would not need a lawsuit if the NFL were willing to give its approval to the Raiders' move."

In the *Herald-Examiner*, Doug Krikorian added: "As the Raiders' dramatic odyssey toward Los Angeles has unfolded, it has become apparent that Pete Rozelle is within the Rams sphere of influence, a rubber-stamping stooge for their whims."

On February 22, Judge Pregerson issued a ruling temporarily barring the NFL from enforcing the three-quarters vote rule. "This is [also] a great day for two organizations, the Los Angeles Memorial Coliseum and the San Francisco 49ers [who apparently would become the Bay Area's sole NFL representative]," said Joe Alioto.

The courts in Oakland were also getting their share of Raider business. On February 22, Mayor Wilson announced that Oakland was preparing an "eminent domain" suit to keep the Raiders home. If enacted, the principle of eminent domain would take the Silver and Black away from the control of Al Davis and the limited partnership of the Raiders and place the organization in the hands of the City of Oakland bureaucracy. Governments used eminent domain to condemn private land when freeways or subways were built. Or as Mel Durslag derisively wrote, eminent domain also was "used by the

Nazis to confiscate paintings." Alioto called it "a dishonest lawsuit." It was really a long shot, but judicial action was the only device left to Oakland if the Raiders were to stay put.

On February 23, Alameda County judge Alan Broussard issued a temporary order until March 6, preventing the Raiders from moving until the eminent domain suit was heard. Oakland formally filed its eminent domain suit on February 25. In Los Angeles, the temporary injunction against the NFL was to expire but was extended by Pregerson on February 29.

If there was any suspense about the future whereabouts of the Raiders, it promptly ended on Saturday, March 1, in the offices of Mayor Tom Bradley of Los Angeles. Al Davis signed a 20-page memorandum of agreement with Bill Robertson and announced his intentions to play in Los Angeles in 1980. He was asked why the Raiders were moving. "This city [Los Angeles] has always been a challenge to me. Pro football in the 1980s must have comfortable stadiums. In Oakland, we didn't have any of the conveniences necessary to go forward in the eighties. I don't mean to demean Oakland, but I'll say they are lagging behind." And Al, what about those Oakland fans who gave you 10 years of sellouts? "We owe them a great deal. They did a lot for me and the Raiders, and the Raiders did a lot for Oakland. I'm sure this is a traumatic time for them. I hope we can win the same kind of fan support here. But in life, you learn to live with sorrow."

Oakland Raider players were interviewed by the media in both areas. Most players said nothing. But tight end Dave Casper took some parting shots at Oakland. "Oakland had its chance. But they are cheapskates. The whole thing could have been solved. I think it's a good thing that we're moving." Casper did move. But not to Los Angeles. The Raiders traded him to Houston during the 1980 season.

Was Oakland really doomed in this entire episode? Many of Al Davis's biggest critics insist that once Rosenbloom moved to Anaheim, Davis set his sights on Hollywood and was intent on moving. Many think that he wanted the confrontation with Rozelle that was to follow. Al had been sore at Rozelle since the merger and sought revenge on the commissioner for Rozelle's banishment of him from NFL committee assignments after the "criminal element" trial. Certainly not considered an insider, Davis was never comfortable with the partiality within the league, where Rozelle favorites like Max Winter could be allowed to move their teams without a whimper from the commissioner, and was hell-bent on beating Rozelle down once and for all. There certainly is validity to all of the reasons why Davis would eventually go to the mat with Rozelle.

But there seem to be many more logical arguments for why the Raiders really wanted to stay in Oakland. Although Al Davis haters say he played Oakland as a stalking horse to up the ante in Los Angeles and vice versa, there is solid evidence that points the other way. For example, after his meetings with Mayor Wilson and Cornell Maier, Davis traveled to Dallas to observe the luxury box seat configuration at Texas Stadium and told Cowboy president Tex Schramm that he wanted a similar arrangement for the Oakland Coliseum. (Years later, Davis used the same architects who designed Texas Stadium for the planned stadium in Irwindale.) Other evidence was presented in *Hey Wait a Minute, I Wrote a Book,* the bestseller by former Raider coach John Madden. In the chapter titled, "My Friend, Al Davis," Madden describes how Davis excitedly told him in a Beverly Hills hotel lobby that "We're going to stay in Oakland. I met with Mayor Wilson and Cornell Maier, [and] it's going to work out."

Al Davis wanted the amenities that were needed to compete in the 1980s, and he gave Oakland every opportunity to produce. He knew that Oakland probably couldn't match what Los Angeles could offer monetarily, but this would be equalized by the rabid Raider fans. It seems that Al Davis truly wanted to stay in Oakland. But when Rozelle arrogantly pulled the rug out from under the Raider negotiations in Oakland, the biorhythms of Al Davis went haywire. He would defiantly move to Los Angeles and challenge anybody who stood in the way.

On Monday, March 3, the NFL convened a special meeting in Dallas to deal with Al Davis. Rozelle appointed special committees to investigate the move. They would meet with all principals in Los Angeles and Oakland and with the television networks. They were giving Al Davis every chance to ask for a vote. But Davis obviously knew that there was no hope of a league-approved move and never asked for a ballot.

The NFL lawyers were busy on the next day, filing a suit in Oakland, charging breech of contract and asking that the Raiders be restrained from moving. On March 6, a temporary restraining order was issued barring the Raiders from operating in Los Angeles. The sheriffs who arrived at the Raider headquarters to impound the place were too late. Al Davis already had all the records and furniture physically moved south. Oakland city attorney Michael Lawson was furious. "I'll seek the court's full authority to impose fines and imprisonment," he said. "I feel the conduct has been outrageous enough to warrant both."

On the same day that the posse in Oakland was trying to arrest Al Davis, the Los Angeles Memorial Coliseum Commission voted 7–1 to approve the memorandum of agreement that Al Davis signed with Bill Robertson.

For his Sunday audience of March 9, 1980, Doug Krikorian kept the *Herald-Examiner*'s swords pointed toward the NFL. "The owners are allowing Pete Rozelle to keep up his crusade because a majority of them detest Al Davis with the same intensity of Rozelle. It's just a case of pure unadulterated jealousy. Al Davis is everything they aren't—and would like to be."

The NFL owners started their regular winter meetings in Palm Springs on March 10. NFL lawyers determined that a formal ballot on the Raiders move (read: rejection) would help them legally. New England's Chuck Sullivan asked for a vote. The tally was 22–0 against with five abstentions and Al Davis absent.

On March 12, the *Herald-Examiner* first reported that the real reason for the commissioner's vehement opposition to the Raiders' relocation was that Pete Rozelle wanted a Los Angeles expansion franchise for himself when he retired. Rozelle denied it. In the *Herald-Examiner*, Doug Krikorian was quick to add his personal zinger. "Please, Mr. Commissioner, no more morality hymns. It not only makes one nauseous, but also insults the intelligence of even the most naive human being."

Perhaps because of NFL pressure, two members of the Los Angeles County Board of Supervisors were becoming nervous about going to bed with Al Davis and sparring with the National Football League. Another supervisor, Kenneth Hahn, was waiting until the Olympic Committee fulfilled its part of the bargain. Al Davis had a nervous reply. "I hope Mayor Bradley and Supervisor Hahn live up to their promises and stay in the fight. We're ahead, we're going to win. . . ." He could not inspire the Board of Supervisors. On March 18, they postponed the vote to approve the Raider memorandum of agreement. Doug Krikorian then took a swipe at the politicians. "Al Davis says he will continue his determined battle to bring the Raiders here until he's left with no legal recourse. It's too bad some Los Angeles politicians aren't displaying the same courage."

Attorneys for all sides were busy on March 25, 1980, setting the stage for the next two years of battle. In Los Angeles, the Raiders filed a $160,000,000 antitrust suit against the National Football League and joined the

LAMCC suit against the NFL. The Raiders action specifically attached the names of Pete Rozelle, Georgia (Rosenbloom) Frontiere, and San Diego owner Gene Klein to their action. As part of the eminent domain suit, an Alameda County Superior Court judge issued another preliminary injunction blocking the Raiders' departure from Oakland. A few days later, the same judge issued an order preventing the Raiders from selling tickets in Los Angeles. And in San Francisco, the NFL filed an instrument saying that their three-quarters vote approval for franchise shifts was valid.

So while the lawyers were ensuring that everyone would have their day in court, the newspapers in both areas hardened their positions. On March 26, Dave Newhouse blasted Davis in the *Oakland Tribune*. "What's Davis doing to Oakland and the East Bay? He's taken our time, money, and emotions and is sneaking out of town. Then he asks that we stand in line at the city limits and cheerfully wave good-bye and then self-destruct. No way."

The Raiders had set a deadline of June 15 for moving to Los Angeles for the 1980 season. But the eminent domain case and the Raiders/LAMCC versus NFL suit were not immediately coming to trial, so the Raiders signed a one-year agreement to play in Oakland. The terms were similar to the 1979 lease.

And almost by some preordained miracle, the Oakland Raiders proceeded to win Super Bowl XV in New Orleans. The highlight of the day was not on the playing field but in the Raider locker room when Commissioner Pete Rozelle presented the Super Bowl trophy to his archenemy, Al Davis. Although Rozelle looked uneasy, the trophy was accepted by the Raiders' managing general partner without incident.

The lawsuit in Los Angeles was moving toward a trial, and all attempts for an out-of-court settlement were futile. On March 17, 1981, Judge Pregerson denied the request of the NFL for a change in venue. Much to

Rozelle's chagrin, the case would be heard in Los Angeles.

The trial began on May 11, 1981. In the *Oakland Tribune,* Ralph Wiley speculated on the strategies of the combatants. "If the trial should come down to the simple matter of the NFL versus Al Davis, Davis may not lose. He has a strong case against the NFL restricting trade and free enterprise, with the Sherman Antitrust Act of 1890 as a buffer. . . . It must appear that the NFL must make paramount the social and economic deprivation the City of Oakland would suffer."

The courtroom ordeal dragged on for the next three months. There was really no earth-shattering testimony by any witness, although the media was fascinated with the personalities. They included Lamar Hunt of the Kansas City Chiefs, Tex Schramm of the Dallas Cowboys, Cleveland's Art Modell, and Coach Don Shula of the Miami Dolphins.

Following four grueling hours on the stand on May 27, 1981, San Diego owner Gene Klein suffered a heart attack and was rushed to a hospital. He would later sue Al Davis for $10 million because of the heart attack. In 1984, Klein sold his interest in the Chargers to developer Alex Spanos and started developing race horses. Ironically, Klein died of another heart attack on March 12, 1990, the day that Al Davis announced he wanted to return to Oakland.

During his stint in the witness chair, Al Davis was to win admiration from lead NFL attorney Patrick Lynch. "Al Davis is a very ringwise witness—the best I've ever been up against. He's a very cagey strategist and a very challenging adversary." Davis was prepped daily by Alioto and his associate Moses Laskey. The most interesting testimony by Davis concerned questions about an alleged boyhood fascination with Adolf Hitler: ". . . I didn't hate Hitler. He captivated me. I knew he had to be stopped."

Given five categories, Al Davis was also asked on the witness stand to choose his preference among love, power, glory, achievement, and money. "Some men say love. For me? Not money. It was something I never had to strive for. My father had it. Achievement came easy. In college it was glory. Now ... it's power. I don't mean ruthless power. I mean control of my destiny. . . . to have the feeling that I can dominate. President Carter was not a dominator."

And why does he speak with what *Los Angeles Times* writer Mark Heisler later called a "Brooklyn-Dixie" accent? "It comes from my days at Fort Belvoir and The Citadel. It still changes, depending on what mood I'm in. I can charm anyone if I want," Davis said.

A significant part of the NFL strategy was broken on July 24 when Judge Pregerson ruled that the NFL was not a "partnership" of 28 teams, but instead consists of "vicious competitors," as described by Davis. Other peripheral issues were removed, including the separate actions against Gene Klein, Georgia Frontiere, and Pete Rozelle. After two weeks of deliberations, the jury was deadlocked 8–2 in favor of the Raiders when it was discovered that one of the jurors, Thomas Gelker, was a cousin of a former owner in the United States Football League. All of the jurors were supposed to be ignorant about football, but Gelker somehow slipped through the selection process. The other jurors reported that Gelker was vehemently against Davis in deliberations. The Raiders charged that Gelker was an "NFL plant." The result: On August 13, 1981, Judge Pregerson declared a mistrial. The Raiders/LAMCC versus NFL would have to be heard again.

The Raiders played the 1981 season in Oakland and slumped to a 7–9 record. During the next few months, there were attempts to reach a compromise and avoid the second trial. The NFL also tried to influence the Los Angeles County Board of Supervisors to abandon Al

Davis. After turning a deaf ear to Los Angeles in 1978, the NFL was now dangling an expansion franchise in their face. Another scheme would return the Raiders to Oakland and give Davis an expansion franchise in Los Angeles. Or was it the other way around? Fortunately, these preposterous schemes were rejected. Oakland also tried to renegotiate with the Raiders, but a December 1981 lease proposal was rejected.

Trial two began March 29, 1982, in Los Angeles. An interesting story that appeared in the newspapers on April 3 had Joe Alioto talking to New York City about the Raiders moving to either Shea Stadium or Yankee Stadium to replace the Jets, who were moving to the Hackensack Meadowlands in New Jersey. It was denied by all parties.

With many side issues removed, trial two lasted only six weeks. Most of the significant testimony was the same as in the first trial. One notable exception was an admission by Pete Rozelle that an expansion team in Los Angeles would be more lucrative to the NFL than having the Raiders move. "The league has a corporate right of all the owners to share in the benefits of an expansion team going into Los Angeles." The testimony would prove fatal for the National Football League and the City of Oakland.

It was finally over on May 7, 1982. And this time there was a verdict. A six-woman jury ruled in favor of the Raiders and the Los Angeles Memorial Coliseum Commission and against the National Football League. Antitrust damages of $49 million were awarded.

Outside the courtroom, Joe Alioto was ecstatic. But Al Davis was subdued. "I don't look at it as a victory. I'm not emotionally elated." And what about Oakland, Al? "I have a lot of love for the fans in Oakland. The people are excellent, the community is excellent. They [Coliseum Board] ruined it; they destroyed it."

The press reacted predictably. Alan Malamud spoke

for Los Angeles. "Justice prevailed and now the way has been cleared for the largest county in America to have major league professional football. Established football, not expansion football, which belongs in Indianapolis, Phoenix, Memphis, or Jacksonville, not Los Angeles." Mel Durslag took another swing at Rozelle. "The war is his baby. His distaste for Al Davis inspired it. He despises Davis, and bursting his moorings altogether, he has to despise anyone who agrees with Davis." In Oakland, Dave Newhouse came right to the point: "Kick Al Davis out of football for good."

The NFL was not done. On May 12, they filed another injunction preventing the Raiders from moving. And Oakland thought it received good news when a California Supreme Court ruled that their eminent domain suit would be heard.

Al Davis began looking at practice sites in the Los Angeles area and on July 7 signed a new memorandum of agreement (not a lease) to play in Los Angeles Coliseum for the next 10 years. Nine days later, the California Supreme Court extended the motion on eminent domain into 1983 and the Federal Ninth Circuit Court declined to hear the NFL appeal of the Raider decision until April 1983. Thus, the Raiders could legally play their 1982 home games in Los Angeles.

An interesting development was unveiled by the *Oakland Tribune*. A mutual friend of Al Davis and *Tribune* editor Robert Maynard brought both men together for secret negotiations in a last-ditch attempt to keep the Raiders in Oakland. They met on numerous occasions in May and June of 1982 and, as Maynard later described, the Raiders were "first and goal" toward signing a new lease with the Oakland Coliseum. On the night of July 7, 1982, after announcing that the Raiders had signed an agreement to play in Los Angeles, Davis tried to call Maynard to continue negotiations, but the *Tribune* editor refused to cooperate. Davis claimed that he only "initialed his intentions" and did not sign a contract, but Maynard thought he had been "used" and would not return calls. The Raiders did not deny the story, but LoCasale claimed that the Raiders were never close to remaining in Oakland. Maynard has not spoken to Davis since this incident, and not coincidentally, the *Tribune* gave only lukewarm support to the 1990 attempt to entice the Raiders back to Oakland.

With the Raiders now physically playing their home games in Los Angeles, there was little likelihood that Al Davis could ever be forced back to Oakland. In February 1983, Judge Pregerson denied a request by the Oakland Coliseum Board to overturn the jury verdict of the previous May. Two months later a jury set damages at $49 million for the Raiders and the LAMCC. The eminent domain suit was heard by Judge Nat Agliano in Monterey, California, in June 1983. Oakland mayor Lionel Wilson was eloquent in his description of the Raiders' relationship with the City of Oakland. "I have never seen a phenomenon such as that in my lifetime. I know of nothing in the city that's contributed more to improving the image of the city and to improving the morale of the city among many thousands of people in the city than the Raiders."

On July 23, 1983, Judge Agliano rejected the eminent domain suit. An appeal was denied in June 1986, and the City of Oakland was ordered to pay the Raiders' legal fees of $4,000,000. By the time the City of Oakland and the Raiders agreed to a payment schedule in October 1988, compounded interest had increased the debt from the eminent domain case to $7.7 million.

During 1983, Pete Rozelle and his lawyers launched a furious fourth-quarter drive in Congress to attempt to overturn the court defeat. Leading the effort was Paul Tagliabue, now the NFL commissioner. The league was trying to gain its long-desired antitrust exemption and was lobbying for a bill that would restrict franchise transfers. By making the legislation retroactive to 1981, the Raiders would be forced to return to Oakland. The crusade was directed at, among others, senators Howard Baker of Tennessee and Dennis DeConcini of Arizona. Interpretation: If they would cooperate with Rozelle, expansion teams would be given to Memphis, Tennessee, and Phoenix, Arizona. Al Davis blasted Rozelle for "dangling franchises in front of senators."

The open vendetta of Pete Rozelle against Al Davis coupled with the NFL owner arrogance displayed during the eight-week player strike of 1982 probably doomed the congressional lobbying effort. Also, both California senators at the time, Democrat Alan Cranston and Republican Pete Wilson, had ambivalent feelings about entering into a north-south factional fight that was not politically winnable. So the NFL assault on Congress to punish Al Davis died on the vine.

The NFL was also unsuccessful in overturning the Raiders/L.A. Coliseum verdict. On February 27, 1984, the Ninth Circuit Court of Appeals upheld the decision of May 1982 in Judge Pregerson's courtroom. The Eighth Circuit Court of Appeals issued a similar ruling against the NFL in June 1984. They then filed their appeal with the U.S. Supreme Court, but in November 1984, the highest court in the land, without comment, refused to hear the case. In June 1986, the Los Angeles Coliseum Commission was awarded $21 million in damages. The judgment for the Raiders was reduced, and in March 1989 the NFL finally paid Al Davis $20 million. Thus, Rozelle's attempt to "put Al Davis in his place," instead ended as a futile and expensive folly for the 27 other owners.

There are two footnotes to this story. In March 1984, the Baltimore Colts suddenly moved to Indianapolis. Colts owner Robert Irsay turned down a generous Baltimore offer of a $15 million loan at 8% interest, $6 millon to build a new training facility, and a guaranteed attendance of 43,000 and accepted a similar offer from Indianapolis. Irsay did not ask for NFL approval and Pete Rozelle blamed the court decision in the Raiders case for an inability to stop the Colts. Mel Durslag used the Colts' transfer as another reason to blast Rozelle. "But it's all crazy now, and it all can be traced to the football commissioner who, after 50 years of franchise moving in this country, decides he doesn't like the style of Al Davis and is going to teach him a lesson."

The St. Louis Cardinals moved to Phoenix in January 1988 and asked for and received NFL approval. Owner Bill Bidwell accepted a package that included $17 million in guaranteed income for sellouts and a $6.4 million loan for construction of 60 skyboxes. Mel Durslag reminded his readers that the Cards, Colts, Jets, and Vikings all voted against the Raiders' move to Los Angeles.

In May 1990, while discussing what may be another illegal NFL rule, the edict against corporate ownership, *San Francisco Examiner* writer Frank Cooney accurately recalled the foolishness of the Al Davis versus the NFL episode: "Ten years ago, when league officials believed one of their precious rules was being violated, the reaction was to attack rather than reason. So they tried to prevent the Raiders from moving to Los Angeles. It cost them time, energy, and about $70 million to learn it would have been easier just to rewrite their rules; after all, the rules were unconstitutional anyway."

So Al Davis won it all. In court, in Congress, and on the playing field, as evidenced by the win of January 1984 in Super Bowl XVIII. He beat down his archenemy Rozelle, defeated the NFL buddy-buddy system where owners such as Gene Klein and Art Modell reigned supreme, but most important of all, was victorious on the playing field against the teams of the Kleins and Modells of the NFL. But was it really worth it? Subsequent events would indicate it was not.

Following the verdict in the eminent domain suit,

Dave Newhouse gave the Raiders a fitting epitaph in the *Oakland Tribune*. "Why did the Oakland Raiders expire? They were winners on the field and at the ticket office. Why? Because the team owner has a homicidal heart. There is no sense pressing charges, he is on the NFL's wanted list but is too elusive to be caught. . . . The Raiders are gone, undeniably gone. In the background a dirge is playing. . . . Oakland Raiders R.I.P."

Do you believe in exorcism, Dave?

Chapter 12

FOUR GREAT
SEASONS IN L.A.

*F*rom 1982 to 1985, the Raiders gave their new fans in Los Angeles four seasons of winning playoff football. The 1983 team won Super Bowl XVIII. The regular season records were 8–1, 12–4, 11–5, and 12–4. The 1982 squad lived and practiced in the Bay Area amid local hostility but flew to Los Angeles for home games. The 1985 team played nearly the entire season without its starting quarterback but won the last six games to capture the AFC Western Division title.

It was a great time to be a Los Angeles Raider. And the Raiders quickly developed a new set of stars for their Los Angeles audience. Defensive end Howie Long, a rookie in the last season in Oakland, became an All-Pro performer in Los Angeles. Tight end Todd Christensen, a former running back who primarily played on special teams in Oakland, became the most prolific pass receiver in the NFL. Free safety Vann McElroy, the number two draft choice of 1982, was installed as a starter in 1983 and was to star for the next seven years. Another 1982 rookie, defensive back James Davis of Southern University, became an effective "nickel" back in the defensive secondary. And with their first draft choice in 1982, the Raiders were to choose a man who had a combination of flair, class, talent, and leadership who would lead the Silver and Black throughout the 1980s. He was also a hometown hero too.

The Raiders were probably lucky to select Marcus Allen with the tenth overall pick in the 1982 draft. Allen won the Heisman Trophy while playing tailback for John Robinson at the University of Southern California in 1981. Many pro scouts considered Allen too small to be a productive running back in pro football. The Raiders had not selected as high as tenth since 1966, the year before the merger. Sequestered in their "war room" on the day of the draft, the Raiders nervously watched the other teams select the first nine college players. Denver, drafting ahead of the Raiders, needed a running back and so did Minnesota. The Broncos selected Gerald Willhite of San Jose State. The Vikings traveled about 25 miles from San Jose up the Bayshore Freeway to nab Darren Nelson of Stanford. The Raiders first breathed a collective sigh of relief and then chose Allen.

What a steal for Al Davis and Company! In nine games of the abbreviated 1982 season, Marcus Allen scored 14 touchdowns. Many were on short goal line plunges where "Air Allen" would fly over the defensive linemen and linebackers. Some were on breakaway runs. Others were as a receiver. He threw one touchdown pass on an option play. Oh yes, the man can also block. Marcus Allen showed his teammates that he was a born leader both on and off the field. An active member of the community. A winner. In 30 years of Raider football, Marcus Allen is the best running back ever to wear the Silver and Black and arguably perhaps the best overall player in team history. Allen now holds the Raider career rushing and touchdown records. A four-time winner of the annual Commitment to Excellence award given to the team's Most Valuable Player. The standards are now in place for Bo Jackson or other future Raiders. Established by Marcus Allen.

The 1982 season started well with two road wins against NFC West opponents. In their first game as the *Los Angeles* Raiders, the Silver and Black upset the world champion San Francisco 49ers 23–17 in hostile Candle-stick Park. Allen was magnificent in his debut, gaining 116 yards and scoring once. Jim Plunkett was sharp, and the defense stopped Joe Montana and his offense when it mattered. Scott Ostler of the *Los Angeles Times* sang the praises of Allen the following day in a column titled "After one game, a nomination for the NFL's Hall of Fame."

In Atlanta, it was a 38–14 cakewalk on a hot and humid day. Wide receiver Cliff Branch had 138 yards receiving, and defensive tackle Archie Reese, acquired from San Francisco, ran back a fumble 75 yards for the final touchdown. Veteran defensive tackle Lyle Alzado and kick returner Greg Pruitt, both acquired from Cleveland, were also impressive.

The first NFL players strike shut down football for the next eight weeks. When play resumed, the Raiders played their first home game in Los Angeles on Monday night, November 22. The "pride and poise" boys were rusty as the Chargers raced to a 24–0 lead. But led by Allen, Christensen, and fullback Frank Hawkins, the Raiders rallied for a 28–24 victory, sending their 55,060 new fans home happy.

The only loss of 1982 came the following Sunday in Cincinnati when the Bengals shut down Allen and the running game. Plunkett threw for 321 yards, mostly after the 31–17 outcome had been decided. Quarterback Ken Anderson and fullback Pete Johnson starred for the Bengals, and defensive end Eddie Edwards overpowered right tackle Henry Lawrence of the Raiders.

Five consecutive victories were to follow. Allen rushed for a regular season high of 156 yards and two touchdowns in a 28–23 triumph over Seattle. Safety Burgess Owens chipped in with two interceptions of Jim Zorn. Next Plunkett had 303 air yards and three TD passes in a 21–16 win at Kansas City. Wide receiver Calvin Mohammad caught a 35-yard scoring pass with 35 seconds to play to win it. The Rams returned to their old stomping grounds at the Coliseum for a nationally televised Saturday afternoon game and jumped out to a 21–7 advantage. They were leading 30–21 when Plunkett and Allen took over. Air Allen scored in the final minute for an exciting 37–31 victory.

Wins over Denver and San Diego pushed the record to 8–1, tied with Washington for the best in show for 1982. The defense recorded seven sacks, and Plunkett fired a 51-yard touchdown to Allen and found Malcolm Barnwell for a 52-yard score in a 27–10 win over the Broncos. In San Diego, the Davis boys, not Al but Mike and James, returned errant Dan Fouts passes for touchdowns in a 41–34 decision. Allen gained 126 more yards and scored twice.

To compensate for the strike, the playoffs were expanded to include eight teams in each conference. In the AFC, the No. 1 seeded Raiders met the No. 8 Cleveland Browns. With the defense putting the pressure on quarterback Paul McDonald, the Raiders were the winners 27–10. Plunkett passed for 386 yards and Allen added two more touchdowns. Next up: the New York Jets.

There were 90,688 at the Coliseum for this bicoastal battle. A touchdown pass from Richard Todd to Wesley Walker helped the Jets to an early 10–0 lead. The Raiders tallied twice in the third quarter to forge ahead but New York scored again and ultimately won 17–14. It was one interception and an almost interception that doomed the Raiders. Late in the game, a Todd pass landed in the hands of Raider linebacker Ted Hendricks. He dropped it. And in the last gasp comeback, a Plunkett pass was pilfered by Lance Mehl of the Jets, his third of the game.

The loss to the Jets exposed two 1982 Raider weaknesses that would have to be remedied if the team were to seriously entertain thoughts of a Super Bowl. Following the retirement of Gene Upshaw, second-year player Curt Marsh was installed at left guard. He was unable to handle the pass rush of the talented New York defensive line, featuring the obnoxious Mark Gastineau. On defense, the Jets stayed away from Lester Hayes and Todd threw in the direction of second-year defensive back Ted Watts. Wesley Walker took Watts to the cleaners in the playoff loss. Al Davis's teams always had good cornerbacks, but this Raider club had a glaring problem on one side.

On draft day 1983, the Raiders drafted USC offensive lineman Don Mosebar with their first pick. Thinking he was the offensive lineman to replace Marsh, the Raiders instead discovered that Mosebar needed back surgery and wouldn't be of much help in the coming season. Veteran guard Charlie Hannah was acquired from Tampa Bay for defensive tackle Dave Browning and proved to be the missing link in the offensive line.

Halfway into the 1983 season, the other weakness was corrected. Unable to come to contract terms with New England, All-Pro cornerback Mike Haynes was a season-long holdout. He was finally acquired by L.A. for the Raiders' No. 1 pick of 1984. With the final piece of the puzzle in place, there was no stopping the Silver and Black.

There were other impressive newcomers in 1983. Receiver Dokie Williams of UCLA became a starter in 1984 and played five years with the Silver and Black. Defensive end Greg Townsend was once a gang member on the streets of the Watts section of L.A. Reformed at Texas Christian University, Townsend quickly became a pass-rush specialist. In 1989, he was moved to left outside linebacker and was credited with 10½ sacks. Al Davis returned to his roots and drafted New York City native Bill Pickel of Rutgers. A valuable spare part in 1983 and 1984, Pickel eventually replaced Reggie Kinlaw at nose tackle.

The 1983 season opened in Cincinnati with the Raiders avenging their only 1982 loss in a 20–10 victory. Marcus Allen scored early, and the defense limited quarterback Ken Anderson and shut down the Bengals running game. The home opener was a 20–6 win over Houston before 37,526, smaller than any 1982 crowd. Although Kenny King and Pruitt scored the touchdowns, the defense held the Oilers to only two third down conversions, and quarterback Archie Manning was sacked five times.

Next the Raiders raced to a 27–0 lead on a Monday night before rookie quarterback Dan Marino made his debut by directing the Dolphins to two late touchdowns. The highlight of the 27–14 win over Miami was a touchdown run with a fumble recovery by rookie defensive end Greg Townsend. Plunkett was sharp and Allen added 105 yards. The Raiders made it 4–0 with a 22–7 win at Denver. The defense completely befuddled rookie quarterback John Elway, who was knocked unconscious by Bill Pickel. Cliff Branch had both scores, Chris Bahr kicked two field goals, and Townsend sacked Steve De-Berg in the end zone for a safety.

The 4–0 Raiders traveled to Washington to meet the 4–0 Redskins in what was probably one of the most exciting NFL games ever played. Marcus Allen sat out the game with a hamstring pull and he was missed as Washington jumped to a 20–3 lead. Plunkett connected with Branch for a team record 99-yard touchdown pass, Pruitt returned a punt 97 yards for a score and Mohammad reached the top of the mountain with two touchdown receptions as the Raiders built a 35–20 lead. Washington coach Joe Gibbs replaced fullback John Riggins with tailback Joe Washington, who caught a 66-yard pass from Joe Theismann to lead the Redskins to a come-from-behind 37–35 win.

The loss in Washington was followed by a listless 21–20 win over Kansas City. Ted Hendricks blocked a 45-yard field goal try by Nick Lowery to save the game. The first of a series of "chamber of horror" games in Seattle followed. The Raiders had the early lead but committed eight turnovers in a 38–36 loss to the Seahawks. Plunkett was sacked eight times, had three passes picked off, and was replaced by Marc Wilson, who became the starting signal caller for the next four weeks.

A pivotal game for the 5–2 Raiders was a Sunday night contest in Dallas. In one of his best games as a Raider, Marc Wilson threw for 318 yards and three touchdowns in a 40–38 victory, the first loss of the year for the Cowboys. Frank Hawkins gained a career-high 118 yards, and a Ted Watts interception of Cowboy quarterback Danny White led to the winning Chris Bahr field goal. The Seahawks next visited the Raiders and won 34–21 for their second decision over Los Angeles. David Krieg replaced the slumping Jim Zorn for Seattle and piloted the Seahawks to victory. It would not be the last time that Mr. Krieg beat Los Angeles. Wilson was sacked five times and had three passes intercepted.

With Plunkett back at the controls, the Raiders won the next five games and wrapped up the AFC West title. Victories at Kansas City and Buffalo were sandwiched around a 22–20 win against the Broncos. Attempting to make a tackle after throwing an interception, Wilson broke his shoulder in Kansas City and was replaced by Plunkett. A 40-yard pass interception by Rod Martin clinched the 28–20 victory. The last-second hero against Denver was kicker Chris Bahr with a 39-yard field goal. Christensen caught four passes from Plunkett on the final winning drive. Bahr made the difference the following week in Buffalo after the Raiders squandered a 24–3 lead. Two fumbles by Allen in the fourth quarter had allowed the Bills to rally. The Giants were then beaten 27–12 as the defense applied seven sacks on New York quarterback Scott Brunner. Reserve tight end Don Hasselbeck caught a 10-yard touchdown in the game.

The Raiders then visited San Diego for a Thursday night contest. The Chargers assumed a 10–0 lead before an unanswered 42-point blitz in the second and third quarters broke the game wide open. Christensen caught three touchdowns, one from Allen, and Hawkins also hit pay dirt twice. At 11–3, the Raiders clinched the AFC West. The offense, defense, and special teams were never better than they were in this game. Never.

In typical Raider fashion, the Silver and Black had a 24–7 lead over St. Louis in week 15 before falling asleep in a 34–24 loss. Only 32,111 watched Plunkett get sacked six times. The Raiders needed a win in the finale against San Diego to secure home field advantage in the playoffs. A 30–14 win over the Chargers was led by Plunkett, Allen, Branch, Bahr, and the defense. The Raiders accumulated 480 yards of total offense.

Following a week off, the 12–4 Raiders entertained the 10–6 AFC Central champion Pittsburgh Steelers in the first round of the playoffs. Early in the game, Lester Hayes picked off a Cliff Stoudt pass and returned it for a touchdown. Marcus Allen scored two touchdowns, and the newly-acquired Haynes also starred in the 38–10 rout.

Seattle upset the favored Dolphins in Miami, so it would be the Seahawks versus the Raiders for the right to represent the AFC in Super Bowl XVIII at Tampa Bay. Could Seattle beat Los Angeles three times in one season?

No! The Raiders stopped rookie running back Curt Warner and shut down quarterback David Krieg. Strong safety Mike Davis had two interceptions. On offense, Allen rushed for 154 yards on 25 attempts and fullback Frank Hawkins scored twice. The Raiders controlled the line of scrimmage in the 30–14 decision, which gave the "pride and poise" boys their fourth AFL/AFC Championship.

Super Bowl XVIII was a rematch of the fifth game of the season: Washington versus L.A. The Redskins finished with a 14–2 record and were slight favorites to repeat their Super Bowl victory of 27–17 over Miami in Super Bowl XVII. Washington had struggled against San Francisco in the NFC Championship game, but a couple of questionable pass interference penalties late in the game aided and abetted the Redskins in a 24–21 win.

The oddsmakers and many football experts were emphatically proven wrong. From the opening kickoff, this world championship game belonged to the Raiders. First the defense, led by nose tackle Reggie Kinlaw and linebackers Bob Nelson, Matt Millen, and Ted Hendricks, stifled Riggins. Midway in the first period, Derrick Jensen blocked a Washington punt and Lester Hayes recovered in the end zone for a touchdown. Later Plunkett hit Branch on a TD pass for a 14–3 lead. Just before halftime, Joe Gibbs committed the ultimate coaching faux pas. With 12 seconds to go before halftime, on its own 15-yard line, common sense dictated that Washington have Riggins run out the clock, go into the locker room trailing 14–3, and regroup. But Gibbs called time-out and replaced Riggins with Joe Washington, who had burned the Raiders in the 37–35 regular season game. Defensive coordinator Charlie Sumner and his players were ready. Theismann tried a screen pass, but reserve linebacker Jack Squirek stepped in front of Washington, intercepted, and walked into the end zone past the stunned Theismann. It was 21–3 Raiders and the Redskins were demoralized. As they say on television: For all intents and purposes, the game was over.

The rest of the contest belonged to Allen and the defense. The Redskins finally scored a touchdown but missed the extra point. Late in the third quarter at the Los Angeles 25-yard line, Plunkett gave the ball to Allen. The play was supposed to be off tackle but the running lane was blocked. Marcus cut the other way, found a hole, and sprinted 75 yards for a touchdown, the longest run from scrimmage in Super Bowl history. Allen had another touchdown in the fourth quarter and almost scored a third time when he was stopped at the Redskin one after another "reverse the field" scamper. Chris Bahr completed the scoring with a field goal, and Tom Flores won his second Super Bowl as Raider head coach in a 38–9 pasting of Washington.

The 1983 Raiders have never been mentioned when the experts discuss the all-time great NFL teams. The 12–4 regular season record looks inferior when compared to the 15–1 or 14–2 teams that were to follow. It even looks paltry when contrasted to the 13–1, 1976 world champion Oakland Raiders. The 1983 squad was not respected in the 1989 NFL Dream Season tournament shown on ESPN when the computers handed them three losses against other championship clubs. But make no mistake, the 1983 Los Angeles Raiders were a great team, solid in all departments. They outscored their opponents 106–33 in the three playoff games and never really broke a sweat. Plunkett, Allen, Long, Hayes, Haynes, Christensen, Rod Martin, and Vann McElroy never played better. Veterans like Bob Nelson, Ted Hendricks, Lyle Alzado, Dave Dalby, Mickey Marvin, Bruce Davis, and Henry Lawrence were solid. Mosebar, Townsend, and wide receiver Dokie Williams were blue-chip rookies. Overall assessment: The 1983 world championship squad was the best team that Al Davis has ever produced.

The Raiders attempted to win back-to-back Super Bowls in 1984 with basically the same cast of characters. Mosebar replaced Mickey Marvin at starting right guard, and Dokie Williams beat out Malcolm Barnwell for the wide receiver position opposite Cliff Branch. But when Branch was hampered by injuries, Barnwell returned to the starting lineup. The Raiders acquired veteran linebacker Brad Van Pelt as a replacement for the retired Ted Hendricks.

Three useful rookies from the class of 1984 were Sean Jones, Stacey Toran, and Andy Parker. Jones, from Northeastern University, was a strong pass-rushing defensive end. Toran spent most of 1984 playing on special teams and eventually became the starting strong-side safety, specializing in hard tackles and blitzes. Driving while allegedly intoxicated, the Notre Dame alumnus died in an automobile accident in August 1989. Parker, a tight end from the University of Utah, became a good special teams performer and also was an understudy to Christensen.

The Raiders won the first four contests, beating Houston, Green Bay, Kansas City, and San Diego. After sleepwalking through the first half in Houston, Allen, Hawkins, and Plunkett reached the end zone to beat the Oilers. The defense knocked Green Bay quarterback Lynn Dickey out of the game and then made life miserable for substitute rookie Randy Wright. Derrick Jensen scored one of the four Raider touchdowns in the 28—7 victory. Three Chris Bahr field goals helped overcome a 13–0 Chiefs lead. The final score was 22–20. The 33–30 come-from-behind win over the Chargers was witnessed by 80,674 on a Monday night at the Coliseum. Plunkett was spectacular, passing for 363 yards, and Marcus Allen scored four touchdowns.

In their history, the Raiders had never won the first five games of a season. 1984 was no different. Inspired Denver stopped the Raiders 16–13. The Broncos held the Raiders to only 12 first downs and kept the ball away from L.A. for the last 4:34 of the game.

The Raiders won the next three games to raise the record to 7–1. Plunkett tore an abdominal muscle against Seattle and would be sidelined for most of the remainder of the regular season. Wilson came off the bench and combined with Allen on a 92-yard pass-and-run play and a 55-yard touchdown pass in the 28–14 win over the Seahawks.

Wins over Minnesota and San Diego followed. The Raiders were assessed an unbelievable 16 penalties for 140 yards against the Vikings and needed a 20-yard, final-play field goal by Chris Bahr to score a 23–20 win. Wilson had the best day of his career at San Diego, passing for five touchdowns including a 51-yard toss to Barnwell that won the 44–37 game.

The return match with the Broncos was a pivotal game in the season for both teams. The Raiders were nursing a 19–12 fourth-quarter lead when an Allen fumble with 2:15 to go was recovered by Denver and converted into the game-tying points. In the overtime period, the Raiders drove to the Bronco 11 when Tom Flores eschewed a field goal on first down. Frank Hawkins then fumbled the ball away. On the last play in the extra period with the clock running out, Rich Karlis kicked a game-winning field goal for Denver. The victory helped catapult the Broncos toward the AFC West title with an eventual 13–3 record. Tom Flores reached for the Maalox.

The next Raider game was in Chicago. The Bears, who were rapidly improving and would win the Super Bowl the next season, were ready for the current world champions. Both Marc Wilson and his backup, David Humm, were knocked out of the game by the ferocious Chicago defense, led by rookie Richard Dent. The Raiders returned the favor by injuring Jim McMahon, finishing the Chicago quarterback for the remainder of the season. The Bears won 17–6.

A 17–14 loss in Seattle gave the Raiders a 7–4 record. David Krieg picked on Lester Hayes for both Seahawk touchdowns. The division crown was becoming remote but a wild card berth was within grasp. The Raiders responded by winning the next four games. The highlight of a 17–7 yawner over Kansas City was a 77-yard fumble return by Rod Martin. Allen gained 110 yards against Indianapolis, and the defense limited the Colts to 158 yards as the Raiders prevailed 21–7.

The Silver and Black traveled to Miami to meet the 12–1 Dolphins. Early in the game, with the Dolphins threatening to blow out the Raiders, Mike Haynes intercepted a Dan Marino pass and raced 97 yards. Marino brought the Dolphins back with a 470-yard passing day and four touchdown passes, but the game belonged to Marcus Allen, who rushed for 156 yards. Late in the game, on a third-down-and-six play with the Raiders nursing a 38–34 lead, Allen broke past the Miami secondary and ran 48 yards into the end zone to ice the 45–34 victory. When New England lost the following Sunday, the Raiders clinched a wild card playoff berth.

Plunkett returned in the second half of a 24–3 Monday night win over Detroit and combined with Allen on a 73-yard pass-and-run touchdown. Punt returner Cle Montgomery also reached the end zone. After 15 games, the Raiders had an 11–4 record, the same as in 1983. If they could win the finale against Pittsburgh, Los Angeles could host the wild card game the following Sunday against Seattle.

But the boys came up flat against the Steelers. Wilson was horrible in the first half. Plunkett completed a disputed fourth-quarter touchdown pass to Dokie Williams but it wasn't enough in a 13–7 loss. "It looks like we were out watching Wally and the Beaver this week," remarked Millen. Pittsburgh won their division and now the Raiders would be playing at Seattle on Saturday in the wild card game. Plunkett started against the Seahawks but the team played one of its typical bad games in the Kingdome. Allen scored a TD, but the defense could not stop the Seattle running game, particularly journeyman Dan Doornick, and suddenly the dream of a repeat Super Bowl winner was gone in the 13–7 setback.

Cliff Branch retired (or was forced to), so the Raiders selected wide receivers in the 1985 college draft. The top choice was Jessie Hester of Florida State, and Tim Moffett of Mississippi was the second pick. But the best selection for the Raiders was No. 10 choice linebacker Reggie McKenzie of Tennessee, who won a starting job for 1985. Rusty Hilger of Oklahoma State, selected No. 6, found a home as the third-string quarterback. Running back

Steve Strachan proved to be a special teams titan. During the season, veteran linebacker Jerry Robinson was acquired from Philadelphia to replace the disappointing Brad Van Pelt. Free agent tight end Trey Junkin provided depth. Mosebar eventually moved to center for the injured Dave Dalby and Mickey Marvin was reinserted at right guard.

The 1985 campaign started nicely with a 31–0 trouncing of the New York Jets. Strong safety Stacey Toran scored a 76-yard touchdown by intercepting a Ken O'Brien toss. Plunkett was accurate and Dokie Williams caught five passes for 131 yards.

But tough times lay just around the bend. Four days later, the Raiders lost to Kansas City 36–20. Nick Lowery connected on five Kansas City field goals and wide receiver Carlos Carson burned both Hayes and Haynes. A crowd of 92,487 then witnessed a 34–10 pummeling by the World Champion 49ers. Plunkett suffered a dislocated shoulder against San Francisco and would not see any action for the remainder of the season. The offense could move the ball when it wasn't allowing nine sacks.

So it was Marc Wilson, come hell or high water. The next week in New England was a crucial game for the Silver and Black. The Pats were ahead early, but the defense starred in the 35–20 comeback. Lyle Alzado scored a touchdown on a fumble recovery, and Hayes and Sam Seale also reached the end zone for the defense. Wilson was hurt, so Hilger made his debut. After missing on his first six passes, Rusty found Christensen in the end zone for the final score of the game.

The Raiders also won the next four games, beating Kansas City, New Orleans, Cleveland, and San Diego. Chris Bahr kicked four field goals and Allen ran through the Chiefs for 126 yards. For the first time in Raider history, the bench started calling all the offensive plays. And for the remainder of the season, most of the calls were to give the ball to number 32, Marcus Allen. In 1985, Allen led the NFL in rushing with 1,759 yards and was named Most Valuable Player. Marcus rushed for more than 100 yards in each of the last nine games of the season.

A Wilson-to-Williams pass broke open a 23–13 victory over the Saints. Allen had the other two scores. A last-minute touchdown pass from Wilson to Christensen made the difference in the 21–20 victory over the Browns. The defense sacked quarterback Dan Fouts six times in a 34–21 decision over the Chargers. Jessie Hester opened the scoring with a 13-yard reverse.

Wilson was intercepted four times, and a Raider field goal attempt was converted into a Seahawk touchdown in another snake-bitten loss in Seattle. It was followed by a 40–34 defeat in San Diego when diminutive Charger running back Lionel James broke loose for a touchdown in overtime. A missed extra point and a failure to stop Dan Fouts and Charlie Joiner in the last minute of regulation time were other lowlights. The Raiders were now 6–4 and fighting with Denver for both the AFC West crown and a playoff berth.

Allen gained 135 yards and caught a touchdown pass in a 13–6 win over Cincinnati before the Broncos came to town. Denver held the early lead on a rainy Sunday but the Raiders fought back to a 28–28 tie. After missing a 40-yarder in regulation time, Chris Bahr kicked the winning field goal for a 31–28 overtime win. Among the 173 yards that Allen gained on the ground was a 61-yard touchdown run. Both the Raiders and Broncos were now 8–4.

Marcus outdueled Gerald Riggs of the Falcons in a 34–24 triumph over hapless Atlanta. The Raiders next traveled to Denver for the rematch. The Broncos were ahead 14–0 at the half but Wilson, Christensen, and Allen brought the Raiders even at 14–14. Snow began to fall over the Rockies during the overtime period, when Howie Long and Greg Townsend caused John Elway to fumble on the Bronco eight-yard line. The Raiders recovered the ball and Chris Bahr won it with another clutch field goal. Final score: Raiders 17, Broncos 14.

The 10–4 Raiders were now in the driver's seat. A 13–3 win over the Seahawks clinched the AFC Western Division title. The defense held Seattle to 201 net yards. Allen again scored the only touchdown of the contest. "Take away Marcus Allen and basically we have nothing," said Matt Millen after the game. A 16–6 Monday night win at Anaheim over the Rams gave the Silver and Black a 12–4 record and home field advantage in the AFC playoffs. Allen closed his brilliant season with another 123 yards to outgain Eric Dickerson. It was the fourth game with only one touchdown, this time scored by Dokie Williams on a 23-yard pass from Wilson in the fourth quarter. Sitting on the bench in street clothes, Jim Plunkett appeared to be healthy and ready to play. But he was not activated. First playoff opponent: New England.

Perhaps the Raiders didn't take New England seriously. They had beaten the Patriots during the season. But Millen's remark after the clincher over Seattle proved to be prophetic. At halftime of the first-round playoff game, the Raiders were ahead 20–17 and Allen was having a great day. Early in the third quarter, the Raiders were near midfield when Wilson suddenly called a time-out to discuss strategy with the coaches. After an unsuccessful play, he called another time out, much to the dismay of the 88,000 fans in Los Angeles Memorial Coliseum. Another incomplete pass. The Raiders punted. Following a tying New England field goal, Sam Seale fumbled the ensuing kickoff, giving the Pats another touchdown. Late in the game with no time-outs remaining, the Raiders stood by helplessly as New England easily ran out the clock. Showing his frustration after the game, linebacker Matt Millen confronted and shoved a heckling Pat Sullivan, the son of Patriots' owner Billy Sullivan, a longtime antagonist of Al Davis. Perhaps he should have attacked Wilson, the coaching staff, or Davis. The offense, led by Wilson, was the actual cause of the defeat. The 27–20 defeat to New England ended the Raiders' dream of playing the Bears in Super Bowl XX.

It was a productive and exciting first four years in Los Angeles and perhaps with some lucky bounces, it could have been three or four world championships. Who would have thought that the winningest team in pro football would not play in a post-season game for the remainder of the decade?

Chapter 13

1986–1989:
A PLUNGE
TO MEDIOCRITY

"If it's a late December day in the last half of the
1980s, the Raiders must be on vacation."
    —*Mark Heisler,* Los Angeles Times

*I*n 1986, the Los Angeles Raiders actually wrapped three seasons of football into one campaign. They started horribly, then rallied into contention. But in the final four games, with the playoffs in sight and a relatively easy schedule, the Raiders collapsed and finished 8–8, their worst mark in five seasons in Los Angeles and the start of a prolonged absence from the upper echelons of the National Football League.

After a halfhearted attempt to obtain a quarterback, the Raiders opened the 1986 season with the same cast of signal-calling characters: Marc Wilson, Jim Plunkett, and Rusty Hilger. Stacey Toran replaced Mike Davis at strong safety. Don Mosebar was permanently moved to center to supplant the retired Dave Dalby, and Mickey Marvin reclaimed the right guard position. The draft produced next to nothing. Defensive back Stefon Adams would see more action on special teams than in the secondary. Running back Vance Mueller spelled Marcus Allen in the lineup but made larger contributions to special teams.

Then there was the strange case of Napoleon McCallum. A star at the Naval Academy, McCallum was the Raiders' fourth draft choice. But Napoleon was scheduled to serve four years in the Navy as an officer. Using his influence, Al Davis managed to have McCallum stationed aboard the *U.S.S. Peleliu,* which was docked in Long Beach harbor, about a 30-minute car ride from the Raider practice field. So after being an officer and a gentleman for the Navy each morning, McCallum played for the Raiders in 1986. However, President Ronald Reagan installed a new Secretary of the Navy in 1987 who must have been a Bronco fan. He wouldn't allow McCallum to play while serving Uncle Sam. The Raiders eventually traded Napoleon to San Diego. He saw limited action with the Chargers. To complete this bizarre tale of the high seas, the Raiders reacquired McCallum from San Diego. His Navy duty ended in July 1990, so the Raiders may yet realize full-time dividends on McCallum. "He started with us as an ensign and comes back as a lieutenant," said Al LoCasale.

The season opener was against the Broncos in Denver. The Raiders were ahead through much of the game, with a highlight being a long touchdown pass from Wilson to former track star Rod Barksdale. But two plays turned the opener toward Denver. Toran was called for a questionable pass-interference penalty in the end zone, which led to one touchdown, and another score came on a trick play with quarterback John Elway on the receiving end of a TD pass. When the dust had settled, the Broncos had a 38–36 victory.

Week two was an entirely different affair. The Redskins and Raiders engaged in a defensive struggle. In the second half, Washington quarterback Jay Schroeder set up the only touchdown of the game with a 59-yard pass to tight end Clint Didier in a 10–6 Raider loss. Next was the home opener against the Giants and again the offense disappeared. The Giants beat the Raiders 14–9 for their first-ever victory over the Silver and Black. Marcus Allen suffered a sprained ankle, which ended his 12-game streak of 100-yard rushing performances. The Raiders were now 0–3, their worst start since 1964.

Some Los Angeles Coliseum fans were wearing paper bags for the San Diego home game. The Raiders struggled, but a 40-yard Wilson-to-Hester touchdown pass made the difference in a 17–13 win. Allen didn't play.

The next four games were all Raider victories, beginning with a 24–17 triumph at Kansas City, which featured a controversial Dokie Williams touchdown reception. It started the Raiders back from a 17–0 deficit. Seattle fell next, 14–10. McCallum gained 75 yards as a replacement for the injured Allen. Then the Raiders won at Miami, 30–28, in a game that was not as close as the final score indicated. Allen celebrated his return with three touchdowns and 96 yards. In a 28–17 victory at Houston, Wilson threw four touchdown passes, three to Todd Christensen. The defense sacked Warren Moon six times and had four interceptions. So the Raiders, who started at 0–3, now were 5–3 and in the chase for first place. The next game against Denver would determine if the rejuvenated Raiders could catch the first-place Broncos.

The Denver game attracted 90,153 fans. Wilson passed for 367 yards, a career best, but also threw four interceptions which sank the Raiders 21–10. The final errant pass was picked off by safety Mike Harden for a touchdown.

Tight end Todd Christensen caught 11 passes in the Denver loss. In 1986, Christensen led the National Football League with 95 receptions, 8 for touchdowns. No tight end has ever caught more. Al Davis teams have always had productive, primarily pass-catching tight ends. Originally a running back, Christensen was converted to tight end in 1981. Christensen is not unique to Raider history, because Billy Cannon, Bob Mischak, and Derrick Jensen have also been converted tight ends. But the colorful graduate of Brigham Young University became the most efficient tight end in Raider annals. After being drafted in the second round by Dallas in 1978 and then released by the Cowboys and then the Giants, Christensen joined the Raiders midway through the 1979 campaign. He scored a touchdown in the 1980 wild card playoff game against Houston and gradually started seeing more action at tight end. In 1982, Christensen began making large contributions to the Raider offense. There were 92 receptions and 12 touchdowns in 1983, 80 catches in 1984, and 82 more in 1985. The strike of 1987 and injuries in 1988 curtailed production. Christensen was released following the Oakland preseason game in 1989 in an unpopular move for Raider fans. The articulate No. 46 is now behind the mike in television and should have a fine future as a broadcaster. Along with Marcus Allen and Howie Long, Christensen was probably the most popular performer in Los Angeles during the 1980s.

Refusing to die, the Raiders rebounded from the Denver loss by winning the next three games. Plunkett replaced Wilson in the second half and threw two touchdowns to Dokie Williams for a 17–13 victory at Dallas. The Plunkett-Williams battery produced two more scores against Cleveland. The 27–14 victory over the Browns was probably their best performance of 1986.

The history books say that the decline of the Silver and Black began in the thirteenth week of the 1986 season, when the Raiders lost to a weak Philadelphia team in overtime. But the decline actually began in the overtime victory over the Chargers, the game played prior to the Philadelphia contest. The Raiders cruised to a 31–14 lead in the third quarter behind defensive touchdowns by Jerry Robinson and Lester Hayes and the pass catching of Christensen. Then third-string quarterback Mark Herrmann started picking the Raider defense apart in a San Diego comeback that forced overtime. Marcus Allen ran 28 yards for a touchdown to win that game but the collapse in the third and fourth quarters against the last-place Chargers was a preview of what was to come.

The San Diego game was a close call, but the Raiders were now 8–4 and had three of the last four games at home against losing teams. A playoff berth seemed all but certain and many experts thought they were now the best team in the AFC. While many Raider fans were thinking about the miracles of 1980, the season quickly duplicated the collapse of 1978.

With 10 days rest, the Raiders next met the 3–9 Philadelphia Eagles. Quarterback Randall Cunningham was sacked 10 times by the defense. But Greg Garrity returned a punt 76 yards for a touchdown and Mike Quick caught three TD passes from Cunningham. Jessie Hester caught two touchdown passes from Plunkett but dropped another. A holding penalty on Henry Lawrence negated another Raider score. The game was tied 27–27 at the end of regulation. In OT, the Raiders drove down to the Eagle 12. Coach Flores declined an immediate field goal try. Allen then fumbled and Andre Waters returned it to the Raider four-yard line. Dokie Williams seemingly came out of nowhere to save the touchdown. But two plays later Cunningham scored and the game was over. Despite the defeat, the Raiders were still 8–5 and appeared to be in good shape.

Next was the annual debacle in Seattle: 37–0 Seahawks. The Raiders played with only one tight end and Plunkett, Wilson, and Hilger were all rendered helpless by the lack of offensive line blocking, which allowed 11 sacks. The 8–6 record was still good and the panic button hadn't yet been pushed.

But it would be after the next week. Benefiting from a softer schedule than the Raiders, Kansas City came into

Los Angeles Coliseum with the same 8–6 record as the home team and with playoff possibilities. Surely the Raiders would beat this team. So what happened? Another pitiful performance, marred by two early Marcus Allen fumbles. There were four Plunkett interceptions, and McCallum coughed the ball up to the Chiefs at their 16-yard line in the fourth quarter. The Chiefs won 20–17 and went on to the playoffs. The Raiders were barely hanging by a thread, with almost all hope gone.

By the time the regular season finale started against Indianapolis and the games in the East were completed, the Raiders had been eliminated from playoff contention. So what the hell, let's go out and beat the hapless Colts. The Raiders led 17–6 at halftime with Plunkett at the controls. Flores played Hilger in the second half but the Colts rallied for a 30–24 win, their third in a row following thirteen losses. With time running out, Hilger moved the Raiders toward the Indianapolis goal line, but on the last play of the game, a pass to rookie Mark Pattison was caught just out of the end zone. The nightmarish 1986 Raider season had mercifully come to an end. "I've got nothing to say except Merry Christmas to everybody," said Davis to a reporter. What he said privately was another matter.

But wait, sports fans. It gets worse. Much worse. In the 25 years that Al Davis had been associated with the Silver and Black, the Raiders had never lost 10 games in a season. They did in 1987. And they had one less game to accomplish this ignominious feat.

It was obvious that changes were needed to return the Raiders to their winning ways. Al Davis signed wide receiver Mervyn Fernandez, who was once drafted by the Raiders but instead defected to the Canadian Football League and became a superstar performer. The Raiders also traded for capable wide receiver James Lofton of Green Bay. Then there was the offensive line, which disintegrated in the collapse of '86. Tackles John Clay of

Missouri and Bruce Wilkerson of Tennessee were drafted No. 1 and No. 2 respectively. Former All-Pro guard Brian Holloway was acquired from New England during the preseason.

Jim Plunkett, Marc Wilson, Rusty Hilger, and Notre Dame rookie Steve Beuerlein were the quarterbacks in training camp. Plunkett was quickly exiled to the "physically unable to perform" list and after hurting his shoulder, Beuerlein was hidden away on injured reserve. Hilger was awarded the starting job, with Wilson as the backup.

In July, Al Davis stunned the sports world by signing former Heisman Trophy winner Bo Jackson. In 1986, Tampa Bay had made the Auburn running back the first pick in the entire draft, but Bo opted to play baseball in the Kansas City Royals organization. In 1987, he was the starting left fielder for Kansas City. After drafting Bo in the seventh round, the Raiders gave Jackson a huge contract to play football after the baseball season was over. Bo called football a "hobby." The Royals were fuming. Al Davis looked like a recovered genius.

1987 was also the year that many old favorites were phased out. Lester Hayes was placed on injured reserve but wanted to play. Hayes claimed that the Raiders did not want him to break the team career interception record, which he shared with Willie Brown. Hayes was inactive during the entire season and never played for the Raiders again. He was replaced by veteran acquisitions Ron Fellows and Lionel Washington.

The offensive line was to undergo further upheaval. During the season, Bruce Davis was traded to Houston and Henry Lawrence was released. Free agent veterans Dean Miraldi and Steve Wright eventually became starters. Longtime San Diego Charger Linden King became a starting outside linebacker.

The 1987 season opened with a 20–0 victory at Green Bay; "winning ugly," said broadcaster Charlie Jones, who covered the game for NBC. Hilger was replaced at half-time by Wilson, who with Allen and the defense led the Raiders to victory. Game two was a 27–7 decision over Detroit, with Hilger rallying the Raiders to three second-half touchdowns.

Then came the strike. The president of the National Football League Players Association was former Raider Gene Upshaw. Al Davis, still ostracized by Commissioner Pete Rozelle, was not involved in the negotiations. Unlike in 1982, when there was no football for eight weeks, management was ready this time. Now the NFL would hire substitute or replacement players. "Scabs," said Upshaw. The regular players were enraged. There was violence at some team offices. Who can ever forget Jack Del Rio and Dino Hackett of Kansas City arriving for their daily walk on the picket line carrying shotguns in the back of a pickup truck?

At the Raider headquarters in El Segundo, California, a few regular players who were on injured reserve went inside for medical treatment. Rather than forfeit his $1 million salary, Marc Wilson also broke ranks with his teammates. The Raiders were one of the most divided teams during the three-week strike, which probably affected their performance later in the year.

After a game at Houston was canceled, the Raider replacement team led by quarterback Vince Evans beat up a Kansas City replacement roster 35–17. Although the attendance was only 10,708 at L.A. Coliseum, the game counted and the Raiders were 3–0.

For the next game in Denver, the Raider replacements were bolstered by the return of defensive linemen Howie Long and Bill Pickel. Long played as if he were still on strike. Evans showed flashes of his Chicago Bear days by passing erratically and the Broncos won 30–14. The third replacement game was a loss to San Diego. Late in a tie game, Evans threw a football right into the arms of Charger defensive back Elvis "Toast" Patterson, who returned it 75 yards for a touchdown. Were the Raiders impressed? They signed Patterson as a free agent in April 1990.

Once the hemorrhaging began, it was not easily stopped. All of the regulars returned for the next game against Seattle. But dissension abounded, as strike leaders Christensen and Holloway and the other players who stayed away were not enthralled with playing next to Long, Pickel, Fernandez, Wilkerson, Hilger, Wilson, Bahr, and the others who crossed the picket lines. The Raiders were belted 35–13 by Seattle as Hilger suffered through a horrible first half. Jackson made his debut in New England the following week. In the fourth quarter, Hilger led the Raiders back to a 23–23 tie with the Patriots. With time running out, New England kicker Tony Franklin missed a field goal, but Lionel Washington was offside. Franklin's second field goal attempt was good. Another loss.

Then there was Minnesota. The Raiders dominated the first half statistically but scored only three points. In the third quarter, Hilger threw an interception and fumbled as the Vikings scored three times. Al Davis reportedly called Flores from the press box and ordered Wilson into the game. The Raiders lost 31–20 and Hilger spent the remainder of the season on the bench.

Two more horror shows were to follow. In San Diego, two late touchdowns could not prevent a 16–14 loss. However, a 23–17 loss to Denver, the seventh in a row, did have one memorable moment. Jackson, beginning to see more action, scored on a 35-yard run in which he flattened Bronco safety Mike Harden on the way to the end zone. Again the Raiders must have been impressed with Harden's portrayal of a tackling dummy, because after he was released by the Broncos they signed him for the 1989 season.

Next stop: Seattle. A "Monday Night" game. The Seahawks were favored by 9½ points. The Raiders, who always seemed intimidated by the Kingdome crowds, had lost their last five times in Seattle. Early in the game, Jackson scored on a 14-yard pass from Wilson to give the Raiders a 14–7 lead. The Seahawks then punted and the Raiders were deep in their own territory. On third down, Jackson broke to the outside off left end and ran 91 yards for a touchdown. Bo was to gain a team-record 221 yards on 18 carries and score three TDs. On the final jaunt into the end zone, Bo blasted Seattle rookie linebacker Brian Bosworth. Even Seattle native Marc Wilson played well in the 37–14 Raider rout.

And when the Raiders followed with a 34–21 win over improving Buffalo to bring their record to 5–7, there was actually some hope for a wild card playoff berth. Wilson played well against the Bills, with three TD passes.

In Kansas City, the large crowd that came to cheer Bo Jackson could have gone home early. Bo suffered a mysterious foot injury (nobody saw it) and only carried the ball three times, his final action of the 1987 season. Wilson reverted to his usual woeful ways and the Chiefs prevailed 16–10. Losses to Cleveland and Chicago followed, the latter a 6–3 loss in which the Bears sacked Wilson nine times. It was an unbenevolent end to a pitiful season.

Big changes were in order. On January 20, 1988, head coach Tom Flores retired, or more accurately "was retired." Just a few days earlier, he was scouting players at the East-West Shrine game in San Francisco. When asked why he was stepping down, he could not give a valid reason. "I'm tired," said Tom.

Although assistant coaches Charlie Sumner and Art Shell were mentioned as likely successors, Al Davis was determined to go outside the Raider organization for a new head coach. You know, bring in some new blood but adhere to the basic Raider philosophy. Something like that.

Washington assistant coaches Dan Henning and Joe Bugel were both interviewed. San Francisco assistant

Dennis Green and San Diego offensive coordinator Jerry Rhome were among the finalists. But Denver quarterback coach Mike Shanahan got the job. Hiring Shanahan also accomplished another goal, disrupting the Denver offense. Shanahan brought along Alex Gibbs and Nick Nicoli, two other Bronco assistants. At the February 29, 1988 press conference introducing the new coach, both Davis and Shanahan spoke of a 10-year tenure to match John Madden. But Shanahan was only given a three-year contract.

There were also three number one draft choices for 1988. Heisman Trophy winner Tim Brown was the sixth overall pick and the Notre Dame wide receiver was also adept at returning kicks and punts. Terry McDaniel of Tennessee was selected to start at cornerback. And hopefully, Scott Davis of Illinois was going to be the defensive end that 1986 number one draft choice Bob Buczkowski never was.

Things were much different in the 1988 training camp. Upon completion of his five-year contract, Marc Wilson was unceremoniously released in May. Plunkett returned but played poorly in the second preseason game and was waived. Hilger never saw action in the preseason and was released. There were only two quarterbacks left, Steve Beuerlein and Vince Evans, neither of whom had ever played for the Raiders in a "real" game.

During camp, Al Davis pulled off a grand heist worthy of Bonnie and Clyde. The disappointing John Clay was dealt to the Chargers for offensive tackle Jim Lachey, an All-Pro who was engaged in a nasty holdout. The trade appeared to solve some offensive line problems. Don Mosebar was being moved to right guard and Bill Lewis would play center. With Brown joining Lofton and Fernandez, the wide receiver position was also looking good. If they only had a quarterback.

"You have to know when to hold 'em, know when to fold 'em, know when to walk away when the dealing's done," sang Kenny Rogers. Maybe Rogers doesn't know football but Al Davis can't sing either. But the Raiders could not have done worse if Kenny Rogers were calling the shots. Or Dolly Parton. In Chicago, speedy wide receiver Willie Gault was a holdout. Gault wanted to be traded to Los Angeles to start a movie career. He also knew that Al Davis paid his employees better than the McCaskey family did the Bears. Gault may have made a nice addition to the Raider passing game. But Al, why give up a No. 1 pick in 1989 and a No. 3 in 1990? Nevertheless, the trade was made and Davis expected Gault to be the second coming of Cliff Branch. Gault actually became more reminiscent of Jesse Hester, frequently dropping passes and rarely being the breakaway threat the Raiders wanted.

Trading disaster number two followed the opening game. San Diego versus the Raiders. Beuerlein against Babe Laufenburg. But hey, it counted. The Raiders prevailed by 24–13 and Shanahan matched Flores, Madden, and Davis as Oakland/L.A. coaches who won their first game. The next day a long-rumored trade was made. Washington sent disgruntled QB Jay Schroeder to the Raiders. The price: Jim Lachey plus a No. 2 pick in 1989 and two more draft choices in 1990.

In week two, the Raiders played the Oilers in Houston. Free agent Rory Graves replaced the departed Lachey at left tackle. Beuerlein passed the Silver and Black to an early 21–7 lead, but reserve quarterback Cody Carlson rallied the Oilers to a 37–35 victory. Terry McDaniel broke his leg on an out-of-bounds play and was gone for the year.

Mosebar was injured in the Houston game as the now paper-thin offensive line awaited the visiting Los Angeles Rams. Beuerlein was sacked nine times and the Rams won 22–17. Steve threw for 375 yards, mostly after the Rams were nursing a 22–10 lead.

Schroeder was not acquired to sit on the bench and

the new Raider quarterback started the Monday night game in Denver, a homecoming for Shanahan. It was 24–0 Broncos at halftime as everything that could go wrong did. But in the third quarter, Schroeder completed two touchdown passes to fullback Steve Smith as the Raiders started a comeback. The Broncos suddenly could do nothing right and the Raiders tied the score 27–27 at the end of regulation. In overtime, reserve safety Zeph Lee intercepted an Elway pass to set up a winning field goal by Chris Bahr. The 30–27 win with a new quarterback appeared to be just what the doctor ordered to return the Raiders to the good old days.

It was not to be. Undefeated Cincinnati and then Miami came into the Coliseum and scored their first-ever road wins against the Raiders. Boomer Esiason chewed up and spit out the defense in a 45–21 rout. Then Miami jumped to a 17–0 lead and held on 24–14. Long, Christensen, and Allen were hurt in these games. After the Miami game, Al Davis held an emergency meeting with the coaching staff, which was now divided into factions. It was Shanahan's men against the holdovers of the Flores regime. Davis nearly fired everyone right there.

Bo Jackson then returned and the Raiders beat the Chiefs 27–17. Beuerlein replaced the ineffective Schroeder late in the game. The next match at New Orleans was another forgettable experience. It must have looked like Seattle to Jackson, who carried the ball for 45 yards on the first two plays against the Saints. But it was more like Kansas City circa 1987, as Jackson suddenly pulled up lame on the sidelines and took himself out of the game. The Raiders were nursing a 6–0 lead until New Orleans rookie Craig "Ironhead" Heywood lumbered through the Los Angeles secondary on a long TD run that broke the game open. Schroeder was ineffective and Beuerlein finished up. The 20–6 loss left the Raiders at 3–5. But Denver and Seattle were only 4–4, so miraculously, the AFC West title was still a possibility.

And just when the Raiders seemed to be down for the count, they won the next three games. Beuerlein was installed as the starting QB, and Bo gained 85 yards in a 17–10 win over the Chiefs. The offense struggled but the defense was outstanding in a 13–3 Sunday night game at San Diego. And then in San Francisco, with many Bay Area Raider fans in the stands, three Chris Bahr field goals and a great defensive effort, including four sacks of Joe Montana, made the difference in a 9–3 upset of the 49ers. The Raiders were now in first place with a 6–5 record. The Niners were also 6–5. One of the two teams went on to win the Super Bowl. It wasn't the Raiders.

And what *did* happen to the 1988 Raiders? Well, they lost four out of the last five games to finish 7–9 and out of the money again. Shanahan was horribly outcoached, and the team looked unprepared in a 12–6 loss to Atlanta, as Beuerlein called three premature time-outs in the second half. Beuerlein and Allen were guilty of costly fumbles. In a 35–27 loss in the Kingdome, Beuerlein was replaced by Schroeder, who became the starter for the remainder of the season. The most futile series of plays of the entire season, and maybe four seasons, occurred in the last minute of the second quarter. Following a Seahawk touchdown, Tim Brown returned the kickoff 95 yards to the Seattle three. On first down, Beuerlein apparently threw a TD pass to Jackson, but reserve tight end Trey Junkin was caught holding. Backed up to the Seattle 13, Beuerlein's next pass was incomplete. With nine seconds left, Shanahan went for a field goal on a third down play, but Bahr missed. A 95-yard kickoff return had astonishingly turned into mush.

A crowd of more than 64,000 witnessed a 21–20 squeaker over Denver. Schroeder was sharp in the first half, and Greg Townsend intercepted Elway for a touchdown in the third quarter. Denver, Seattle, and the Raiders were all 7–7 and tied for the top.

The Bills beat the Raiders 37–21 in frigid Buffalo.

The defense could not contain quarterback Jim Kelly and running back Thurman Thomas. The most vivid memory of the loss was a frozen Shanahan feebly trying to call a time-out in the third quarter. Schroeder didn't see his coach and threw a touchdown to Steve Smith. Denver was annihilated in Seattle, so the 8–7 Seahawks would meet the 7–8 Raiders in the final game of the season. Winner take all, or at least the AFC West title.

The Raiders have faced many All-Star players over the years. They rarely have made average players look good. But one glaring exception is Seattle quarterback David Krieg. In the 35–27 loss in the Kingdome, Krieg burned the Raider secondary for five touchdown passes. In the rematch, he threw three more. The Raider defense came unglued in a 43–37 defeat. Early in the game, the less-than-speedy Steve Largent flew past Mike Haynes into the end zone for a touchdown. Later, fullback John L. Williams made safeties Vann McElroy and Russell Carter look like slow-falling bowling pins on a long TD run through the middle of the defense. Schroeder was nearly as hot as Krieg, hitting Gault and Fernandez in the end zone. In what was to be his last hurrah in the NFL, Todd Christensen caught four consecutive fourth-quarter passes from Schroeder, as the Raiders tried to mount a late comeback. The Seahawks won their first-ever AFC West title and the Raiders went home empty-handed again.

Following the disappointing season, there was further uneasiness among the assistant coaches, Shanahan, and the front office. Defensive coordinator Charlie Sumner publicly criticized Shanahan and resigned. Defensive backfield coach Willie Brown was fired. Longtime defensive end coach Earl Leggett went to Denver, of all places. When Shanahan tried to dismiss offensive coaches Tom Walsh and Joe Spinella, Davis intervened. Al then dismissed Nick Nicoli, a Shanahan appointee. Just another happy off-season in El Segundo.

The Gault and Schroeder trades left them with few draft choices available for the 1989 draft, so the Raiders relied on the newly created Plan B free agent draft to bring in new blood. NFL teams were allowed to protect only 37 veteran players, making the remainder free agents who could be signed with no compensation to their former clubs. The Raiders signed 11 Plan B performers and lost six. Some new Raiders were name players, others obscure. Otis Wilson, Mike Richardson, and Jackie Shipp were well known but could not contribute and were eventually released. Colorful Bob Golic was a valuable addition and replaced Pickel at nose tackle. Another find was Thomas Benson, who became a starter at an inside linebacker position.

One blue-chip rookie did come from the collegiate draft. A trade with Dallas led to the selection of Penn State guard Steve Wisniewski, who was immediately plugged into the right guard position. Wisniewski had a fine rookie season and looks like a future Pro Bowler.

A week before the preseason opener, Stacey Toran was killed in an automobile accident. His alcohol level was allegedly three times over the legal limit. The Raiders eventually signed Mike Harden to replace Toran, and veteran Russell Carter also saw duty at strong safety.

Following an 0–4 preseason record, which featured a horrible defense and a shaky Schroeder, the Raiders opened the season with a surprising 40–14 romp over San Diego. Beuerlein replaced an injured Schroeder and was sharp. Tim Brown tore knee ligaments on a kickoff return and was lost for the season. Despite widespread rumors and innuendo that his firing was imminent, Shanahan had survived the first game.

The next three games were losses and the head coaching career of Shanahan prematurely ended after 20 ballgames. In Kansas City, the Raiders blew a fourth-quarter lead. A comeback was aborted because Rory Graves could not handle rookie Chiefs linebacker Derrick

Thomas. The television cameras found Davis on the press box telephone explaining plays to Shanahan. With the NBC cameras fixed on Davis in Denver, the Broncos raced to another big halftime lead, but this time the Raiders could not come all the way back. A Schroeder interception by rookie Steve Atwater ended the last gasp for the Raiders in the 31–21 loss. And at home against Seattle, the defense again could not stop John L. Williams, and the Seahawks scored the winning touchdown in the fourth quarter. The newspaper writers found Davis banging on a table.

With a 1–3 record, the dispirited Raiders were in total disarray. Shanahan was "white as a ghost" during the post-game press conference. Al Davis was not going to let another season go down the drain. On Tuesday, October 4, Shanahan was fired and offensive line coach Art Shell was selected as the replacement. "I'm sensitive to a head coach, which is the toughest job in America, other than the President of the United States," said Al Davis at the press conference. Hiring the first black head coach in 60 years was historic, but Al Davis indicated that Shell had better win or he would go the way of Shanahan. "If this is an historic occasion—and what's happening here is not lost on me—it only will be meaningful and historic if he is a great success." When asked about becoming the first black coach in the NFL since the Roaring Twenties, Shell knew that his true colors really were Silver and Black. "I know who I am and I'm proud of it, but I'm also a Raider," was his answer. Shell talked about how he wanted the Raiders to get back to playing with "power, explosion, and simplicity" as they used to. He was probably thinking about the power of offensive linemen Shell and Upshaw, certainly not to be confused with Graves and offensive guard John Gesek.

For the Raiders, the hiring of Shanahan was obviously a mistake. As an owner, Al Davis operates entirely differently than anyone else in the NFL. Why not? Al has been an assistant coach, head coach, general manager, scout, and all the rest. With George Halas gone, there is nobody else in the NFL running a team with a football background. John Madden and Tom Flores reluctantly understood that this "interference" is an integral part of the Raiders scene. Both John Rauch and Shanahan were never comfortable with Al looking over their shoulders. Shanahan also faced a few other hurdles that had nothing to do with Al Davis. In Denver, Mike was perched in a press box, sending plays down to Coach Dan Reeves and Elway. He had no feel for being on the sidelines. Bill Walsh, who covered the Seattle game as an NBC color analyst, accurately remarked that Shanahan lacked the bench experience to be an effective coach. He appeared to be unsure and easily rattled on the sidelines in 1988.

Another problem was the assistant coaches Shanahan inherited. Charlie Sumner, who had been with the Raiders for the better part of 26 seasons and had been head coach of the USFL Oakland Invaders, was obviously disappointed when he was bypassed in favor of Shanahan. The selecting of assistant coaches by the head man is becoming a very thorny issue in the NFL. In recent seasons, Marty Shottenheimer resigned in Cleveland after owner Art Modell complained about the offensive coordinator position. In New England, the question of who would call the plays led to the dismissal of Raymond Berry. Dan Reeves expressed his displeasure when owner Pat Bowlen reduced the size of the coaching staff from 17 to 11 assistants. Despite winning a Super Bowl in 1986, Chicago coach Mike Ditka openly feuded with defensive coordinator Buddy Ryan, who became the head mentor with the Philadelphia Eagles. Their hostility has continued as NFC rivals.

After packing his belongings, Shanahan later returned to Denver as a personal coach for John Elway. He also was offered a college head coaching position at the University of Kentucky but declined. Although Shanahan is a capable X and O strategist, who deserves some credit for the success of the Broncos, his tenure with the Raiders was an unfortunate mistake for all concerned.

The players immediately responded to Shell, who pledged a return to "Raider football." A Monday night game against the New York Jets was won on a brilliant interception return by Eddie Anderson. Allen was hurt, but thankfully Bo Jackson would be available on the following Sunday. A 20–14 win over Kansas City avenged the earlier defeat to the Chiefs.

Shell tasted his first defeat in a frustrating 10–7 loss in Philadelphia. New kicker Jeff Jaeger missed two easy field goals, and the Raiders were offside on a missed Eagles' field goal, allowing Philadelphia another chance, which was successful.

With Beuerlein back at the controls, the 3–3 Raiders beat the Redskins 37–24 at the Coliseum. Bo ran wild and the defense registered seven sacks against Mark Rypien. Beuerlein partially tore two knee ligaments, so good old Jay Schroeder started the next three games.

By the middle of the 1989 season, Bo Jackson may have been the most popular athlete in America. Nobody had successfully played two professional sports at the major league level since basketball-baseball star Dave DeBusshere in the 1960s. And Bo was excelling at both baseball and football. In three full seasons in the major leagues, he had already become quite a baseball player. Voted to the All-Star game by the fans in 1989, Jackson hit a gigantic home run off Rick Reuschel and was selected as the Most Valuable Player. He was reducing his strikeouts and was improving as a base runner and fielder. Bo also starred in a series of television commercials for the Nike shoe company. "Bo knows baseball" and "Bo knows football" would become the most quoted advertising lines since "Where's the beef?" There was also a mysterious side to Jackson, which added to the folklore and kept the media off-stride. He wouldn't discuss football in the baseball season and vice versa. And Bo would not reveal to anyone how long he would continue to play both sports.

Jackson's best performance of the season was against Cincinnati. Early in the game, Jackson raced down the left sideline 93 yards for a touchdown, making Bo the only man ever to have two 90-yard jaunts in a career. In the first quarter, the defense knocked Esiason out of the 28–7 game. For his 159-yard, two-touchdown day, Jackson was selected as NFL Player of the Week. In a Freudian style typographical error, *USA Today* saluted him as "Bo Jackson, RB, Oakland Raiders." The 5–4 Los Angeles Raiders were now in playoff contention.

The annual Sunday night encounter in San Diego was a 14–12 loss, with Schroeder unable to move the offense. But the worst game of the season was a 23–7 defeat in Houston. An immobile Beuerlein returned, but the Raiders defense could not stop Oiler quarterback Warren Moon, who shredded the Raider secondary with precision passing.

The 1989 Los Angeles Raiders were repeating the pattern of the 1979 Oakland Raiders: great at home, terrible on the road. The next three contests at Los Angeles Coliseum were critical and they responded with victories against New England, Denver, and Phoenix. In the Bronco game, tight end Mike Dyal caught a fourth-period pass from Beuerlein and rambled into the end zone to tie the score. Jaeger's field goal in overtime made the difference in a 16–13 triumph. It was the first time since 1978 that the Raiders and Broncos had split their two meetings. Against Phoenix, a questionable pass-interference call against the Cardinals helped sustain a last-minute drive. Allen returned to action and contributed an "Air Marcus" special, a dive over the Cardinal defensive line for the winning score.

On to Seattle for the 8–6 Raiders. Again the problem was stopping David Krieg. On this Sunday night, the Seahawks burned the Raiders with short passes. Early in the game, the Raiders were on the Seattle one when Shell, perhaps under orders from Davis, bypassed Allen for Jackson. Bo couldn't get in and the Raiders settled for a field goal. The failure to score seven points would be important later. Beuerlein moved the club toward the Seattle end zone in the last seconds. Trailing by six points, the Raiders had to go for a TD to win. On a fourth down from the Seahawk 13, Beuerlein overthrew an open Fernandez in the end zone and, for the seventh time since 1983, the Raiders had lost in the Kingdome.

The Raiders played the favored New York Giants to a standoff in the first half, but a total collapse after the intermission led to a 34–17 loss in the finale, leaving the Raiders at 8–8 and with no cigar again. Shell was 7–5 after replacing Shanahan, and perhaps with a break or two the Raiders could have won 9 or 10 games and made the post-season party. Although many advocates of an Al Davis move out of Los Angeles say the Raiders had no home field advantage in L.A. Coliseum, the "pride and poise" boys were 7–1 at home but a pitiful 1–7 on the road.

The year 1989 ended with the chronic problems at offensive left tackle, lack of a standout pass rusher on defense, a collection of aging linebackers, and an unsettled quarterback position. In the 1990 Plan B free agent sweepstakes, the Raiders signed veteran guard Max Montoya of the Bengals and tackle James Fitzpatrick of San Diego. Montoya will compete with 1989 Plan B signee Dale Hallestrae and holdover John Gesek for the left guard job. Fitzpatrick, who flopped as the Chargers' Number 1 draft choice in 1986, will be given an opportunity to challenge Rory Graves at left tackle. Another candidate for Graves' job is Bruce Davis, who was re-signed by the Raiders in July 1990 after being released by the Houston Oilers.

The pass rush should be helped by the addition of

Number 1 draft choice Anthony Smith from the University of Arizona. Smith, who had a troubled youth, will get a chance at defensive end or outside linebacker. The second draft choice of 1990 was Aaron Wallace of Texas A&M, who is also viewed as an outside linebacker.

Two new inside linebackers are Plan B veterans. Bruce Klostermann of Denver and Joe Campbell from San Diego have been primarily special teams players. Although technically not a Plan B player, Riki Ellison of San Francisco was made a free agent by the 49ers. Hampered by injuries in 1989, he was replaced in the San Francisco lineup by Matt Millen. Based on the so-so results of the 1989 Plan B signings, it is not a good idea to bet the mortgage on any of these guys having a major impact.

Seeking more veteran help, Davis surprisingly turned to Anaheim. Running back Greg Bell was acquired from the Rams for a middle-round draft choice. The Raiders obviously hope that Bell will be more receptive to accepting the unique full-time/part-time role as caddy to Bo Jackson than Marcus Allen was. Kickoff returner/receiver Ron Brown also came over from the Rams, and the plan was to convert the world-class sprinter into a defensive back, a position he played in college. Another new 1990 wide receiver was Jamie Holland, late of San Diego.

The biggest news in the quarterback sector of Silver and Black land was the hiring of Mike White as assistant coach for special projects, or something like that. A disciple of Bill Walsh, White has helped develop many quarterbacks, including Jim Plunkett and Steve Bartkowski in his college and pro coaching career. He will be assigned to work with Beuerlein and get Schroeder out of his prolonged funk. A new $1 million contract should also help Schroeder's disposition. Major Harris, a star college quarterback from West Virginia, was drafted in the twelfth round by the Raiders. He signed a contract to play in the Canadian Football League but has hinted he would eventually like to play in the NFL.

Nobody likes to lose and things have not been very copasetic in Raiderland in recent years. Despite four less-than-successful seasons, Al Davis always reiterates that the Raiders have the best record in professional sports since 1963. But a few more seasons like 1986, 1987, 1988, and 1989 and the Raiders and their "winningest record" distinction will be gone.

What will Al Davis say then?

Chapter 14

WHAT GOES UP MUST . . .

*T*he most obvious recent sign of the decline of the Raiders has been the snarling face of linebacker Matt Millen in a San Francisco 49er uniform. Millen was a steady and spirited if unspectacular performer for nine seasons with the Silver and Black. He played on two world championship Raider teams and finally made it to the Pro Bowl after the 1988 season. Presumably because of a salary dispute, Millen was no longer a favorite with Al Davis. Despite a pronounced weakness at inside linebacker, the Raiders released Millen following the last preseason contest of 1989. Matt didn't stay unemployed for long. Both the Rams and 49ers suffered key injuries to their linebacking corps and came calling. Millen signed with San Francisco, quickly became a starter, and was an integral part of the 49er Super Bowl champions. As someone who started the 1989 season in the nervous and chaotic Raider camp, Millen must feel as if he had died and gone to heaven!

What is ironic about the Matt Millen saga is that throughout the Raider glory years, the Matt Millens of the NFL usually would land in Oakland or L.A., not San Francisco. The Raiders always seemed to find players that nobody else wanted and meld them into the mix. No more.

Although the Raiders won world championships in 1980 and 1983 and were close in 1982, 1984, and 1985,

245

the seeds of decline were actually sown in 1980 in the form of a wasted number one college draft pick, quarterback Marc Wilson. It probably represented Al Davis's biggest and costliest failure in all his years as mentor of the Raiders.

When drafted by Oakland, it appeared that Wilson had all the qualities that separate the great from the mediocre. As a collegian at Brigham Young University, Wilson broke all the NCAA passing records. At a height of 6 feet, 6 inches, Wilson had the physical stature to see his receivers over the arms of charging defensive lineman. He had a strong arm and could throw long, which would fit nicely in the Raiders' passing scheme. It seemed like a wise choice. It was not to be.

The year 1983 saw the emergence of the United States Football League. The owners in the USFL agreed not to spend large amounts of money for players. The agreement lasted about two weeks. The New Jersey Generals signed University of Georgia running back Hershel Walker to a large contract. Walker was a junior who won the Heisman Trophy in 1982. The floodgates were now open for a bidding war between the USFL and NFL.

Following a losing inaugural season for the Generals, the team was purchased by New York billionaire real estate developer Donald Trump. Immediately, Trump started seeking NFL talent. He signed All-Pro defensive backs Gary Babaro and Kerry Justin. Trump actually inked star linebacker Lawrence Taylor of the New York Giants. Later the Giants matched the offer and kept L. T. The first big-name quarterback to join the new league was Jim Kelly of the University of Miami, who signed with the Houston Gamblers. Kelly had been the first draft choice of the Buffalo Bills in 1983. Trump started looking for a quarterback. Somehow he found Marc Wilson.

Wilson was without a contract in 1983. As most fans know, the NFL offers limited movement within the league for free agents. If another NFL team had signed Wilson, the Raiders would have been compensated with two number one draft picks in return. Nobody would even touch the best players in the league for that price. When Chicago's Walter Payton was also a free agent, he received no offers. So who could be interested in Marc Wilson?

But the USFL was another matter. Trump offered Wilson a contract that would have paid about $900,000 per year. Because the Raiders usually had the highest payroll in the NFL, they had previously been immune to USFL offers. Al Davis was now faced with a decision that was to have a greater impact on the future performance of the Raiders than anybody realized at the time. Rebuffed in his attempts to trade for rookie quarterback John Elway, Davis decided to exceed Trump's offer. Marc Wilson was given a five-year deal at an annual salary near $1 million. "I played Al Davis like a drum" was Trump's reaction to the signing. At the NFL headquarters on Park Avenue in New York, Pete Rozelle had to be smiling.

Trump turned his "loss" of Wilson into a gain. The Generals eventually signed Brian Sipe, an experienced and successful quarterback who had led the Cleveland Browns to the AFC Central Division title in 1980. Sipe played one season for New Jersey and was later traded to Jacksonville when Trump signed Heisman Trophy winner Doug Flutie in 1985. In Jacksonville, Sipe suffered a career-ending shoulder injury and did not return to the NFL when the USFL folded.

In time, the contract given Wilson became an albatross that was tightly wrapped around the neck of the Raiders. Al Davis should have bitten the bullet, admitted his mistake, and unloaded Marc Wilson while he may have had trade value. But Al was determined to collect his million dollars' worth of performance from Wilson. He never received it. Wilson's presence on the Raider roster also seemed to prevent Davis from acquiring the quarterback the Raiders needed.

The Raiders' extended pursuit of a quarterback (besides Wilson) to eventually replace Plunkett started with John Elway in 1983. The Stanford star was the first choice in the NFL collegiate draft in 1983 and was selected by the then Baltimore Colts, who did not win a game in 1982. However, Jack Elway, John's dad, who was a college coach at San Jose State, did not want his son playing for the controversial and volatile Frank Kush, who was the coach at Baltimore.

When the Elway clan announced that they wouldn't play for the Colts, a quiet bidding war started within the NFL. When the Colts first declared that they wouldn't trade Elway's draft rights, George Steinbrenner responded with an offer for him to play major league baseball for the New York Yankees. At a press conference, John Elway said he would only play for a West Coast team and advised the Colts not to accept a deal for three number one draft picks that was reportedly offered by New England.

Al Davis got busy in a hurry. He knew that Jim Plunkett wouldn't last forever and was already skeptical about Marc Wilson. The Raiders were planning to make a deal with Chicago for their top draft choice and would also offer Baltimore the top pick of the Raiders in 1983 (University of Southern California offensive lineman Don Mosebar) and/or the 1984 first draft choice. Shockingly, the name of 1982 Rookie of the Year Marcus Allen was also mentioned in the talks.

It is obvious that the Raiders offered Baltimore a much better deal than what the Colts eventually accepted to rid themselves of Elway. The Denver Broncos traded their first pick of 1983 (Northwestern University offensive tackle Chris Hinton, the fourth overall choice) and reserve quarterback Mark Herrmann for the rights to Elway. Seven years later, Hinton was shipped to Atlanta in a trade for another quarterback, who was the first pick in the draft: Jeff George of the University of Illinois. Elway has lived happily ever after in Denver, becoming one of the most exciting players in pro football, three Super Bowl losses notwithstanding. Back in L.A., the Raiders were forced to live with Wilson and Plunkett.

Al Davis reacted bitterly to the Colts accepting less from Denver than what was offered by the Raiders and accused Commissioner Pete Rozelle of interfering in the negotiations. It seemed that Al was being punished for the move to L.A. and the subsequent lawsuits. The thought of having the most glamorous collegiate quarterback of 1983 play for the hated Raiders was probably too much for the commissioner to handle. Al Davis had been foiled where it hurt the most: on the playing field.

A year later the Raiders could have helped themselves again but declined. And they couldn't blame the commissioner this time. As an unheralded collegian, Warren Moon led the University of Washington to a 28–0 victory over Iowa in the 1981 Rose Bowl. It may seem like ancient history now, but in the early 1980s, black quarterbacks were as rare in the NFL as an embrace between Pete Rozelle and Al Davis. Moon was ignored in the college draft and signed with the Edmonton Eskimos of the Canadian Football League. He then led the Eskimos to the Grey Cup championship. When his Canadian contract expired, the NFL came calling. The Raiders were not seriously interested. Moon signed a big contract with the Houston Oilers. Perhaps as part of the deal, former Edmonton head coach Hugh Campbell assumed the same position with the Oilers. Moon has been a star in Houston and led the Oilers into the playoffs in 1987, 1988, and 1989. He started for the AFC in the 1990 Pro Bowl. And at the Oiler controls, he picked the Raiders apart in a 23–7 Houston win in a November 1989 game.

Another available quarterback who would have been a decided improvement over Wilson, Hilger, and the aging Plunkett was Bobby Hebert. After a collegiate career at small Northwestern Louisiana College, Hebert was also not coveted by the NFL. He eventually signed with the Michigan Panthers of the new USFL and became their starting quarterback. Hebert and wide receiver Anthony Carter soon became the most potent pass-catching duo in the spring league. In 1983, Hebert and Carter led the underdog Panthers to the USFL Championship with a victory over the Philadelphia Stars. They were a playoff team again in 1984. The Panthers merged with the Oakland Invaders for the 1985 season and Hebert again played for a championship.

When the USFL went out of business in 1986, Hebert and his agent threw themselves open to NFL bids. Hebert eventually returned to his Cajun roots and signed with the New Orleans Saints. In 1987, Philadelphia/Baltimore Stars head coach Jim Mora became the main man in New Orleans. With Hebert as his starting quarterback, Mora led the Saints to a 12–3 record in 1987 and their first-ever playoff appearance. In 1988, Hebert passed the Saints to a 20–6 victory over the Raiders, the first time that New Orleans had ever beaten Oakland/L.A.

After Mora replaced him as the Saints starting quarterback late in the 1989 season, Hebert announced that he did not covet a return to New Orleans and wanted to play for the Raiders, especially if they moved back to Oakland. Hebert said that the Raiders were not seriously interested in his services in 1986 because Oakland Invaders head coach (and former Raider assistant) Charlie Sumner did not like his attitude and recommended against his signing by Al Davis.

Another instance where the Raiders were either asleep at the switch or victims of league interference in trade talks involved Steve Young. In 1984, the Brigham Young quarterback bypassed the Cincinnati Bengals of the NFL and signed a $40 million deal with the Los Angeles Express of the USFL, owned by financier William Oldenburg. As a rookie in 1984, Young led the Express into the playoffs. When Oldenburg's financial empire collapsed in 1985, the Express was taken over by the league. Young was already looking to the NFL for a life raft. Cincinnati traded his draft rights to Tampa Bay and Young joined the Buccaneers in late 1985. Tampa Bay finished the 1986 season with the worst record in the NFL and planned to make University of Miami quarterback Vinny Testaverde their number one pick in 1987. This meant that Young would be traded. In February 1987, the San Francisco 49ers traded their second- and fourth-round picks to Tampa Bay for Young. Although Young has primarily been a backup to Joe Montana for three seasons, he has won a few big games for San Francisco and has been a part of two Super Bowl championship teams. For the 49ers, Young represents a valuable insurance policy if Montana should be injured. It seems that the Raiders could have (and should have) offered more than San Francisco for Young. After getting burned with Marc Wilson, perhaps Al Davis didn't trust anybody from BYU.

The Raiders were offered Doug Williams by the Redskins before the 1987 season. Washington wanted a Number 1 draft pick in return. Al Davis declined. The erratic Williams replaced the even more inconsistent Jay Schroeder in the Redskins lineup and was the Most Valuable Player in their Super Bowl XXII rout of Denver. Williams has since been plagued by injuries and personal problems and was released by Washington in March 1990. Perhaps the Raiders will finally take a flyer on the 34-year-old Williams.

It is an old sports axiom that "sometimes the best trades are the ones that you never make." The case of Neil Lomax of the St. Louis/Phoenix Cardinals is a prime example of Al Davis wisely backing off. Lomax had enjoyed a checkered career in St. Louis. In 1984, he nearly led the Cardinals into the playoffs, losing to Washington on the last day of the season. Bothered by injuries, both Lomax and the Cardinals stumbled in 1985 and 1986. There were rumblings in St. Louis that Lomax was being offered around with no takers. With the sixth pick in the 1987 draft, the Cardinals surprised the football experts by selecting quarterback Kelly Stouffer of Oregon State. Surely Lomax would be traded. But a funny thing happened on the way to market. The Cardinals and Stouffer never agreed on a contract and he sat out the 1987 season. He was traded to Seattle in 1988. Lomax gave the Cardinals two outstanding seasons before a hip injury abruptly ended his career. It is not known whether Al Davis was ever seriously interested in Lomax.

In his prime, Jim McMahon would have been the perfect quarterback for the Raiders. But only for the Raiders in *their* prime, when they were in Oakland and intimidated everybody. The flamboyant McMahon would have been a perfect complement to John Madden's teams. Even though McMahon won a Super Bowl for the Bears, he always seemed to be at loggerheads with Chicago coach Mike Ditka. McMahon was constantly bothered by injuries and Ditka always seemed to be looking for a new quarterback. There were continuing rumors of McMahon trading his Chicago Blue for Raider Silver and Black. It never happened. During the 1989 preseason, the Bears finally traded McMahon. He was sent to the San Diego Chargers for a Number 2 draft pick in 1990. McMahon suffered through an inconsistent and injury-riddled 1989 season. His San Diego career did not exactly get off to a flashy start. After appearing confused and passing poorly, McMahon was benched by Charger coach Dan Henning during the 1989 season-opening loss to the Raiders.

The end of McMahon's San Diego career came in April 1990. While he may have realized the dream of many fans by blowing his nose on a sportswriter, the Chargers were not impressed. New San Diego general manager Bobby Beathard had seen enough. McMahon was released outright by the Chargers. In July 1990, McMahon was signed by his old friend Buddy Ryan to back up Randall Cunningham in Philadelphia.

On Labor Day, 1988, the Raiders finally traded for a quarterback. Prior to joining the Raiders, Jay Schroeder had an interesting career. After starring at nearby Pacific Palisades High School, Schroeder was a competent if unspectacular quarterback at UCLA. However, Jay also played baseball and signed with the Toronto Blue Jays organization. After an undistinguished minor league baseball career, Schroeder was invited to the Washington Redskins training camp in 1985 and won the backup job behind Joe Theismann. When Theismann suffered a career-ending broken leg against the Giants, Schroeder was thrust into action. He beat New York and then led Washington to an 11–5 record. It was to be a preview of the following season. In 1986, Schroeder threw for over 4,100 yards as the Redskins finished at 12–4. Jay was named to the Pro Bowl.

But Schroeder's quick rise to the elite of NFL quarterbacks was matched by a rapid fall. Schroeder's performance in 1987 was sub-par and he was replaced by Doug Williams as the Washington starter. Except for one play, Schroeder watched from the sidelines as Williams destroyed Denver in the Super Bowl. Schroeder started complaining about his backup role and fell out of favor with head coach Joe Gibbs. A trade seemed inevitable. Initially the Redskins wanted two of the Raiders three number one draft picks in 1988. Al Davis said no and selected Tim Brown, Terry McDaniel, and Scott Davis instead. When the 1988 training camp opened, former replacement player Vince Evans and the untested Steve Beuerlein were the top signal callers for new coach Mike Shanahan. Wilson was gone and Plunkett and Hilger were later released. There was certainly a need for a quarterback with experience in Raiderland.

In the Redskin camp, Schroeder was persona non grata with Gibbs. The Super Bowl champs had two impressive young quarterbacks in Mark Rypien and Stan Humphries, who could understudy Williams. In a preseason game in Los Angeles, Schroeder sat on the Washington bench as the Redskins routed the Raiders 45–21. Both Rypien and Humphries were impressive. On the other side, Beuerlein was still learning and Evans was overthrowing receivers. The trade that was waiting to happen had still not happened.

During the preseason, the Raiders acquired holdout All-Pro offensive tackle Jim Lachey from San Diego. The price was 1987 number one pick John Clay plus draft choices. Clay was selected by the Raiders despite having a reputation as lazy at the University of Missouri. The personal tutelage of then assistant coach Art Shell did not help Clay; the overweight player had a lousy rookie year. So the trade for Lachey appeared to be a Raider heist, reminiscent of Al Davis deals of the good old days.

The Redskins and Raiders started the 1988 regular season with Schroeder still in Washington. It was rumored that Washington was still demanding a high draft choice plus either Howie Long, rookie Tim Brown, or Lachey. Long threatened to retire rather than accept a trade and Heisman Trophy winner Brown looked like an instant star. Lachey played at offensive left tackle in the Raiders' opening win over San Diego. On the day following the opening game, the Raiders acquired Schroeder for Lachey, their number two pick in the 1989 draft, and two 1990 fourth-round draft choices.

The trading of Lachey to the Redskins has been even more devastating to the offensive line. In the game following Lachey's departure, the Raiders lost two offensive linemen to injuries. Eventually journeyman Rory Graves "won" the left tackle position. He has had some good moments in his two years with L.A., but Graves has been plagued by both holding and offside penalties and cannot handle some of the quicker linebackers and defensive ends in the league. Although Lachey has suffered some injuries in Washington, he is still a star performer. He signed a huge new contract with the Redskins in early 1990. Chalk up the Clay/Lachey/Schroeder deal as a Raider fiasco of the worst kind.

And then there is Willie Gault. But to properly tell the story of how and why the Raiders acquired this wide receiver with world-class speed, we have to go back to 1985.

As everybody in pro football knows (even Bo), Al Davis has always been an advocate of throwing the long pass. He calls it the vertical game. Stretch the defense, etc., etc. And the Raiders have always had good, fast receivers. Everybody knows that too. Ten days after Al Davis came to Oakland in 1963, his first player move was signing free agent Art Powell of the then New York Titans to catch the long bomb. Later the Raiders had Warren Wells and then for 13 seasons, Cliff Branch. The Raiders always complemented their speed burners with the slower possession-type receivers like Hall-of-Famer Fred Biletnikoff, Rod Sherman, and Bob Chandler. But Al loved that speed.

When Branch retired (or *was* retired) after the 1984 season, the Raiders were going to use their number one pick, the 23rd overall, to draft a wide receiver. The top three receivers of the year were Al Toon, Eddie Brown, and Jerry Rice. Toon and Brown were gone early, and World Champion San Francisco traded up to the 14th spot and took Rice. Drafting just before the Raiders, the Chicago Bears selected William "Refrigerator" Perry, who would become the most celebrated rookie of 1985. L.A. then picked Jessie Hester of Florida State. His agent was Mike Blatt, who would later be tried for the murder of a business associate. It was a bad omen. Just to be sure, the Raiders took another wide receiver: Tim Moffett of the University of Mississippi in round 2.

It will pain Raider fans to summarize what has happened to these players since draft day 1985. Hester seemed to have a bad case of "dropsies" from his very first game. He rarely displayed the speed that was expected and also seemed to suffer those nagging minor injuries. Three years was enough. In 1988 he was traded to Atlanta for a fifth-round pick. Hester was in the training camp of the Indianapolis Colts for the 1990 season. Moffett also spent parts of three seasons in L.A. He couldn't cut it at wide receiver so the Raiders tried to convert him into a defensive back. It didn't work. Moffett has disappeared from the football scene.

Even the casual football fan in the audience knows that Jerry Rice may be the best receiver who has ever played the game. In Super Bowls XXIII and XXIV, Rice caught five touchdown passes from Joe Montana. The difference between Rice and Hester may be the primary reason Bill Walsh replaced Al Davis as the resident "genius" of the National Football League.

The Chicago Bears have always been known for ferocious play. They have never been known for paying their players generously. Former Bears owner George Halas was once described as someone who "throws around nickels like manhole covers," and his heirs had done little to change the penny-pinching reputation. After five good seasons with the Bears, Willie Gault was holding out for more money in 1988. That's a no-no in Chicago. Head coach Mike Ditka started offering Gault around the NFL. Al Davis took the bait. In August 1988, the Raiders traded their No. 1 pick for 1989 and No. 3 selection of 1990 for Gault. Davis now had another wide receiver for his collection.

To call Willie Gault a disappointment is like saying Chicago is windy or that Gorbachev is bald. Gault was bothered by minor injuries in 1988 and caught only 16 passes. Healthier in 1989, Gault improved to 28 receptions, or 1.67 per game. Gault's vaunted breakaway speed was good for only four touchdown receptions in 1989. Meanwhile, Tim Brown had a spectacular rookie year in 1988, and Fernandez caught more than 1,000 yards in passes in 1989. Low-round draft choice Mike Alexander also showed potential. The Bears used the No. 1 given by the Raiders in 1989 to select promising defensive back Donnell Woolford, the eleventh player overall. The dream of Schroeder throwing bombs to Gault is not to be confused with Bradshaw to Swann, Montana to Rice, Lamonica to Wells, or Stabler to Branch. The Gault acquisition was certainly not one of Al Davis's shining moments at the bargaining table.

We have casually discussed the Raiders' failure on draft days during the past decade. In the NFL, the teams that continually draft successfully will usually win on the field. The trick is to constantly bring in young talent to replace aging veterans. A Number 1 pick must eventually become a starting player and enough of the lower-round picks must make the team each year to keep the new blood pumping. The competitiveness of professional football makes successful drafting compulsory. The NFL is so well balanced that one or more consecutive washouts on draft day can break a team for years to come. That is what happened to the Dallas Cowboys. And it is also what happened to the Los Angeles Raiders. Unfortunately, the trades that were made to correct the failures have only aggravated the problems they were supposed to solve.

Wilson, Hester, and Clay, failures all. But wait, there have been two other miserable first-round Raider picks in recent years. Following the Super Bowl year of 1980, the Raiders had two first-round selections for the first time in their history. One Number 1 pick was defensive back Ted Watts of Texas Tech. In three seasons, the Raiders painfully learned that Watts could play neither cornerback nor safety with any skill. Mike Haynes was acquired in the middle of the 1983 season to replace Watts in the lineup. Ted was eventually traded to the New York Giants.

The other prime choice in 1981 was Curt Marsh, a huge offensive lineman from the University of Washington. The often-injured Marsh became more famous for victories in the NFL arm-wrestling competition than for stellar play on the field. Marsh was handed the starting offensive left guard position when Gene Upshaw retired in 1982. He was the weak link in the offensive line and was consistently overpowered by bigger defensive lineman. During the 1983 season, the Raiders acquired guard Charlie Hannah from Tampa Bay, and Marsh was only a reserve player for the rest of his career.

Bob Buczkowski of the University of Pittsburgh was the top pick in 1986. This defensive end was considered a "sleeper" or a "reach" by the draft experts. A "sleeper" really means that he was not considered a first-round pick by many scouts and that the team selecting Buczkowski was taking a large risk. The results of Buczkowski's Raider career indicate that Al Davis and player personnel director Ron Wolf were sleeping on draft day. Hampered by a bad back, Bob rarely played and was finally released before the 1988 season. He spent most of 1989 with the Phoenix Cardinals as a reserve lineman and will play with Cleveland in 1990.

To add insult to injury, the second choice in 1986 never played a down of pro football. Brad Cochran had been an All-American defensive back at Michigan and the Raiders penciled him in at cornerback to eventually replace Lester Hayes. However, Cochran was hurt in training camp in 1986 and never returned.

Yes, the Raiders did have some very good Number 1 picks in the 1980s: Marcus Allen, Don Mosebar, Tim Brown, Terry McDaniel, and Scott Davis. Bo Jackson was a top pick of Tampa Bay. And there have also been some successes with lower-round picks. The trade of a Number 1 pick for Mike Haynes led to a Super Bowl victory.

But look closer. Haynes was acquired because Watts flopped. Gault was obtained because Hester was a bust. Lachey was picked up when Clay couldn't perform and Schroeder came west after eight years of Marc Wilson proved to be too much. The trades that were completed attempted to solve immediate problems but created voids elsewhere. Unfortunately, the Gault and Schroeder trades have not solved anything. As 1990 began, the Raiders were still not a solid club, with ongoing problems in the offensive line, too many miles on the linebackers, and an unstable quarterback situation. It will probably take more than one draft and a few quality free agents to correct all the problems. Hopefully, the roof won't start leaking elsewhere in the interim.

The abysmal performance at the draft table and with trades have led skeptics to ask many questions. Are the days of continuing Raider dominance on the field a thing of the past? Did Al Davis lose his magic touch in the evaluation of talent? Why have the Raiders drafted so poorly and made such unsuccessful trades? Has the Davis infatuation with the long pass become passé in the NFL? Has Al spent too much time in the courtroom and in confrontations with stadium authorities and left the Raiders neglected?

In order, the answers to the above questions are: maybe, probably not, probably yes, and definitely yes. The biggest change in pro football in the past decade has been in the players, not strategies. Big money has adversely infected many players now coming into the NFL. That has led to other evils such as cocaine abuse and alcohol. The Raiders have had some substance abuse problems (Warren Wells, Art Whittington, Greg Townsend, Jerry Robinson, Cliff Branch, and the late Stacey Toran) but probably no more, no less than anybody else.

In their salad days, much of the Raider mystique came from the acquisition of players who were either problem children or underachievers elsewhere. But in recent years, the Raiders have not always pursued this kind of performers. Two recent examples involve Mossy Cade and Chip Banks. Cade was a Number 1 draft pick of the Green Bay Packers, who instead chose the Memphis Showboats of the USFL. Following the USFL demise he joined the Packers and looked like a star cornerback. But then he was convicted of forced rape and spent time in prison. Upon release from jail, Cade was also released by the Packers. The Minnesota Vikings were going to sign him but backed off when there was an outcry from the community. Nobody else in the NFL, including the Raiders, was interested.

A more obvious absence of interest by the Raiders involved Chip Banks. An All-American linebacker at the University of Southern California, Banks became a star with the Cleveland Browns, playing in a few Pro Bowls. During a salary dispute with the Browns, Banks asked owner Art Modell for a trade to the Raiders. And with their starting linebackers rapidly reaching the geriatric ward, the Raiders could have used the speedy Banks. Instead, Cleveland dealt Banks to the San Diego Chargers in 1987 for a No. 1 draft pick. He was soon arrested for drug possession in San Diego and was also convicted of a felony in Atlanta. Chargers owner Alex Spanos announced that Banks would never again play for San Diego. After release from both jail and a drug treatment center, the Chargers traded Banks to Indianapolis for a middle-round draft choice.

Although the Raiders have helped players like Robinson and Townsend already on their roster, they have backed away from taking on somebody else's drug problems. The last player with a known drug problem who joined the Raiders was New England offensive tackle Shelby Jordan, who was arrested in 1975 for selling cocaine. He played for the Silver and Black from 1983 to 1986. The unwritten Raider rule used to be: "As long as you showed up and played like hell on Sunday, we don't care what you do during the week." But the drug epidemic in America has changed the philosophy. Al Davis has made some strong public comments about substance abuse problems in America, advocating that drug education commence in kindergarten and "make it like a police state" to clean up the nation. The painful experience of losing wide receiver Warren Wells to a federal penitentiary during the season in 1971 because of a rape charge probably made the acquisition of Cade a high-risk venture. It seems that the old Raider way of taking on malcontents has been lost to the war on drugs.

With the San Francisco 49ers' recent success, many NFL people are wondering how and why they have escaped the parody of the rest of the teams in the league. There has to be a reason why the Niners continue to have successful drafts and keep finding good athletes in the middle and lower rounds while the Raiders and others get burned. Although Al Davis is still a brilliant football mind, it may be time for some changes. For example, the Raiders have always prided themselves on ignoring the NFL scouting combines and going it alone. The recent draft failures are not exactly an endorsement for continuing to fly solo.

Just like the latest designer jeans, strategy changes in the NFL are like fads. They come and go. Shotgun formations, nickel backs, I formations, flexes, and 3-4 defenses were not handed down on Mount Sinai. After one club had success with these nuances, the rest of the league unabashedly played follow-the-leader. The team that wins the Super Bowl is more important than who is first at the patent office. For that reason, the success of the 49ers offense in the 1980s should not go unexamined. And other NFL teams are starting to copy this style. Joe Montana is a master at throwing the short pass of 10 to 20 yards. The Niners rarely throw the bomb. But Jerry Rice can catch long or short passes. The 49ers are masters of "taking what the defense gives you."

The theories of offensive football that Al Davis put into place in 1963 are still valid. When you see Mervyn Fernandez drop a pass, Beuerlein overthrow an open receiver, or Rory Graves called for holding that nullifies a Bo Jackson sweep, you realize that the plays still work, it is the performances that are wanting.

When Art Shell succeeded Shanahan in October 1989, both Davis and the new head coach happily proclaimed that there would now be a return to "Raider football." As described by Shell when he was hired: "We will take what we want, not what the defense gives us." That sounds nice, but there are one or two obvious problems to playing what was once known as "Raider football." Has the NFL caught up to the Raider style that was so successful in days of yore, or does Al Davis lack the personnel to make it work anymore?

It is probably a little bit of both but definitely the latter. The best players on offense are probably better suited for the "take what the defense gives you" philosophy rather than the long passing game that Davis craves. Both Marc Wilson and Jay Schroeder could throw long but lacked the leadership qualities that were an integral part of the makeup and psyche of Lamonica, Stabler, and Plunkett. Schroeder frequently overthrows the short spirals. Steve Beuerlein may be the key to a successful short passing game. Al knew that Wells, Branch, and Biletnikoff could catch the ball. What about Willie Gault, Jessie Hester, and Tim Moffett? Although Gault may have world-class speed, he is not dependable catching the short pass in traffic. Fernandez has good speed and moves well in traffic, but Swervin' Mervyn may not be in a class with Branch, Wells, and Rice as a game-breaker. The hope for the 1990s rests with Tim Brown, who spent most of 1989 on injured reserve. Gene Upshaw and Art Shell were superior pass blockers, who have been replaced by the likes of Rory Graves and John Clay.

Is this the job you really wanted, Coach Shell?

Chapter 15

THE RAIDERS AND
THE MEDIA

*"The press and the television is microscopic
today. Ten years ago, it was just an overview, but
this is micro. You're right on top of every event
that takes place. ESPN ... CNN ... you guys are on
top of it daily. You're on top of it every minute so
everything that's being done is being critiqued
and criticized, and I'm not so sure by people who
are capable of doing it, but anyhow, it's being done
regularly and we have to live with it."*
—**Al Davis, 1988**

Al Davis has been critical of the "media microscope" in recent years. Instead of the newspapers, his indirect criticism has been aimed at the broadcast television
networks and ESPN and CNN. Although many in both
the print media and the national television networks are
slow to digest the changes, the cable networks have radi-
cally altered the coverage of sports in America. Both
CNN and ESPN have 30-minute "sports wrap-up" shows
every night and ESPN has a one-hour "Sportscenter" on
Sunday evenings. While not as widely available as CNN
and ESPN, FNN/Score now runs a continuous 30-minute
sports scoreboard program on weekends. Sort of a
"Headline News" for sports buffs. ESPN also has both
"Gameday" and "NFL Primetime" programs during the

football season that thoroughly dissect every game. The cable networks are also attuned to all off-the-field activities and provide thorough coverage in the off season if warranted. A good example of this extensive coverage was the ability of ESPN to broadcast live from the news conference that announced the hiring of Art Shell.

With the advent of cable, more games are being seen by more people than ever. The Sunday night coverage by ESPN and TNT has added 17 more national telecasts than were available in 1986. That also means more pre-game, halftime, and post-game analysis shows. The NFL will play its schedule over 18 weeks in 1991 and has added two more playoff games. More football on television is more entertainment and additional knowledge and awareness for the fans.

In 1989, Davis discussed the information explosion with Pete Axthelm on ESPN and carried his remarks one step further: "The microscopic scrutiny of the press and the lack of patience of the press and the media, the whole group, is gradually going to a confrontation, whereby someone is going to turn it around and start to take on the press and the media. And I think the first group that is going to be taken on are the TV announcers and people like that, because there are a lot of them who are doing it who have never really won. They've played but have never really won. But [they] are making statements about players, about coaches, about what's going on in the field that I'm not sure they have the right to do. Now [I] so far have not reached a point where I have been offended at any time."

Al Davis made one mistake is his remarks. The first group that is going to be taken on will not be television announcers but the sports columnists of the San Francisco Bay Area for their hypocritical stances toward Al Davis and the Raiders. And it will be done right here, in Chapter 15.

To tell this story properly, let us go way back to the

USC days in 1957. Rah-rah, sis-boom-bah. Al Davis was a baseball fan who closely followed the exodus of the Brooklyn Dodgers to Los Angeles. It didn't take a Perry Mason to realize that the most influential sportswriters in Los Angeles at the time were Melvin Durslag and Vincent X. Flaherty of the *Examiner* and Bud Furillo of the *Herald*. Flaherty and Durslag were instrumental in mating Dodger owner Walter O'Malley with the movers and shakers of Los Angeles. The *Los Angeles Times* sports department was somewhat bland in those days. When Davis joined Sid Gillman with the new Los Angeles Chargers in 1960, the *Times* was not the most receptive to the new AFL club and appeared to more attuned to the Rams. These impressions were filed in Davis's noggin for future reference.

When the Chargers were enticed to move down the road to San Diego in 1961, columnist Jack Murphy played a major role. Just like Durslag and Flaherty in Los Angeles, Murphy brought all the key players together and watched over the proceedings like a mother hen hovering over her young. They do have a damn good reason for calling it Jack Murphy Stadium. When Al Davis signed Lance Alworth for the Chargers in 1962, Mr. Murphy was impressed. Eventually Jack Murphy was to join Mel Durslag in the favorite writer club of Al Davis. Durslag was one of the few writers who conversed with Davis after the proposed move back to Oakland was announced.

Al knew the score when he took the Oakland job in 1963. He was a new coach, with a new team in a new league, in a new big league city. On the other side of the bay was an established team that was somewhat adored by the San Francisco newspapers. While the *Oakland Tribune* would send a writer to Raider road games in the early years of the AFL, the San Francisco dailies saved their money and used wire service reports.

If the Oakland Raiders franchise was to succeed with

Al Davis as coach and general manager, the *Oakland Tribune* would have to play more than a bit part. Al quickly became good friends with *Tribune* sports editor George Ross and developed a strong rapport with football writer Gordon (Scotty) Stirling. He was also impressed with the knowledge of San Francisco Chronicle writer Michael Berger, who covered the Raiders from 1963 to 1966. But the other San Francisco guys could not crack the nut of favored status. As the pro football wars were heating up, Al Davis didn't trust them or their intentions.

Glenn Dickey became the Raiders beat writer for the Chronicle in 1967 and intermittently covered the team through 1977. Darrell Wilson and Jack Smith also sometimes had the Raiders for their assignments. Many of Dickey's game summaries were lively, entertaining, and irreverent stories, which were unusual for the times. Dickey started doing daily commentary in 1971 and gradually became the most widely-read sports columnist in Northern California. Many of his columns seemed to be intended to "stir the pot," i.e., take the adversarial position on any issue no matter how absurd it would be. For example, after the 49ers sank to a 6–5 record in 1988, Dickey urged quarterback Joe Montana to retire. Luckily for the Niners, nobody took the suggestion seriously.

After Dickey was ordained as star columnist at the *Chronicle,* Ira Miller handled the day-to-day doings of the Silver and Black in 1978 and 1979 and C. W. "Chuck" Nevius was the Raider beat writer for the *Chronicle* in 1980 and 1981. Another *Chronicle* writer who frequently found himself in the press box during Raider games of the 1970s was Art Spander.

Over at the *San Francisco Examiner,* Don Selby, Phil Norman, and Will Connelly were the original beat writers. Later Walt Daley came over from the defunct *News– Call Bulletin* in 1965. Daley and Frank Cooney were the primary Raider reporters at the *Examiner* for most of the

1970s. After Al Davis hired Stirling as the Raiders public relations director in 1964, Bob Valli started covering the Raiders for the *Oakland Tribune* on a daily basis. Bob and Al developed a good rapport that still exists today. When Valli was promoted to sports editor, Tom LaMarre, Blaine Newnham, Dave Newhouse, and finally Ron Borges covered the Raider beat in the *Trib*.

Why am I telling you this? Because the biggest enemies of Al Davis when the Raiders moved to Los Angeles in 1982 were many of the gentlemen named above. Most of these people became so enamored with the success of the San Francisco 49ers that they made like the Oakland Raiders never existed. The Raiders moved to Los Angeles in 1982 but many Bay Area fans still watched the Silver and Black on television or listened to popular announcer Bill King on radio. The television ratings in the San Francisco area for Raider games were still good. But the newspapers and local television stations refused to cover the team. Never mind the quest for high ratings or greater circulation. They were going to teach Al Davis a lesson.

Many of the above-mentioned "journalists" soon became prolific cheap-shot artists who would delight in taking nasty little digs at the Raiders' owner and his team. Of course, with the Raiders in Los Angeles, they would only come face-to-face with Davis on rare occasions, such as when the Raiders played the 49ers in an annual exhibition game. The cheap shots were administered fearlessly because they never imagined that Al Davis might permanently return.

Glenn Dickey was particularly vicious. After assistant coach Charlie Sumner left the Raiders, Dickey proceeded to lash out at Davis in a particularly nasty column on January 5, 1989. Because he and his colleagues at the *Chronicle* were so consumed with the 49ers march to the Super Bowl, he could not fathom that there might still be some Raider fans hiding in the bushes. Presumably

speaking for the 6,000,000 inhabitants of the San Francisco Bay Area region, Dickey concluded the column by
saying, "The question of whether the Raiders will return
is less important than this one: Do we want Davis back? As
a winner, Al Davis was barely palatable. As a loser . . .
forget it."

The next time Dickey addressed the subject of the
owner of the Raiders was three months later, after tickets
to the August exhibition game sold out within 2½ hours.
Dickey begrudgingly admitted that there was still Raider
interest in the Bay Area but feared that the quick ticket
sales for the preseason game would undercut efforts to
get an expansion team. "But let the dream go. They will
never be Oakland Raiders again," he wrote.

The "chasing a dream" theme was repeated by Dickey
on July 19, 1989, when he cautioned the Oakland negotiators about dealing with Davis. "Al Davis is the most un-
sentimental man I know. He will pretend to the emotion
when he's involved in a public ceremony, but he soon
turns any speech into a self-serving message."

Dickey certainly reached the summit of his one-man
campaign to stop the Raiders return on the morning of
August 28, 1989, when he minimized the importance of
the capacity crowd that reacted wildly for the Silver and
Black at the Oakland exhibition game. Dismissing the
crowd as having a "rock concert mentality," he proceeded to dispel the notions that 1) the Raiders had
unique support in Oakland and 2) Los Angeles never
supported the Raiders. Four days later, many of the ideas
were repeated. "The crowd for last Saturday night's
exhibition against Houston was a disgrace, drunken and
disorderly, hardly better than a British soccer crowd"; although Dickey grudgingly admitted, "I think it's very important to the city that it get the Raiders back."

But on September 13, 1989, Dickey was back to insert-
ing the cheap shots: "It feels strange to use the word principle and Davis's name in the same sentence. . . . Paying

for the dubious privilege of getting Al Davis doesn't make sense."

We next hear from Glenn on February 14, 1990. No significant Al Davis bashing here, only a grudging realization that "the Raiders are good for the city, psychologically and economically." And on the morning of March 12, 1990, in typical Glenn Dickey fashion, was a prediction that Al Davis would pass on the deadline to announce a decision on Oakland and "let the politicians bluster and rationalize once more." Good prediction, Glenn. The announcement came a few hours later.

Dickey has behaved relatively well since March 12, 1990, and is somewhat supportive of a "sensible" Raider return to Oakland. But his May 4, 1990, column couldn't be completed without one more dig: "These are not the championship Raiders of old, but a mediocre team with many question marks, starting with the big one: Has the game passed Al Davis by?" Glenn Dickey did not return our telephone calls to be interviewed for this book.

Art Spander, who is currently the reigning sports columnist at the *San Francisco Examiner,* has always had a good rapport with Davis. But Spander and his paper have occasionally slipped into the "San Francisco is superior to Oakland" syndrome. Caught up in the euphoria of the 49ers initial Super Bowl win in 1982, Spander proclaimed "The 49ers are San Francisco's team, the Bay Area's team." Well, yes and no, Art. The Raiders still belonged to Oakland in January, 1982. In 1987, while the Oakland A's hot rookie Mark McGwire was burning up the American League, Spander mused about how nice it would have been for McGwire to be playing for the San Francisco Giants. A column expressing the desire for the Giants' Will Clark to be playing in Oakland never came. On August 24, 1988, with the Raiders' owner safely out of sight, Spander wrote a "bash Al Davis" column, under the title of "Al Davis's Return to Oakland Is Pure Fantasy." Spander derisively referred to

Davis as Mr. Al, similar to Mr. Boll Weevil. A sample from the column: "Mr. Al and [the] Raiders are where they are through a series of circumstances involving misjudgment, egomania, and gold-digging." But Spander reached the pinnacle (or the depths) of his anti-Raider passions while he appeared on an ESPN "Sportslook" program in June 1989, shortly after John Matuszak died. Spander was ostensibly promoting his latest book when host Roy Firestone asked him if the Al Davis credo of "just win, baby" was somehow responsible for Matuszak's death. "I'm afraid so, Roy," was the reply.

But Spander regained his grip on reality on March 14, 1990, in his second column after the announcement of the return to Oakland. "Don't blame Al Davis for looking for the best deal. That's the American way—hell, the way of the world. But Al isn't going to just take, he wants to give—give the fans and himself a winner if possible."

Al Davis is often portrayed by his critics as being vindictive and unforgiving when he is crossed. But he has always liked Spander and still freely converses with the *San Francisco Examiner* columnist.

Dave Newhouse of the *Oakland Tribune* is an enigma. In the past 15 years, he has gone from a happy Raider beat writer to a columnist and radio talk show host with an open disdain for Davis, to being totally forgiving of the Raider owner. When murmurings about a Raider move to Los Angeles were first heard, Newhouse originally sided with the Silver and Black and blamed the Coliseum Board. All that changed when the Raiders announced their intentions to depart. On the day that the Raiders won their court case against the NFL in May 1982, Newhouse proclaimed that it was time to "throw Al Davis out of football."

Through most of the 1980s, Newhouse would take his shots at Davis. If listeners wanted to discuss the Raiders on his talk show, it was better to wait until Newhouse went on vacation and Ralph Barbieri was the guest host. In

1986, when the Raiders and the United States Navy came to an agreement that would allow Ensign Napoleon McCallum to play for the Raiders and simultaneously fulfill his military obligations, Dave ranted, raved and wondered how Al Davis could have pulled off such a deal. Wonder what the Newhouse reaction would have been if Bill Walsh had maneuvered the same ploy?

Newhouse discussed the Al Davis candidacy for the Pro Football Hall of Fame in print in 1986 and speculated when he would be elected. "I hope it isn't too soon," was his sentiment. After Tom Flores retired as Raider coach, Newhouse launched into another attack on Davis on January 21, 1988, and went down memory lane to do it. Discussing the retirement of John Madden, Newhouse said, "Davis lost control of Madden, like a puppeteer who watches a puppet jump out of its strings, then can't tolerate it when the puppet demands an identity of its own."

Next, Newhouse started a campaign to try to get an expansion team in Oakland. He began a letter-writing campaign and asked his readers to write to both NFC president Wellington Mara and his AFC counterpart, Lamar Hunt. Fewer than 100 letters were received at the NFL office. The expansion "movement" started by Newhouse was abandoned in embarrassment.

But Dave can be forgiven. When the rumors of a Raider return to Oakland started, Newhouse jumped on the bandwagon and was one of the few sportswriters totally supportive of the negotiators and their offer. He stuck to his guns during the period when the offer was being attacked. Newhouse was virtually the only Bay Area writer who constantly supported the return of the Raiders through the entire process.

And surprise of surprises. On March 14, 1990, just two days after Al Davis announced his intention to return to Oakland, Newhouse wrote his column under the incredible title of "It's Time to Stop Blaming Davis, City of Oakland." And the man who once wanted Al Davis

thrown out of football wrote, "So, Al Davis, no one's perfect. We'll forgive your mistakes if you forgive ours. Just
don't ride back into town high-handed."

There have been other slights by the Bay Area media
heaped on Al Davis, his team, and its fans. Sometimes
they must be uncovered by a microscope. In February
1990, the *San Francisco Chronicle* added a 125th anniversary supplement with the Sunday edition, detailing the
growth of the newspaper against the backdrop of events
of since 1865. When discussing sports in the Bay Area,
the *Chronicle* proceeded to rattle off the world championships of the Oakland Athletics, Golden State Warriors,
and the San Francisco 49ers. In a display of cutting that
would make the editors at *Pravda* proud, the *Chronicle*
failed to acknowledge the two Super Bowl triumphs of
the Oakland Raiders.

Ira Miller of the *Chronicle* also zinged the Raiders by
the process of omission. Remember that Miller was the
beat writer for the Silver and Black in 1978 and 1979. Before Super Bowl XXIV was played, Miller listed his 10 all-
time Super Bowl thrills. The Raiders played in 4 of the
previous 23 championship games. That calculates to
17.3913% of the Super Bowls, so we might expect the
17.3913% of Miller's list to mention a Raider game.
Maybe Marcus Allen's run or Willie Brown's interception, perhaps the Kenny King reception from Jim Plunkett. Nope. Nothing. Incredibly, he included the bumbling Super Bowl V game between Dallas and Baltimore
as one of the 10 best.

He started writing a simple commentary. But as he developed the topic, Mark Heisler was becoming increasingly angry. When it was finished and printed in the *Los
Angeles Times* on March 13, 1990, what started as a criticism of the abandonment of Los Angeles turned into the
form of tirade, a sort of a Bronx cheer to dear old Al.
Some excerpts: "This is a man who won't stand for being
crossed, who won't be held accountable. In five years cov-

ering his team, I have never interviewed him once, despite repeated requests. His replies ranged from insincere modesty . . . to mention that he knew my publisher personally but hadn't complained to him about me yet, to profanity.

"I was beginning to suspect that he didn't like me. However, it put me at a little competitive disadvantage. He rarely allowed himself to be interviewed by any beat writer, preferring instead long confidences with out-of-town writers who were directed never to use his name, or quote a Raider source or even apparently to use the word *source*. When A. D. was your source, you were out there alone."

In Southern California, "the Los Angeles Raiders versus the media" has been an entirely different ballgame than in San Francisco. The *Los Angeles Herald-Examiner* was front and center in their unabashed support of enticing the Raiders, and all of their writers were united in the effort. Sort of like the Bay Area journalists for the San Francisco Giants' downtown ballpark in 1989. From 1978 until 1982, the *Los Angeles Times* was "out there somewhere" in the Raider effort, but it was unclear where. Because the *Times* sees itself as more of a national/international paper, it prefers to use its influence on city hall for other issues. Al Davis was certainly an admirer of Jim Murray, but the Pulitzer Prize-winning columnist and his paper played no role in bringing the Raiders to L.A. After initially viewing him as an "NFL writer" in the AFL days, Davis developed a good relationship with *Times* football expert Bob Oates. And perhaps Oates' famous "rogue elephant" column of 1978 was influenced by a talk with Al Davis. There were also no problems with either Mike Downey or Scott Ostler of the *Times*. Ostler now is toiling for the *National*.

But the Raiders always perceived the *Times* as a "Rams paper." In 1988, in the first edition of "The Los Angeles Raiders Newspaper," "executive editor" Al LoCasale criticized the *Times* for their coverage of the Marc Wilson release and Heisler's use of unidentified sources in the Raider organization for his stories.

When asked about the *Times'* relationship with the Raiders and their coverage, sports editor Bill Dwyre replied, "If I read Al Davis right, he's a man who likes to have a little more influence in what is printed than he has with the *L.A. Times*." Dwyre also maintains that the *Times* must cover the Rams, Chargers, Angels, Dodgers, Lakers, Clippers, Kings, USC, UCLA, and other teams, so that the Raiders get less attention than Davis would like. "The pie gets sliced up a bit more here," said Dwyre.

The strain between the Raiders and the largest newspaper on the West Coast was not helped by the three years that the team was covered by Alan Greenberg, who is now a star columnist for the *Hartford Courant*. "He often had a flippant attitude," said a fellow reporter. Although Greenberg developed a close friendship with Matt Millen, other players did not care for him. Lyle Alzado once threw something at Greenberg after a game.

Mark Heisler replaced Greenberg in 1985. Of all the writers who have ever covered the Raiders, Heisler has probably written the best and most detailed stories. Even the Raiders will grudgingly admit that the guy knows how to write. For all home and most road games, the *Times* usually assigns a second reporter to file a "sidelight" story. Occasionally Murray, Durslag, or Mike Downey will also cover the game. The Rams also receive similar treatment.

The first evidences of the Heisler-Davis differences of opinion occurred immediately after the final game of the 1986 season. Perhaps everybody was a tad testy after the Raiders had dropped the final four games to miss the playoffs. On December 24, 1986, Heisler wrote the following: "So what's on Coach Davis's mind?

Approached after last Sunday's game (a loss to Indianapolis that concluded an 8–8 season) and asked about the possibility of an interview in the coming week or ever, Davis demurs. He embarks on the customary review of the reporter's treatment of the Raiders (deemed wholly negative), posture towards same (malicious), knowledge of Raider history (inadequate), and his publication's stance since the move from Oakland (perceived to be hostile)."

One of his problems with the Raiders front office was that Heisler occasionally became more fascinated by what was going on in the owner's box than the action on the playing field. In Minnesota in 1987, Heisler reported hearing a Raider official upstairs say, "Mr. Davis wants a new quarterback." After a loss to Cleveland, Mark reported that Davis was fuming about the play-calling. On a third-down-and-five play, Flores had Marcus Allen run the ball. He fumbled and Cleveland recovered. "This coach has had it," was the reported overheard reaction of Davis. Heisler also accurately reported some of the warts that the organization would prefer hidden from public view. This included the problems between Davis and Marcus Allen, Vann McElroy, and Bill Lewis. It was honest reporting but certainly not designed to improve rapport between Davis and the *Times*.

Until its demise in December 1989, the *Herald-Examiner* was the main competition for the *Times*. In early 1980, the *Herald-Examiner* assigned Jack Disney to cover all the daily gyrations of Al Davis and officials of Oakland, Los Angeles, and the National Football League. Disney did an excellent job and was assigned the Raider beat when they finally moved to Los Angeles in 1982. Disney usually beat the *Times* to any scoops involving the team. Although Heisler complained that he didn't have access to Davis, neither did Disney or any other beat writers. Not talking to Davis was no excuse for being late with team news. "He [Heisler] could have done better," said another member of the *Times* sports department.

Upon close examination, some of Heisler's charges in his March 13, 1990, commentary probably apply to all 28 teams in the NFL. His complaints included the lack of access to Davis, Raider assistant coaches "who were never to say anything remotely controversial and often begged off interviews altogether," and charges that the head coach "is expected to be ultra-bland and reveal nothing."

Most owners in the National Football League are rarely interviewed. And that group includes Georgia Frontiere of the Los Angeles Rams. With few exceptions, most NFL fans don't really know (or care) who the assistant coaches are and few receive or generate any publicity. Head coaches *always* take the credit for winning. Not many assistant coaches give interviews on any club. Of the 28 head coaches in the NFL at the start of the 1990 season, only Mike Ditka, Buddy Ryan, Jerry Glanville, and maybe Sam Wyche ever utter anything that could be considered glib, unusual, lively, or profound. Rams coach John Robinson is certainly no ball of fire at revealing secrets to the press, and neither is George Siefert of the 49ers. Despite being adored by the Bay Area media, Bill Walsh was constantly at odds with many writers. It reached a peak when the *San Francisco Examiner* exposed the alleged extramarital activity of the former 49er coach. Remember how Giants coach Bill Parcells clammed-up to the media after a controversial pass-interference call cost his team a playoff game against the Rams in January 1990? In their relationship with reporters, Tom Flores, Mike Shanahan, and Art Shell were really no different than most other head coaches in the NFL. Saying little or nothing to the media is the rule of thumb among all 28 NFL teams. In fact, a former Raider beat writer gave both Shanahan and Shell high marks for being more informative and thorough with the press than your average NFL coach.

Mark Heisler won't be covering the Raiders anymore. When the Raiders opened training camp in Oxnard, California, in 1990, Chris Baker was filing daily reports for the *Times*. Heisler was reassigned to the Lakers.

Chapter 16

THE HALL OF FAME

The failure to elect Al Davis into the Pro Football Hall of Fame has become somewhat of a national disgrace among professional football writers. Ever since Will McDonough of the *Boston Globe* first placed his name in nomination in 1986, Davis has been repeatedly rejected. Oh sure, Al usually makes the first cut that whittles the list down to fifteen finalists, but he has never made it to the final seven names that are considered each year.

And whatever people might think of him personally, Al Davis certainly has the credentials. He is the only person, living or dead, who has served professional football as a scout, assistant coach, head coach, general manager, commissioner, and owner. Under the direction of Al Davis, the Oakland/Los Angeles Raiders still have the best record in all of professional sports since 1963, the year that Al came to the East Bay. They are the only football team that has played in the Super Bowl in the 1960s, 1970s, and 1980s. Only Pittsburgh and San Francisco have won more Super Bowls than the Raiders, but the Steeler and 49er victories were accomplished over a shorter span of time.

A look at the roster of the Hall of Fame will show how blatant the omission of Al Davis has become. The best players are chosen, so why not the best owners? Some of the owners who have been enshrined were picked because they were "founding fathers of the National Football League," not because they fielded winning teams.

Some of them were also of dubious backgrounds and stubbornly resisted social change.

Among the owners enshrined are Charles Bidwell, the original owner of the Chicago Cardinals, who under the guidance of his son and nephew became the St. Louis Cardinals and later the Phoenix Cardinals. It has been alleged that "Stormy" had ties to Al Capone. The Cardinals were certainly no ball of fire in their days in the Windy City. Their only NFL Championship came in 1947, after Bidwell died.

Kansas City Chiefs owner Lamar Hunt is in the Hall of Fame, primarily for being a founder of the American Football League. While Hunt was there in the beginning, it can be successfully argued that it was people such as Al Davis and Sonny Werblin who ensured the survival of the fledgling AFL. Hunt doesn't have a plaque on the wall at Canton because of the Chiefs' performance on the field. After fielding an explosive team in the AFL days, which was primarily built by scout Don Klosterman and Coach Hank Stram, the Chiefs have since treated their fans to mostly sorrowful teams and a parade of inept coaches and general managers. In 1986, the Chiefs surprised the experts by making the playoffs and seeing their only post-season action in the last 20 seasons. How did Hunt reward head coach John Mackovic for the achievement? You guessed it. Mackovic was fired.

The selection committee must have been in a forgiving mood when the late George Preston Marshall was inducted in 1963, the year that the Hall of Fame opened. If Marshall belongs in Canton, then perhaps former governor George Wallace of Alabama should be enshrined in the NAACP "Hall of Fame." Marshall was the original owner of the Redskins, who were based in Boston before he moved them to Washington in 1937. Apparently none of the football writers at the time were outraged over the relocation of a franchise, as they would later be when Al Davis moved the Raiders to Los Angeles. By 1961, the

Redskins were an embarrassment to the NFL as the only team that did not have any black players. Marshall didn't want to alienate the white Southern fans who followed the Redskins on their large regional television network. Fortunately the federal government stepped in. Funding was being withheld for the new District of Columbia (later renamed Robert F. Kennedy) Stadium, unless the Redskins were integrated, and fast. Not surprisingly, the segregated Redskins were the worst team in the NFL in 1961. The Redskins had the number one draft choice in 1962 and Heisman Trophy winning running back Ernie Davis of Syracuse was the obvious choice. Marshall eventually traded his draft rights to Cleveland and received superstar running back and wide receiver Bobby Mitchell in return. Mitchell became the first black player to play for Washington. Ironically, in 1983, 20 years after Marshall was enshrined, Mitchell was also inducted into the Hall of Fame.

Why Dan Reeves is in the Hall of Fame is a mystery. Reeves was the owner of the Cleveland Rams, who became the first professional team in the West by moving to Los Angeles in 1946. Another franchise shift, for shame! In his 30 years of ownership, the Rams could only win the championship once, in 1951. The biggest Rams news of the 1950s and 1960s was the feud between Reeves and fellow owner Ed Pauley. In the years between their 1955 Western Conference championship and the arrival of George Allen in 1966, the Rams were regularly in the NFL West cellar. After Allen made the Rams a contender, Reeves rewarded his coach by firing him. After the player's near-revolt, Allen was rehired. At the end of his contract, Allen left for Washington.

Besides Al Davis, there are some other owners who deserve to be considered and elected in Canton. Although he only owned the New York Jets for five years, the influence of Sonny Werblin on the events of professional football was probably greater than Hunt's.

And what about Carroll Rosenbloom? Not only did his money save the Baltimore Colts franchise in 1953, but he built one of the most glamorous and successful teams in NFL history, a team that was regularly in title contention. The Colts of the 1950s and 1960s have placed seven players in the Hall of Fame. In 1972, Rosenbloom moved to Los Angeles, and from 1973 until he died in 1979, the Rams were always in the playoffs.

Of course, part of the problem for the failure of the Al Davis candidacy has been the lack of a public relations effort from the Raiders. Al Davis has been less than cordial with certain members of the press corps through the years and has never "campaigned" for Hall of Fame entry. Another problem is that many of the members of the committee that selects and elects are writers who covered NFL teams prior to the merger and have minimized the contributions of players and owners from the AFL.

Although the balloting is done secretly and the writers rarely disclose their votes publicly, *Oakland Tribune* columnist Dave Newhouse asked ten selection committee members about the candidacy of Al Davis on January 16, 1986. Two of the biggest detractors stepped out front-row-center with opinions on Al Davis. One was John Steadman, now with the *Baltimore Evening Sun*. Said Steadman, "I don't see where he's made any lasting contribution to pro football. He's certainly had an impact, but at this point in a negative way. I go back knowing Al Davis longer than any man on the committee, when he was a coach at Fort Belvoir, Virginia. Although an enlisted man, he rarely wore a uniform. Even then he had connections. Whether he likes or dislikes Pete Rozelle or the City of Oakland has no bearing on whether he qualifies for the Hall of Fame. Personally, I don't think he belongs."

And then there is Ed Pope, who has been with the *Miami Herald* for many years. So what is your beef with Al Davis, Mr. Pope? "I would be much more concerned about people like Paul Hornung, who are more deserving of getting in, than I would be about Al Davis. If it took Pete Rozelle nine years, I think it should take Davis a long time. I'm not going to waste any sympathy on Davis. I don't think he needs it."

After Pope made that remark, he helped Paul Hornung get elected. But it apparently didn't change his feelings about Al Davis. The "class of 1990" was announced on January 27, 1990, in New Orleans, a day before Super Bowl XXIV was played. As usual, it did not include the name of Al Davis. On the Sunday morning before the game, "The Sports Reporters," a discussion program on ESPN, originated from the Superdome. Among the media guests with host Dick Schaap were former 49er coach Bill Walsh, now of NBC, Mike Lupica of the *National*, Mike Downey from the *Los Angeles Times*, and Ed Pope. When the subject of discussion turned to Al Davis, Lupica, Walsh, and Downey, while expressing reservations about his personality, all strongly endorsed the Raiders owner for enshrinement into the Hall of Fame and seemed to chide Pope for his opposition. "If you put Pete Rozelle in the Hall of Fame, Al Davis has to go in the Hall of Fame, or turn it into a gas station," concluded the outspoken Lupica. While not actually revealing his actual vote, Pope launched into the following soliloquy about Al Davis: "He also originated the modern floating franchise system. I personally take violent exception to this business of owners auctioning off their franchises to the highest bidder." Wonder how Ed Pope voted in 1990?

Of course, Al Davis did not invent franchise shifts, veiled threats to landlords, or maximizing your profits, possibly at the expense of a city government beset with urban problems. What Pope conveniently forgot to mention in his diatribe against Al Davis is that the late Joe Robbie, then owner of his hometown Dolphins, threatened to move to Los Angeles Coliseum in 1978 if he didn't get improvements in the Orange Bowl. That was before Al Davis became involved with Los Angeles. Later Robbie was to build a new stadium which contained all of the amenities that Al Davis had originally wanted from Oakland. With the Dolphins now playing in a privately owned stadium in suburban Dade County, the City of Miami lost the rental payments and other revenues that Joe Robbie was generating by playing in the Orange Bowl, funds that could help alleviate urban problems. In May 1990, the Orange Bowl Committee, which stages the annual New Year's Eve college football game, expressed an interest in moving its game from the Orange Bowl Stadium to, guess where? Joe Robbie Stadium. If they do eventually move the game out of the Orange Bowl in downtown Miami, even more revenue is lost to the City of Miami because much of the tourist dollar that both Miami and Miami Beach desperately need will instead transfer to the more affluent areas of upper Dade and Broward counties.

Blaming Al Davis for other franchise shifts is fine and dandy, but what does Al Davis have to do with the Phoenix Cardinals' move? Billy Bidwell asked for and received the affirmative votes needed to move from St. Louis. Al Davis abstained from voting.

After being in and around the Baltimore Colts through their entire existence, John Steadman was justifiably enraged in 1984 when Robert Irsay moved the team to Indianapolis without league approval. Commissioner Pete Rozelle claimed he was powerless to stop the moves because of the Al Davis transfer to Los Angeles. But there are many who disagree with that assessment. After being defeated in court by the Raiders, Rozelle should have modified the rules on franchise shifts, as many lawyers had urged. A more workable and legal NFL Rule 4.3 may have prevented the Colts' departure.

The annual denial of Al Davis is becoming somewhat of an embarrassment for football writers. Perhaps what the opponents of Al Davis are really stating by their negative votes is that they don't possess enough football knowledge to be worthy of such a prestigious assignment as picking Hall of Famers.

Chapter 17

THE DREAM TEAM

*T*he journey through the world of Al Davis continues with the All-Time Raider team. With the talent that has passed through Oakland and Los Angeles in the past 30 campaigns, this is not an easy task but here goes:

Defense

Let's assume a four-man defensive front with three linebackers. No pass-rush specialists, extra linebackers, or nickel backs allowed.

Defensive end: Howie Long
Defensive end: Ben Davidson

Let's forgive Howie for the dropoff in his performance in recent years. The Villanova grad was a pass-rushing terror in his early days. Davidson gave the Raiders a strong defensive presence in the late sixties. Runner up: Greg Townsend.

Defensive tackle: Tom Keating
Defensive tackle: John Matuszak

Hey, its my team and I'll pick who I want. The Tooz never made All-Pro but the Raiders probably couldn't have won those first two Super Bowls without him. Although he often played defensive end on a three-man line, let's put Matuszak at defensive tackle. Keating was probably the best defensive tackle who ever wore silver and black and was also one of Al Davis's best trade acquisitions. Otis Sistrunk is not far behind these two.

Outside linebacker: Ted Hendricks
Outside linebacker: Phil Villapiano

Fortunately for the Raiders, both Hendricks and Villapiano played together from 1975 to 1979. Both were superb pass defenders who also could stop outside sweeps. The Raiders' defense has really not been the same since Hendricks retired in 1983. Some credit also should be heaped on Gus Otto and Rod Martin.

Middle linebacker: Dan Conners

He was the best in Raider history on the inside. In an eleven-year career, Conners scored five touchdowns. As his predecessor, Archie Matsos put in three good years on Al Davis's early teams. And give Matt Millen some kudos for nine seasons as a tough inside linebacker.

Cornerback: Willie Brown
Cornerback: Lester Hayes

If Mike Haynes and Dave Grayson had played their entire careers with the Raiders, they might have been included on the dream team. Grayson also played safety for the Raiders and was All-AFL in 1968 and 1969. Willie Brown played 11 of his 16 pro seasons in Oakland and is tied with "Lester the Molester" for career interceptions. Give a few token votes to Fred Williamson, Kent McCloughan, and Skip Thomas, alias Dr. Death.

Strong safety: George Atkinson
Free safety: Jack Tatum

You really can't get much of an argument about these two. Vann McElroy is just a shade behind Tatum. Ditto Mike Davis at strong safety.

Offense

Left tackle: Art Shell
Left guard: Gene Upshaw
Center: Jim Otto

Very, very obvious. Three Hall-of-Famers and certainly among the best offensive linemen who ever laced shoulder pads.

Right tackle: Harry Schuh
Right guard: George Buehler

Schuh played six years with the Raiders and was a superb pass blocker. Henry Lawrence and John Vella should also receive some honorable mention. George Buehler had many memorable battles with "Mean" Joe Greene of the Steelers and deserves the All-Raider honor. Later Mickey Marvin played a competent right guard. Let's give Wayne Hawkins some brownie points for enduring the 1960–62 teams and also for 11 years of stellar service. Besides, Wayne is a nice guy.

Tight end: Todd Christensen

What a difficult selection! Dave Casper was great but the nod goes to Todd for those spectacular catch totals of the middle 1980s. A smidgen below Christensen and Casper are Raymond Chester and Billy Cannon. Had Cannon started his career as a tight end and played longer than six years with the Silver and Black, he might have been the best.

Wide receiver: Fred Bilentnikoff
Wide receiver: Cliff Branch

It can be successfully debated that Freddie B. was the best "possession" receiver ever to play the game. For 13 seasons Cliff Branch was *the* deep threat for Lamonica, Stabler, Blanda, Lawrence, Humm, Raye, Pastorini, Plunkett, and Wilson. (Did we omit anybody?) Cliff

Branch was steady, but Warren Wells and Art Powell were both probably more spectacular and flamboyant in silver and black, but in a shorter time span.

Halfback: Marcus Allen

It is difficult to slight Clem Daniels, Clarence Davis, or Charlie Smith for their contributions, but Marcus is a true superstar who is in a class by himself on the All-Time roster of Raider running backs.

Fullback: Mark van Eeghen

Mark is the clear-cut choice at fullback, but don't forget Marv Hubbard or Hewritt Dixon and all their big plays in big games.

Quarterback: Ken Stabler

If you ask why not Lamonica or even Plunkett, it really can't be answered. Stabler was the regular quarterback for nearly seven seasons. Lamonica toiled six years as top gun and, subtracting time missed for injury, Plunkett started for about five full seasons. Lamonica was AFL Player of the Year in 1967 and 1969 and had gaudy statistics. Stabler played in a Super Bowl championship, an accomplishment that eluded the Mad Bomber. And Plunkett topped Stabler with two Super Bowls. Until Joe Montana came along, the Snake had no peer in pulling out victories in the final seconds.

Special Teams

Kickoff returner: George Atkinson
Punt returner: George Atkinson

This is another difficult selection but Atkinson is picked because of longevity. Both world-class sprinter Bo Roberson and Claude Gibson were dangerous returners in the early sixties and Rodger Bird was a steady performer later. In his three Raider seasons, Ira Matthews was a terror on special teams. But the best one of all may ultimately be Tim Brown, who was selected to the Pro Bowl as a return specialist in 1988.

Place kicker: George Blanda
Punter: Ray Guy

Period. Exclamation point!

Coach: John Madden

I know that Al Davis is finished coaching, so John is the only choice to coach this talented bunch. And if John's ulcer acts up, bring back Tom Flores from Seattle.

Owner, managing general partner, president of the general partner: Al Davis

Lest there be any doubt.

Chapter 18

THE NEXT AL DAVIS

A question that is sometimes quietly asked among Raider fans and the media is: "Who would take over operation of the Raiders if Al Davis either retires or . . . ?" We wont finish that sentence. The oddity of the bylaws of the Raider organization stipulates that the shares of a general partner are not inheritable. However, the limited shares can pass to a wife or children. So the removal of Al Davis from the scene could leave the Raiders with no general partner.

Al Davis now derives his authority in the partnership under the laws of the State of California, which give a general partner the right to make all business decisions. Before the death of Ed McGah, Davis was operating under a 20-year contract. And unless a new general partner is found or created, it is assumed that a successor to Al would be working under a similar contract. And this is where the guessing game starts. There are four possible people who could emerge as "the next Al Davis."

Mark Davis, Al's son, is the nepotistic possibility. Although Mark has occasionally watched a game with his dad from the press box, the younger Davis has never been closely involved in the team. Mark is presently running his own business.

There are three front office people who seem to have the overall experience and abilities to do the job. John Herrera has spent much of his adult life with the Raiders but was also once employed as a young training camp assistant in Santa Rosa. He has done a little bit of everything

293

for the Silver and Black, including public relations, ticket sales, and scouting. Herrera was once a scout with the Redskins and Tampa Bay Buccaneers and had a stint as a general manager of the Saskatchewan Roughriders of the Canadian Football League, so he has been around the block a few times. Whether his management of the Irwindale project is a positive with Al Davis is questionable, but John Herrera has football credentials that would be tough to ignore.

And why not Madden in charge? Not John, but his son Mike. Although Mike was born in 1963, he is a Harvard graduate and is now serving the Raiders as an administrative assistant. Being the son of a head coach doesn't hurt his resumé either. If Al Davis remains on the scene until about 2010, look for young Madden to become increasingly more prominent and visible in the next few years.

And don't forget Al LoCasale. Nobody else in the Raider organization has been as loyal to the boss as his executive assistant and that is not always an easy task. LoCasale had been a scout and player personnel director with the Chargers and Bengals before joining Al Davis in 1969. "Little Al" has also attended numerous owner meetings, both with and without Davis, and has also been close to the brain trust for both franchise moves. LoCasale is presently the closest thing in the Raider hierarchy to a public relations director.

If Al Davis stays with the Raiders until overcome by "the death business," his last will and testament would probably include some zinger about a successor that would turn the football world upside-down. Al Davis has repeatedly said that "The greatness of the Raiders is in our future." As difficult as it may be to fathom, there will someday be a future for the Raiders without Al Davis.

Chapter 19

AND THE LUCKY CITY IS . . .

"I never got into it [moving] with St. Louis. But New York was very interesting. Their approach was, 'You'd be coming home.' "
            —Al Davis, August 23, 1989

Luxury boxes. It is unlikely you will find that term defined in your typical dictionary. But Al Davis knows what it means and so does every other owner in professional sports. Similar to a lavish hotel suite, a luxury box allows affluent fans to sit in their own private rooms away from the masses. The game is usually viewed through a plate-glass window. There is a fully-stocked bar, a desk, sofa or bed, and many other amenities. The first luxury boxes were placed in the Houston Astrodome in 1965. More stylish luxury boxes were an integral part of Texas Stadium, built by the Dallas Cowboys in 1972. But wealthy patrons for football games are not limited to Texas oilmen. Nearly all arenas and stadiums that have been planned and built since 1972 have included that magical ingredient: luxury boxes.

Owners will kill to get luxury boxes. They can also move their franchises because they don't have them. There is a very logical reason why Al Davis and other sportsmen want luxury boxes in their facilities. Unlike regular ticket receipts, which must be shared with the visiting clubs, all revenues from luxury boxes revert to the home team. For example, if the Los Angeles Rams can rent 100 luxury boxes at $50,000 per season, they will gross $5 million more than a team that doesn't have this amenity. With salaries in the National Football League increasing every year and the total free agency of rookie and veteran players always a strong possibility, the extra $5 million can come in handy. You don't have to be an Einstein or an Al Davis to realize that teams with luxury box seats have a distinct financial advantage over the other clubs in the league. The additional money means that the Rams would have a large financial advantage over the Raiders in signing players. Obviously a man like Al Davis, who is obsessed with winning and producing championship teams, will not take kindly to competing in the marketplace at a pronounced disadvantage.

After Al Davis moved to Los Angeles in 1982 and then won all the legal battles to stay there, it would have been assumed that both the Raiders and the Southland would live happily ever after, locked in holy football matrimony. Certainly the last scenario that any person would expect was that the soap opera titled "Where Will the Raiders Play?" would be repeated. But the sports pages for much of the latter part of the decade were devoted to the same story that made headlines in the early 1980s, as Davis expressed both private and public displeasure with his accommodations at Los Angeles Memorial Coliseum. Why? All together now: It was those "luxury boxes."

Perhaps it shouldn't have been so surprising. Al Davis has always been a precise person who knows exactly what he needs to keep the Raiders on top of the heap. He occasionally had trouble coexisting with the grandstanding politicians and slow-moving bureaucrats who were his landlords. That was proved in Oakland. Los Angeles had a different cast of characters, but their modus operandi was really the same as Oakland's. The nine-member Los

Angeles Memorial Coliseum Commission (LAMCC), which also manages the adjacent Sports Arena, consists of three representatives each from the City of Los Angeles, L.A. County, and the State of California. The turnover on the commission was frequent, with new members often espousing totally different ideas from their predecessors. Even before the Raiders came to town, the Coliseum Commission had accumulated an abysmal track record in their relationships with professional sports teams. During a 10-year period from 1968 to 1978, it had lost the Los Angeles Lakers basketball team, the Kings hockey club, and the Los Angeles Rams as tenants. Later when the Raiders moved to Los Angeles, the UCLA football team left the Coliseum for the Rose Bowl in Pasadena. Perhaps Al Davis should have done a more thorough background check before he came to Los Angeles. History dictated that what eventually happened was inevitable.

The present story really began in 1984, shortly after the closing ceremonies of the 1984 Summer Olympics. After operating in L.A. on a "memorandum of understanding" for two years, the Raiders agreed to a 10-year lease with the Los Angeles Coliseum Commission. It was signed on December 9, 1984, and was retroactive to the 1982 season. The agreement called for the Raiders to construct the luxury box seats that Al Davis had wanted in Oakland but was denied. Now they would finally be installed. Although not a part of the written agreement, the LAMCC would be responsible for other Coliseum improvements including the reconfiguration of the remaining 92,000 seats. The lease included three five year options for the Raiders, who could conceivably enjoy the income from the luxury boxes until 2007 without having to negotiate a new agreement. "It's our hope that the Coliseum and the Raiders have a great marriage," said Davis.

Now let's move to 1986. Two years later and there were still no luxury boxes in Los Angeles Coliseum. It was a hot August night, but the leaves were not hanging down, as Neil Diamond would say. It was the night of the first Raider exhibition game of the season. Construction cranes shared the Coliseum floor with the Raiders and the Dallas Cowboys. It appeared that the kickoff of the long-awaited luxury box seats and other renovations was finally going to occur just as Al Davis was promised when he moved to Los Angeles. Davis was ready to build the luxury boxes but was waiting for the Coliseum Commission to commence with the other work. But Alexander Haagen, the president of the Coliseum Commission, said, "It's not part of the lease, Al." The Raiders felt that the $21 million that the Coliseum received from the NFL in damages from the lawsuit should be used to improve the stadium. Al Davis was not going to engage in a mud-slinging contest with Haagen. He waited a few months. Finally on February 18, 1987, after 1,700 existing seats were ripped out as preparation for luxury box installation, the Raiders ordered the removal of the construction cranes. A week later, a Raiders official was quoted as saying, "The situation in L.A. is becoming hauntingly familiar to the one in Oakland several years ago."

In April, after Los Angeles mayor Tom Bradley made an attempt to settle the dispute, the Coliseum asked the Raiders to resume construction. Haagen, a real estate developer who was admired in Los Angeles for building shopping malls in poor neighborhoods, admitted that the Coliseum didn't have the money. But what about the money you won in court, Walter? Irv Kaze of the Raider front office spoke for his boss. "We question the Coliseum Commission's credibility. They have violated all the previous agreements. They have misled us." On April 24, the Raiders formally canceled the construction of 60 luxury boxes on the north side of the Coliseum.

Enemies of Al Davis have claimed that sports columnist Melvin Durslag is a mouthpiece of the Raider owner. Friends will say that Durslag and Al think alike. On April

27, 1987, under the title of "Look for Davis to Look Around," Durslag accurately sized up the situation in the *Los Angeles Herald-Examiner.* "A distinguished alienator of tenants, driving more away than any landlord in sports, the Coliseum Commission now must figure its next move . . . Some prophets whisper knowingly, 'Davis would never leave L.A. after going to all that trouble to get there.' Obviously, such prophets don't reckon with the Davis philosophy, namely, take your loss and get even next week."

And Davis *did* start to look around. Other potential sites in Southern California, including the county fairgrounds in Pomona, the site of the Hollywood Park Racetrack in Inglewood, and private land in Carson and Hawthorne, both close to the Raiders' training facility in El Segundo, were now being mentioned as alternate stadium sites for the Raiders, but no serious plans or offers appeared. There were also some preliminary meetings with Sacramento interests. The relationship between the Raiders and the Coliseum Commission was cool, but conventional wisdom (Durslag's comments notwithstanding) dictated that the landlord and tenant would settle their differences and that the luxury boxes would eventually be built. They never were.

Enter Irwindale. Irwinwho? On May 18, 1987, this tiny city in the San Gabriel Valley sent a letter to the Raiders indicating their interest in obtaining the Silver and Black. Raider executive John Herrera and a three-man negotiating team representing Irwindale begin talking on June 15. Al Davis toured the stadium site on June 28. Was he impressed with what was soon to become the most famous gravel pit west of the Mississippi? Yes, because serious discussions between Herrera and Irwindale ensued over the next six weeks.

There were more negotiations, including a marathon 10-hour session on August 20 that finalized the deal. At 7:15 that night, Al Davis signed on the dotted line. The

Raiders agreed to move to a proposed new stadium in the wealthy but tiny town at the intersection of the 210 and 605 freeways, about 20 miles east of Los Angeles Coliseum. The City of Irwindale would float about $95,000,000 in bonds to finance the construction of the stadium, which would be ready in 1991, maybe sooner. The money would be given to the Raiders, who would supervise the construction. "Raiders Stadium" would have luxury boxes. "If they are a renegade team, then we are a renegade city," said Xavier Hermosillo, the chief negotiator for Irwindale, who promised that the mostly Hispanic city would bid for the 1992 Super Bowl. And Mr. Davis, how solid is this deal? "We have committed to Irwindale. There is no alternative. You got that?"

Interesting reactions came from within the NFL. "Having a new place, his own stadium, sounds just like Al," said New Orleans general manager Jim Finks. Dallas president Tex Schramm, probably echoing the feelings of close friend Pete Rozelle, was more pessimistic: "I don't know if he [Davis]) will ever be happy." Bill Robertson, no longer a member of the LAMCC, blamed his successor. "Alexander Haagen is the true villain," he said.

To quiet the pundits and cynics (which probably included Al Davis) who questioned how a small town of about 1,000 people could satisfy a difficult man and his team by building a stadium in a gravel pit, Irwindale gave Al Davis $10,000,000 of non-refundable, good faith money to secure the deal. Another $10,000,000 was to be delivered to Davis when the stadium was completed. "Raiders of the lost park!" "Just dig, baby!" So much for conventional wisdom.

All was well in Irwindale, which was suddenly attracting favorable national attention. In an era of large budget deficits, Irwindale was seen as a model of a fiscally-sound and well governed city with virtually no urban problems. This little bump on the freeway had succeeded in making the larger city of Los Angeles look foolish and inept.

But the euphoria in Irwindale was not to last. Even in a small town, the usual problems of people, politics, and money can get in the way of progress. Not to mention Los Angeles city and county politicians who were embarrassed and jealous of the Irwindale deal. Los Angeles was not going to lose the Raiders without a fight and started looking for loopholes in the agreement to dig that proposed hole in the ground.

They didn't have to look very far. Because the parking lot for the Irwindale stadium would require filling federal wetlands with dirt, the U.S. Army Corps of Engineers had to issue a permit, which would be predicated on an environmental report. Irwindale apparently did not include the planning and filling of the 40-acre parcel in their package presented to the Raiders. Los Angeles city councilman Ernani Bernardi filed suit against the Raider move and on September 29, 1987, Judge Ricardo Torres issued a preliminary injunction, temporarily halting the project. The issuance of bonds was blocked and Irwindale was forced to prepare an expensive ($3 million) environmental impact statement. Three days later, the LAMCC filed a $57 million breach-of-contract suit against the Silver and Black.

On November 24, 1987, Dave Newhouse of the *Oakland Tribune* wrote the most perceptive column of his career. Quoting Oakland Coliseum Board president George Vukasin, who stated that "Irwindale is a tough row to hoe," Newhouse came to a logical conclusion. "Let's say Oakland tries to beg for another NFL team, to avoid chancing expansion. It should beg in a southerly direction. Why not? Los Angeles stole the Raiders from us, why shouldn't we steal them back?" Vukasin admitted he had talked to Al Davis about the expansion of the Oakland Coliseum, but not about the possible relocation of the Raiders.

While the environmental impact statement was being prepared, the natives were growing restless. In June 1988, Irwindale voters elected two new city council members who were less than enthralled with the Raider deal. The original team of three negotiators was quickly eradicated. Irwindale fired Hermosillo, the $8,500-a-month consultant who was their primary negotiator. Next to be excused was Frederick P. Lyte, another consultant and the number two man in the Raider pact. That left Charles Martin on the Irwindale staff as the lone Raider negotiator. He was both city manager and city attorney. However, a court order related to another deal barred Martin from involvement in the Raider stadium agreement.

It was now obvious that the Irwindale accord, which seemed flimsy to many from the git-go, was in serious trouble. The Los Angeles Memorial Coliseum Commission filed a separate lawsuit against the Raiders for back payment of a $6.7 million loan, which was part of the 1982 Memorandum of Agreement. The team was also precluded from exercising the three five-year options on their lease. The court was told that the Coliseum Commission wanted to be legally free to find another team after the Raiders left. In August 1988, the Raiders filed a countersuit against the Los Angeles Coliseum Commission and claimed that they had no further obligations to move, because "Irwindale did not furnish either the promised building sites or the $115 million loan" and that any deal had lapsed. Although Raider officials were still publicly committed to Irwindale, Davis knew that the 1987 agreement was legally dead. The Raiders quietly started exploring all their options.

During the 1988 season, Al Davis was also silently starting to question whether he wanted to spend his football future in Southern California. The Los Angeles Rams, who were playing in modern Anaheim Stadium, were also having trouble filling 65,000 seats. The Rams only had two sellouts in 1988. The passive crowds in

Anaheim didn't appear to affect the outcome on the field: The Rams were only 4–4 at home, but 6–2 on the road for 1988. Raider attendance was also lagging. Although the Raiders announced an opening day throng of 45,171 for 1988, there were actually less than 40,000 present. Two weeks later when the Rams came to the Coliseum, the attendance was 86,007, but a 92,000+ sellout should have been expected to see the two Los Angeles teams square off on a sunny Sunday afternoon. But the real turn-off for Davis came on October 2 against Cincinnati. In the previous week, the Raiders rallied from a 24–0 halftime deficit in Denver to win an exciting 30–27 overtime thriller. New quarterback and local hero Jay Schroeder was brilliant in leading the comeback before a "Monday Night" national TV audience. The opposition Bengals were 4–0 and headed for a Super Bowl. With all of these factors plus good weather, it would have been reasonable for Davis to expect a crowd of 60,000 to 70,000. The attendance was 45,584, minus about 3,000 no-shows. To add insult to injury, the Raiders were routed by Cincinnati, so most of the crowd left early. Al Davis knew then that he might not want to stay in Los Angeles or Irwindale.

The problems with the Irwindale deal attracted the attention of the *Los Angeles Times,* which urged the Coliseum Commission to seriously negotiate with the Raiders. In a December 30, 1988, editorial, the *Times* noted that "there hasn't been a wider window of opportunity to save the hometown team in a long while. For starters, the commission should make good on its offer to build luxury boxes. The blame for driving the Raiders away rests with the commission. The same crowd should now take responsibility in bringing the team back home."

Enter Oakland. Again? In August 1988, just as the pages of the Irwindale agreement were starting to turn yellow, the Fred Edelstein newsletter, a weekly NFL insider and gossip sheet, reported that the City of Oakland, which still owed the Raiders about $9 million in legal costs from losing the "eminent domain" lawsuit which was supposed to prevent the Raiders from leaving in 1981, would concoct a creative settlement with the Silver and Black that would be part of a larger package to move back to Oakland.

Edelstein was partially correct. On October 12, 1988, the Raiders and the City of Oakland announced a settlement of the damages from the eminent domain suit. Oakland would pay the Raiders $4 million plus their attorney fees of $3.2 million. "This settlement marks the end of Oakland's dealings with the Raiders," was the statement issued from Mayor Lionel Wilson and City Attorney Jayne Williams. Speculation that the Raiders might return to Oakland "is just whistling in the wind," said Councilman Wilson Riles, Jr., who added, "I think we will get an expansion franchise before we would ever get the Raiders back."

At about the same time, *Sportspage News*, a Raider newspaper in the Bay Area, was launching a petition drive to ask the East Bay politicians to open negotiations that would bring Al Davis back. In December, Alameda County supervisor Charles Santana met with Don Maroney, the publisher of *Sportspage News*, to feel out the possibility of getting the Raiders back. Also expressing an interest in a Raiders return to Oakland was Don Perata, chairman of the board of supervisors in Alameda County. Perata and Santana next met with Ed DeSilva, a local construction contractor, about the prospects of the Raiders returning to Oakland. DeSilva then talked to his close friend Jack Brooks, who was the second largest holder of Raider stock. Brooks discussed the likelihood with Davis, who apparently did not discourage the possibility of moving back. George Vukasin, the chairman of the Oakland–Alameda County Coliseum Board, was told by Perata and Santana to prepare a proposal. There were indications that Vukasin was also encouraged to submit a proposal by Al Davis during a secret meeting at Lake Tahoe in February 1989. Secret discussions soon began. It was leaked to the press in May. DeSilva and Brooks were representing Al Davis in the talks.

The Bay Area effort was fueled by a scheduled exhibition game at the Oakland Coliseum in August between the Raiders and the Houston Oilers. Perhaps Al Davis was cunningly re-testing the waters of support in Oakland. When tickets went on sale for the game on March 26, 1989, the fans made like Moby Dick and swallowed 50,000 seats (priced at $15, $25, $30, and $35 each) within 2½ hours. Neither Michael Jackson, Madonna, or anyone else ever produced a faster sellout in Oakland. The fan support was obviously still there.

Sacramento was also reentering the picture. Considering both the personality of the Sacramento representatives and the Oakland history of failed negotiations with the Raiders, a bid from the capital city of California was not totally unexpected. Developer Gregg Lukenbill, who originally made a mark in his father's construction business, was a symbol of the new money in Sacramento. In 1984, Lukenbill and his group purchased the Kansas City Kings basketball team and one year later moved them to his hometown of Sacramento. He first built a temporary arena to house the Kings and then constructed Arco Arena, a 16,000-seat permanent facility next door. Sacramento now had a "big league" image and Lukenbill was being hailed as a local hero in the capital city. Because all of the land at a proposed stadium site was owned by Lukenbill's real estate development group and private financing could be utilized, the rezoning of this farmland would be the only governmental involvement in the construction process.

Why stop at basketball? Lukenbill and his associates from the Sacramento Sports Association contacted Davis in 1987, after the breakdown between Davis and the Los Angeles Coliseum Commission. Talk of attracting a baseball team to Sacramento also started in 1987. On one Sunday afternoon, 20,000 people came by the busload from Sacramento to an Oakland A's home game to indicate their support for a major league baseball franchise in their hometown. Lukenbill started preparing engineering plans for a 42,000-seat baseball park adjacent to Arco Arena. Football in Sacramento? No problem. Scrap the baseball plans and build a 70,000-seat football stadium instead. Meanwhile, Lukenbill heard the rumors about the Raiders talking to Oakland and called Al Davis.

The Sacramento bid for the Raiders was revived in February 1989, on the same day that Vukasin had his secret encounter with Davis. Living 80 miles away from Oakland in Sacramento, Lukenbill certainly remembered the rancor that was part of the Raiders' move to Los Angeles in 1982. He knew that negotiations to keep the Raiders in Oakland in the early 1980s had failed because the three different entities (Oakland City Council, Alameda County Board of Supervisors, and the Oakland Coliseum Board) that must approve any package given to the Raiders were not united and could not agree on a deal. Lukenbill also realized that many of the same cast of characters who were present when Al Davis moved the Raiders to Los Angeles were still in office, including Mayor Lionel Wilson of Oakland. The Raiders had always had a big following in Sacramento and their games were still broadcast and televised there. Lukenbill concluded that Sacramento had a real shot at the Silver and Black. So why not go for it? After some initial feelers, Lukenbill secretly met for four hours with Davis on May 19 at Arco Arena and was encouraged to prepare a definitive offer.

By the middle of May 1989, despite denials by everybody in California and elsewhere, three cities were entered in the race for the Raiders. Although the Los Angeles newspapers were urging that a new proposal be given to the Raiders, the Memorial Coliseum Commission was entangled in litigation against the team. The MCA Music Entertainment Group was now assisting in the operation of the Coliseum and Sports Arena and they hired Spectacor, a company that managed the operation or construction of stadiums and arenas. Spectacor was admired by sports executives for its success with the construction of Joe Robbie Stadium in Miami, which was totally financed with private funds and revenues from future sales of luxury seats. Richard Riordan, the new chairman of the Coliseum Commission; Irving Azoff, the head of MCA, and Joel Cohen of Spectacor met with Al Davis on June 16, 1989. An informal proposal to renovate the Coliseum was discussed. Davis told the group that he would only discuss formal and definite plans. The next step was for the full commission to vote to prepare a formal offer to the Raiders. MCA and Spectacor were only consultants to the LAMCC; they were not even authorized to directly negotiate with the Raiders. It did not appear that Al Davis was prepared to wait for Los Angeles to decide to make him an offer.

Of course, it was all "unofficial." If the Raiders publicly acknowledged that they were "negotiating" with Oakland, Sacramento, or Los Angeles, the City of Irwindale would probably await their turn behind L.A. in court. But Irwindale had other things to worry about. Because of an increase in interest rates on bond purchases and the added expense of building the parking lot, the cost of the Irwindale stadium was now estimated at $170 million. Besides the $10 million of "good faith" money given Davis in August 1987, no funding had ever been produced to finance the stadium. There was a real concern in Irwindale that the $10 million was already down the drain and would never be recovered if the stadium was not built. Hermosillo, now back in the good graces of the Irwindale City Council, announced that there was only a $35 million shortfall and that "there are literally hundreds of proposals dealing with the money situation, and it's just a matter of coming up with the right one."

They never did. In a meeting with the Raiders on June 14, 1989, Irwindale was given 30 days to put together a financing package or the Raiders would abandon the project. Hermosillo was now quoted as saying it would be the end of the year before Irwindale would produce the money. By the end of 1989, Hermosillo was no longer employed by Irwindale and was representing a group that was trying to secure private financing to build stadiums and arenas all over the country. Hermosillo hoped his first client would be Al Davis.

During the next few weeks, discussions between the Raiders and Oakland became more intense. Al Davis made an unexpected visit to the Oakland Coliseum on June 22 and talked to Vukasin by phone four days later, ostensibly to discuss the August exhibition game. Finally on July 12, 1989, a financing package that had been negotiated between Raider partner Jack Brooks and Oakland representatives was presented to the Oakland City Council in a closed-door session. The package included a $32 million "franchise fee" that would be paid to Al Davis before the Raiders ever played a game in Oakland. In the elaborate bond funding proposal, local tax money would have to cover any revenue shortfalls, i.e., if the Raiders didn't sell out. Of course, luxury boxes would be part of an expanded Oakland Coliseum. The city council reportedly expressed "stunned disbelief" according to one source. Two days later the Oakland representatives agreed to resume negotiations with Brooks and DeSilva. Mayor Lionel Wilson called for more studies on the Raider deal, which prompted *Oakland Tribune* columnist Dave Newhouse to warn Oakland not to fumble the ball. On July 16, Newhouse wrote: "This is a first, Oakland, and a last. You blow the Raiders and you don't get an expansion franchise. The National Football League has conveniently written you off as an expansion possibility. So it's the Raiders or nothing, Oakland. Your move."

Newhouse's column had an immediate effect. On July 18 in a letter to DeSilva, Perata stated that East Bay interests had reworked their proposal and submitted a "strong competitive bid" for DeSilva to deliver to Jack Brooks. "We have a formal proposal now on its way to the Raiders," said Perata, who expected a response within two weeks.

While the *Oakland Tribune* was reporting the latest news in the Raider story, the *San Francisco Chronicle* was getting in its shots. Glenn Dickey, never a fan of Davis, wrote on July 19 that "the Oakland negotiators are naive" and are "chasing a dream." In the *Los Angeles Daily News,* Ron Rappaport was also cynical. "Sometimes I think that if Oakland didn't exist, we would have to invent it," chided Rappaport, gleefully calling the Oakland negotiators "suckers."

The Raider exhibition game in Oakland had come and gone, and the many rumors of Davis announcing a move during the festive weekend all proved to be false. "Al Davis Hints Oakland Is in Front" was the headline in the August 24, 1989, *Tribune.* The Oakland negotiators said they expected an answer by the middle of September. Following the wild fan support at the exhibition game, Dave Newhouse wrote, "How could he [Davis] ever say no to this?"

He didn't say no. But he didn't say yes either. While the Raiders were opening the 1989 season before about 41,000 spectators in Los Angeles Memorial Coliseum, it was disclosed that the Oakland bid actually included a $54 million franchise fee, not the $32 million that had previously been reported. The full package, including improvements to the Oakland Coliseum totaled more than $239 million. However, there were three major points of contention between the Oakland negotiators and Al Davis. The Raiders wanted a 10-year lease instead of the 15-year term being offered. Oakland wanted protection against possible lawsuits by Los Angeles, Irwindale, or Sacramento should the Raiders come back. Finally, there was apprehension about advancing a "franchise fee" to the Raiders in June 1990, before a home game was ever played in Oakland. What if Al Davis changed his mind? Obviously the folly of Irwindale giving Al $10 million of non-refundable money and not building the stadium was not lost on Oakland.

The Sacramento front was quiet. Because Lukenbill's proposal included the purchase of 20% ownership of the Raiders and a 20-year lease, it was assumed that Davis was not seriously interested. Next, the Sacramento Sports Association admitted that it needed help from taxpayers to fund the $50 million franchise fee and $100 million stadium costs that were being tendered. On September 13, the Sacramento City Council unanimously voted 9–0 to provide funding of $50 million to assist the Sacramento Sports Association effort. The next day, the Sacramento County Board Of Supervisors gave a similar stamp of approval. The proposal given by Sacramento allowed the Raiders to share potential revenues that would accrue from concessions and parking from a major-league baseball team. Of course, Sacramento didn't have a baseball team. They also didn't have a stadium. "Now we can roll out the red carpet for Al Davis," said Lukenbill, who then ridiculed Oakland negotiator Don Perata: "I wonder who he's negotiating with, the tight end or the quarterback. I'm the only guy negotiating with Al."

In the tradition of an old-time preacher whipping an audience into a frenzy, the populace of the Sacramento area responded to Lukenbill and the political approvals by jamming the telephone lines with orders for season tickets. While putting the ticket requests into a vault, Lukenbill said he expected an answer from Davis within 90 days.

If there were any doubts that the Irwindale bid was all

but legally dead, they were dispelled by Hermosillo's reaction to the events in Sacramento and the Raiders' terse response. "Lukenbill must live in a dream world. Don't deceive the people of Sacramento. They deserve better," said Hermosillo. While not acknowledging negotiations with either Sacramento or Oakland, Raider executive John Herrera, who had previously only spoken positively of Hermosillo, suddenly changed his tune. "Xavier's comments are ludicrous; they don't serve any purpose. They [Irwindale] have failed by not putting together the deal in a timely fashion. Nobody gave Irwindale the right to string this along for an indefinite period of time."

Meanwhile, the Los Angeles Coliseum Commission continued fiddling while the flames were burning up north. Because Al Davis would not sign an agreement stating that anything said in prospective negotiations to keep the Raiders in L.A. could not be used in his lawsuit against the Coliseum Commission, neither MCA nor Spectacor was even allowed to present a formal offer. So while both Oakland and Sacramento were moving very fast, the reconstruction of Los Angeles Coliseum was still languishing in the discussion stages. Al Davis reiterated that the Raiders would only consider a formal written proposal.

Significant opposition to the Raiders' moving back to Oakland came from an unexpected source, the Athletics baseball club. The A's were using their clout as the tenant that stayed home after the Raiders left. They were also a pennant-winning team that had just set an attendance record. An unidentified Coliseum Board member told the *Oakland Tribune* on October 6 that "The deal the way it is now, the A's are going to leave. It's awfully odd that he [Supervisor Don Perata] can negotiate with Al Davis but can't pick up a phone to call the A's." Obviously this led to the public disclosure of the rancor that apparently had been simmering between Perata and members of the

Coliseum Board. Perata threatened to dissolve the board and have Alameda County directly run the Coliseum. The A's delayed any formal talks about the impact of the Raider negotiations until after the World Series. However, because of an unexpected appearance of Mother Nature, the World Series took longer to play than anyone expected.

The earthquake that struck the Bay Area on October 17, 1989, caused damage to the walkway leading from the BART subway to the Oakland Coliseum parking lot. Many observers thought that it might permanently damage the Oakland effort to return the Raiders. There was already some opposition in Oakland based on urban problems such as the homeless, drug wars, and a bankrupt school system. Advocates said that these should be addressed with the money earmarked for the Raiders. Now, because of the earthquake damage in Oakland, which included the collapse of the Cypress Structure of the Nimitz Freeway that killed 41 people and riveted national attention on the rescue effort, the Raiders quickly became a secondary concern. One Oakland official said that "The Raider deal isn't on the back burner, it may be out of the kitchen." Even Don Perata, the leader of the Oakland bid, told C. W. Nevius of the *San Francisco Chronicle* that "This may be nature's way of saying we have to move on to other things."

Los Angeles interests saw the earthquake as an opportunity to seriously reenter the Raider sweepstakes. On October 20, county supervisor Kenneth Hahn, who was influential in attracting the Dodgers in 1957, ordered round-the-clock talks between the Coliseum Commission and the Raiders. Hahn surmised that the Raiders are "worth $50 million to $100 million to the local economy."

The conclusion of the World Series was delayed until October 30, 1989, and the A's finally expressed their concerns in a meeting on November 14. No resolutions or agreements with the A's were consummated. "The A's are not going to stop the deal," said Coliseum president George Vukasin.

Following a November 8 meeting with Al Davis in El Segundo, where the Raiders managing general partner expressed reluctance about selling part of the Raiders to a group of businessmen he hardly knew, Gregg Lukenbill contemplated publicly that he might drop his insistence that the Sacramento Sports Association buy into the Raiders. But the November 8 meeting ended with Lukenbill storming out of Davis's office and the acrimony was obviously not helping the Sacramento effort. Davis actually gave Lukenbill an option to buy Raider stock but refused to give him the opportunity to share in the cash flow for the first five years that the Raiders would play in Sacramento.

On the football field, the Raiders were trying to secure their first playoff berth in four years, and the feeling from all the hopeful cities was that Al Davis would not select his future home until after the 1989 season was over. The apparent timetable did not stop Oakland from sending their "final offer" to the Raiders on November 28. They stuck to their insistence on a 15-year lease, made the Raiders legally responsible for lawsuits, and stipulated that the Raiders would refund the franchise fee if the deal fell through. Both Mayor Wilson and Supervisor Perata were pessimistic. "An answer from Davis should come within two or three weeks," said Perata.

On December 6, lawyers from the Los Angeles Raiders met with East Bay negotiators to discuss their final offer. The pessimism soon faded. "I'm optimistic that it will go all the way," said an Alameda County administrator. The *Oakland Tribune* reported that "a final answer may be only a week away."

Enter Los Angeles. Commission president Richard Riordan and representatives from Spectacor met with Al Davis on December 11 to discuss the details for renovating Los Angeles Coliseum. "I would say I'm still a bit pessimistic," said Riordan. Besides the acceptance of Al Davis, Riordan may have been skeptical about the other problems attached to his informal offer. Because it was the site of both the 1932 and 1984 Summer Olympic games, the Coliseum had been designated an historical landmark by both the State of California and the federal government, which would indicate that nothing less than an act of God would be required before any alterations to the facility could be undertaken. That could mean a lengthy study and approval process. As the fourth horse out of a field of four, and trailing in the home stretch, the last thing Riordan wanted was an obstacle like an environmental impact statement blocking him from the finish line.

Another negative for the last-minute Los Angeles efforts came from columnist Melvin Durslag, who moved to the *Times* when the *Herald-Examiner* went out of business on December 2. Lambasting the Coliseum Commission, MCA, and Spectacor for their tenuous relationship and the informal proposal, Durslag concluded that "a feeling exists here . . . that the Raiders who like to go deep will go 400 miles."

As the new year began, the L.A. Coliseum Commission hired a financial consultant to assist MCA and Spectacor in preparing a "formal" offer to Davis. The decision to present the formal offer was approved unanimously by the L.A. Coliseum Commission on January 10, 1990. "His decision is very close. I think he'll make a decision in January," said Riordan.

Oakland officials were unfazed by the Los Angeles bid and thought that, rather than presenting a viable offer to the Raiders, L.A. was really laying the groundwork toward attracting an expansion team. Don Perata told the *Tribune* that a tentative agreement with Oakland could be completed as early as mid-January. George Vukasin expected a resolution by the end of January. "There is no time to drag this on," he said.

After losing away games in Seattle and New York to finish 8–8, the Raiders missed the playoffs. But Al Davis soon went on a road trip of his own. After attending a funeral near Oakland for Andy Hererra, John's father, on January 5, his chartered plane flew to Arco Arena, where he met with Lukenbill and his associates. Various politicians were also present. Sacramento mayor Anne Rudin was not invited and was annoyed that Lukenbill had not brought her together with Davis. Al was not pleased to be confronted by 27 politicians and had words with Lukenbill. Many who attended the three-hour meeting looked confused when confronted by the media and offered no positive response when asked what happened in the meeting. "He's still very interested in Sacramento," said city manager Walter Slipe.

The following week, Al Davis visited the Oakland Coliseum and met with Mayor Wilson, Supervisor Don Perata, and others. Officials were cautious but upbeat. "On a scale of one to ten, I would place it at about eight," said Wilson when asked about the Oakland chances of regaining the Raiders. During the meeting, the final Oakland offer was handed to Davis. It was reported that it would require another meeting in about two weeks before Davis was ready to make a decision.

The concerns that the baseball Athletics expressed about the Raiders proposal were not previously resolved. During a Democratic Party club meeting on January 18, Mayor Wilson said that the A's were making "unconscionable demands" of the Coliseum Board. Wilson's claim was downplayed by both Vukasin and Perata. Some observers thought Davis would make his announcement in New Orleans during the week of the Super Bowl, before the thousands of national media representatives who were present. They were wrong.

If Al Davis was adhering to NFL rules concerning franchise relocation, he would have formally notified Commissioner Paul Tagliabue of his intentions to move no later than January 15. It was not publicly disclosed whether Al followed this procedure. However, during the annual "state of the league" press conference that preceded the Super Bowl, Tagliabue said, "The stadium situation in Los Angeles is wanting. . . . Al has told me he has found his stadium situation unsuitable." On January 27, Davis told Jon Rochmis of the *Oakland Tribune* that "the Commissioner said that L.A. Coliseum was not a suitable place to play, not a suitable stadium for a National Football League team." When the Super Bowl was over, Al Davis left the New Orleans Superdome, muttered something to San Francisco television reporter Mark Ibanez about how the Denver Broncos embarrassed the American Football Conference (San Francisco routed Denver 55–10) but said nothing about either where or when he would decide the future home of the Silver and Black.

It may be said that if you can't beat Al Davis on the football field or in the courts, beat him in public opinion polls. On February 5, 1990, the *Oakland Tribune* printed the results of a Gallup poll concerning the Raiders. The questions were directed to Oakland residents only. The results indicated that 39% of the respondents said returning the Raiders was "important" and 17% thought it was "very important." Although the Gallup organization acknowledged that about half the population of the United States doesn't follow football and that the 39% reading on the Raiders was good, the *Tribune* was not impressed. In a February 9, 1990, editorial titled "No Mandate for the Raiders," the *Tribune* concluded that "the majority of Oaklanders don't put the Raiders' return on their agenda. So officials negotiating the deal should be more cautious than ever in making sure they don't give away the store to try to restore the glory of the now-mediocre Silver and Black."

Not to be outdone by their newspaper brethren to the north, the *Los Angeles Times* printed the results of a poll on February 12, 1990, that placed the Raiders fifth in popularity among L.A. professional teams, ahead of only the hapless Clippers basketball club and the Kings hockey franchise. Of the Angelenos who participated in the poll, 67% said they would be upset "hardly at all" if the Raiders moved. Most preferred that, rather than satisfying Al Davis, the Coliseum Commission should look for another team. Davis was not pleased. "The poll was a joke. It had no credibility. They went to Orange County," he said.

On February 15, 1990, Oakland mayor Wilson and Alameda county supervisor Perata announced that the Raider negotiators had basically agreed to a deal with the locals. The Raiders agreed to a 15-year lease, would refund the advance payment of $31.9 million, due in June 1990 if they didn't return, and would be liable for damages if the other "suitors" sued the city or county. A joint public hearing and vote was set for March 12. One stumbling block remained: the Oakland A's.

The press delighted in throwing around the number "$602,000,000" as if it were penny candy. *San Francisco Examiner* columnist Rob Morse delighted in adding the additional numbers if the Raiders and the Coliseum Board agreed to a nine-year option. He then threw in the insurance and other miscellaneous costs of stadium operation and made it a "billion-dollar deal."

The agreement included a $54.9 million franchise fee to the Raiders that would be repaid over nine years and $53.5 million in bonds that would be sold by Alameda County and the City of Oakland to renovate the Coliseum, which would be managed by the Raiders, who would be responsible for cost overruns. The city and county would guarantee the Raiders $7.5 million in annual ticket sales and be responsible for the marketing and sales of seats. Although the proposed ticket prices were high, if the Raiders sold out for all the 15 years of the lease, the local governments could earn about $50 million in direct revenue and millions more in indirect benefits.

Although there was much public comment by the A's about dust from construction activities and changes to the sight lines in the outfield, there was only one real concern for the Athletics: money. It was solved on February 26. The A's verbally agreed to an additional $500,000 per year in stadium revenue, bringing their annual haul to $2,000,000 per year. The lease would be rewritten to allow the A's an unrestricted escape in 1996 if their joint occupation with the Raiders was less than successful. Although not publicly disclosed, the six years would also allow the Coliseum Board to buy time to plan and build a baseball-only ballpark for the Athletics. The concept of separate football and baseball stadiums in Oakland is not new: After the Raiders departed in 1982, the Coliseum Board presented the plan to the NFL in its pitch for an expansion team.

In an apparent last-ditch effort to win the Raiders, Lukenbill and his partner Fred Anderson spent four hours talking with Davis and Raider attorney Amy Trask on February 13. They reluctantly increased the annual parking revenues for the Raiders to $5 million. Davis was noncommittal. Meanwhile, the $50 million bonds that were part of the Sacramento offer were due to expire on February 28. Sacramento mayor Anne Rudin set a deadline: "If there is no answer by then, the offer is off the table. Ninety days—three months—is enough time for anybody to make up his mind." Sacramento City Council member Joe Serna, Jr., was more direct: "We're not so anxious for an NFL team that we're willing to prostrate ourselves before Al Davis or anyone else any longer."

February passed without a Raider deal for Sacramento. Lukenbill held a news conference on March 2 to announce that the capital's bid for the team was over. It was later revealed that one of the major problems with the Sacramento bid was the absence of a temporary facility for the Raiders to play in while Lukenbill's stadium was being built. Considered was a 7,500-seat "stadium" at Cal State–Sacramento and the 22,000-capacity Hughes Stadium at Sacramento City College. Also examined was a 30,000-seat field at the University of Pacific in Stockton, located about 40 miles from Sacramento. Al Davis balked at playing there. The Stockton Raiders would have been a bit much for everyone, including Al Davis. The silent rejection of the Sacramento bid infuriated Joe Serna. "I got the council to a first-and-goal, then I look up and he [Davis] is taking the ball for the other goal post. He may know his football, but I know my politics. If he gets turned down in Oakland, I'll remind him that it takes five votes on this council, and if he comes back this way, he better not come knocking on my door." But Serna was also conciliatory toward Oakland. "Well I guess you guys [Oakland] got 'em. I really do wish Oakland well," he said.

Although there continued to be rumblings in Los Angeles, Oakland was now the obvious front-runner. Davis met with East Bay officials on March 6 and nearly agreed to a move that evening, but it was discovered that there were additional construction costs of $6 million for stadium improvements for baseball that had not previously been considered. The next day Davis called Perata and consented to pay the additional costs. But Perata and Wilson were clearly getting jittery. They had a public meeting scheduled in five days but still had not received an affirmative sign from Al Davis. Their nervousness reached a peak when a March 8 *Los Angeles Times* story reported that Al Davis had demanded that L.A. investors pay the Raiders $15 million to delay a move. Donald Sterling, the owner of the basketball Clippers and a tenant at the Sports Arena, also managed by the Los Angeles

Memorial Coliseum Commission, told the *Times* that an agreement by the Raiders to stay in L.A. "could be very close." However, it was learned that the Los Angeles Memorial Coliseum Commission voluntarily offered the money to the Raiders but it was rejected by Davis.

On March 8, the East Bay negotiators gave Al Davis an absolute "deadline" to either agree to move to Oakland or call the whole thing off. The deadline was 5 P.M. on Friday, March 9, 1990. "If I submit the matter to my council for a decision, you can be damn sure the Raiders are coming," was the statement of an irritated Mayor Wilson.

But the man who doesn't believe in deadlines was not going to be pushed. At about 3:30 P.M., Al called Wilson and Perata and, citing "personal reasons," deferred a decision until noon on March 12. The public meeting was still scheduled but it would be canceled if no answer was forthcoming. Meanwhile, the Oakland Coliseum Board voted 9–1 in favor of the proposal negotiated by Wilson and Perata.

The "personal reasons" were probably twofold. One was to give Mayor Wilson time to swing a few indecisive votes. The other was to give Al Davis an opportunity to discuss developments with NFL commissioner Tagliabue at the owners meeting, which would begin in Orlando, Florida, on Sunday, March 11.

While moves were progressing behind the scenes, the Bay Area newspapers had a field day poking holes in the proposal. The *San Francisco Examiner* ran four consecutive days of negative stories. "Will Bay Area Support Mediocre Team?" was the headline in the Sunday *Oakland Tribune*. And on the morning of March 12, Glenn Dickey again warned his *San Francisco Chronicle* readers that the deal was just too expensive.

High noon finally struck on the big clock on the face of the *Oakland Tribune* building in downtown Oakland, and Al Davis was on the line with a call to Mayor Wilson and

Supervisor Perata. Yes, the Raiders would return to Oakland if the "process" was successfully completed. The "process" included the vote of the politicians and final execution of the documents. At about 12:35 P.M., Mayor Wilson, wearing an Oakland A's baseball cap, held up an Oakland Raiders jacket as Perata cheerfully looked on. It was exactly 10 years and 11 days removed from the time of another memorable press conference, held by Al Davis in the office of Mayor Tom Bradley of Los Angeles. The Raiders would be returning to Oakland.

Nobody who attended the joint meeting of the Alameda County Board of Supervisors and the Oakland City Council will soon forget it. Mayor Wilson and Supervisor Perata were cheered by the mostly partisan Raider audience, many clad in silver and black. Wilson Riles, Jr., was booed. Following presentations by the marketing consultants and architects, 141 speakers were given one minute each to express their opinions and feelings about the deal. Most of the speakers were opposed to "giving" Al Davis this large sum of money. The antagonists were jeered lustily by the Raider fans. A black woman who called the Raider proposal "a toy for white boys" was booed off the stage. The Raider partisans included former players Jim Otto and John Vella, who assured the politicians that "the Coliseum will sell out." The proceedings were not without some lighter moments. As the architects explained that a six-feet lower baseball diamond would not be noticeable, somebody from the rear of the Calvin Simmons Auditorium yelled, "[Jose] Canseco knows." After the last of the 141 citizens had finished their remarks, Mayor Wilson asked the audience if anyone else wished to speak. A young man dressed in a T-shirt and Oakland A's hat rushed to the microphones and shouted that he had his car stolen three times and why didn't the Oakland police do anything. He was escorted off but continued to scream through the discussion and voting segments of the meeting.

They did finally vote on the proposal. The Alameda County Board of Supervisors voted 3–1 for the Raider deal with one politician absent. The negative vote came from the Berkeley representative. The Oakland City Council vote was 5–3. Two key swing votes for the Raiders came from Carter Gilmore and Vice-Mayor Aleta Cannon. Gilmore said that many of his constituents were opposed to the deal, but the long-time political ally of Mayor Wilson would not let his friend down.

The headlines in the newspapers were predictable. They ranged from the positive "Raiders Say Yes" in the *San Francisco Examiner* to the "Commitment to Exodus" of the *Los Angeles Daily News*. Of course, every sports columnist in California and elsewhere had *something* to say. The most unusual was a commentary by *Los Angeles Times* beat writer Mark Heisler, who could not contain his resentment for five years of less-than-cooperative treatment by the Raiders' managing general partner. "Are we surprised?" Heisler asked. "If we are, we must be waking from a coma. Check his track record: Lie down with Al Davis. Wake up alone . . . He'd have had to overlook some slights, forget some disagreements, extend some good faith, and do another deal with the Los Angeles Coliseum Commission. This is the way things are done in the real world, where compromise is often a technique for bridging differences between competing interests. Oops, did they have the wrong boy."

Of course, Mel Durslag had a different opinion than Heisler. His theme: Blame the Coliseum Commission. After quoting Davis, who said he tried to give them one last chance, Durslag wrote, "It [LAMCC] has played burlesque for more than 40 years, its faces changing but the dedication to comedy never wavering. It now has lost the Rams, Bruins, Lakers, Kings and Raiders."

As Oakland Raider fans cheered in the lobby and outside the Calvin Simmons Auditorium following the vote, the opposition to Al Davis's return was beginning to plot strategy. Many of the opponents to the Raiders' return to Oakland were politically motivated. After all, it was an election year and five candidates had emerged to challenge Mayor Lionel "King" Wilson, as he was disparagingly called by his enemies. Attorney Frank Russo, who became the leader of the petition drive to place the Raider deal on the ballot, was once chairman of the Democratic Party in Alameda County and was currently a supporter of Elihu Harris, a candidate opposing Wilson. His cochairperson was Natalie Bayton, whose day job was as an aid to Wilson Riles. Many other activists in the movement to "get Al Davis" were involved in either the Riles or Harris campaigns. A second vote of the Oakland City Council was taken March 21 and repeated its approval. Because the deal was actually an amendment to the 1964 agreement that authorized construction of the Coliseum, Oakland city attorney Jayne Williams claimed that the Raider agreement could not find its way to the ballot box. As the opponents were busy looking for loopholes to overturn the deal, it was obvious that Al Davis had found controversy once again and the ultimate destination of his football team was still not certain.

On March 30, in response to the active opposition, the Raiders and Oakland and Alameda counties agreed to modify their agreement. The Raiders would only be "guaranteed" revenue from the higher priced premium seats and not the $30 general admission ducats. The revision was not enough to satisfy Frank Russo and the other opponents. They announced that their petition drive to place the Raider deal on the ballot would be continued and hired Voter Revolt, a professional canvassing organization, to obtain signatures. The previous claim to fame for Voter Revolt was its successful signature drive that placed an auto insurance initiative on the California ballot in 1988.

When the Raiders left for Los Angeles in 1982, spokesperson Scott Summerfeld of the Oakland Cham-

ber of Commerce estimated that the Raiders were responsible for direct annual revenues of $36 million and
$100 million in indirect revenues. But many of the media
critics and legal opposition insisted that because of the
high ticket prices, the Raiders would not sell out, causing
Oakland and Alameda counties to fund the deal with taxpayers' money. Marketing studies indicated that the fan
base was there, and even in the worst-case scenarios, Oakland and Alameda Counties would not lose money. Con-
versely, they would gain revenue. More pessimistic ticket
forecasts "prepared" by the opponents had the taxpayers
covering $23 million in bond payments over 15 years.
But there was a catch or two. Enactment of the new Raiders deal would retire the bonds that built the Coliseum in
1964, which were costing $1.5 million per year. Also, the
baseball A's would eventually be demanding an estimated $25 million in stadium improvements whether or
not the Raiders returned. But those improvements were
included in the construction costs of the Raider package.
So the $25 million cost of stadium improvements needed
to satisfy the A's was greater than their maximum calcu-
lated loss of $23 million with the Raiders in Oakland.
Perhaps playing upon the latent resentment of Davis by
many in the community because of the Raiders move to
Los Angeles, the opponents charged that while Davis was
becoming rich at taxpayers' expense, police and fire personnel would have to be laid off. Perata and Wilson were
criticized for "spending so much time and energy negotiating with Al Davis," rather than using their time to solve
urban problems.

Among the biggest critics in the Bay Area newspapers
was *San Francisco Chronicle* sports columnist Lowell Cohn,
who was also raised in Brooklyn, just like Mr. Davis. In a
January 22, 1990, column, Cohn wrote the following
about the pro football team that plays in San Francisco:
"There's something religious about the 49ers phenomenon. It's a secular religion that binds the Bay Area." The

implication from that statement would seem to be that there was no religion left over for the Raiders should they return. As a resident of Oakland, Cohn was outraged over the deal. He demanded that the public be permitted to vote on the Raider proposition. In the March 15, 1990, *San Francisco Chronicle,* Cohn blasted other sports writers "who have jumped on the Raider bandwagon." Because many of his journalistic compatriots didn't live in Oakland, Cohn surmised that "the writers don't have to come up with the cash, don't have to worry if more classes get dropped from the school curriculum." Yet just a few months earlier, Cohn was a supporter of the China Basin baseball stadium proposal in windy San Francisco, which involved $20 million of taxpayer money. After China Basin was rejected by the voters, Cohn blamed the earthquake for the election defeat and urged San Francisco Giants' owner Bob Lurie to try again. "Of course the earthquake made a difference," wrote Cohn on November 9, 1989, and added, "But before he [Lurie] cuts out on San Francisco, he should give the downtown ballpark one more try. He owes it to himself and he owes it to the City." As an Oakland resident, Cohn apparently was unconcerned about San Francisco taxpayer money.

There seemed to be much hypocrisy among the opponents. In 1985, the City of Oakland gave a $15 million "loan" to the Oakland A's with virtually no interest and a very favorable payment schedule. Where was the "outraged" opposition? In 1988, Oakland provided nearly $30 million worth of concessions to developer Lawrence Chan to build a downtown hotel. Chan then proceeded to buy a hotel in London with his own money. Why wasn't Voter Revolt out in the streets collecting signatures?

Jack Brooks stated that the agreement with Oakland would be withdrawn if there were a referendum and "the Raiders will go someplace else." On April 5, 1990, Commissioner Tagliabue announced that the NFL might expand by four teams no later than 1993. George Vukasin, president of the Coliseum Board, emphatically stated that Oakland would not be in the expansion picture. "If the Raiders don't come back for whatever the reason is, I'm not sure there's any reason to pursue . . . an expansion program, because of the inability for the city, county, and community to recognize what the requirements are to bring NFL football to this area," Vukasin said. Was the Los Angeles Memorial Coliseum Commission listening?

A failure to complete the Raiders deal for whatever reason would also undermine the credibility of Oakland to attract new teams in any sport or keep existing tenants. Thus, it was likely that the NBA Golden State Warriors, who were requesting that a new arena be built in Oakland, would avoid the possible political squabbling and instead find happiness on the way to San Jose. And the owners of the National Hockey League expansion franchise that was awarded to the Bay Area indicated they would prefer to play in San Jose rather than the Coliseum arena.

Obviously, the carefully orchestrated hysteria in Oakland gave the Los Angeles Coliseum Commission renewed hope. On March 25, Al Davis visited the home of Mayor Tom Bradley. The next day the Coliseum Commission finally voted to give MCA/Spectacor a free hand in running the stadium and arena, which included the construction of improvements. With the Oakland deal growing shakier by the moment, Los Angeles could finally make an offer, environmental and historic landmark interests notwithstanding.

The unraveling of the Oakland agreement soon became a battle of numbers. On April 4, 1990, the Oakland Coliseum Board decided to start taking deposits for Raider seats for the 1992 season. The decision was weeks overdue. A rally at the Coliseum kicked off the drive. By April 10, they had taken deposits on 38,000 seats. But on April 12, the opponents delivered 31,072 signatures on petitions. Only 19,000 valid signatures were needed to force a referendum.

Although there were possible legal problems concerning the validity of the petition, because the original Raider agreement was modified, Mayor Wilson was not about to present a challenge to the opponents. After thoroughly discussing the turn of events with his political advisors, Wilson then abruptly did an about-face and recommended that the offer to the Raiders be rescinded. He did not inform Perata of his change of heart. On April 17, the Oakland City Council voted 6–0 to pull the Raider proposal off the table. "The city has acted summarily and you cannot carry on a partnership this way," was Perata's public reaction to Wilson. His private response must have been more interesting.

If Jack Brooks and Al Davis had told Oakland to "stick it" at this point, they would have been completely justified. But they agreed to start over. Mayor Wilson appointed a seven-person advisory committee to oversee the deal and yes, Frank Russo was one of those selections. With the upcoming election in mind, Mayor Wilson excused himself from the negotiations on May 1 and was replaced by city council members Dick Spees and Aleta Cannon.

Wilson's attempted distancing from the Raiders did not help the mayor politically. A Gallup poll published in the *Oakland Tribune* on May 20, showed the incumbent mayor running a poor third in the race, with his support for the Raiders a big contributor to his declining ratings. The following day, another Gallup poll showed that support for the deal had dropped from 39% to 34%. With the *Tribune*'s lukewarm support of the Raiders' return, it was not surprising that the newspaper endorsed Elihu Harris for mayor on May 30.

The pollsters were correct. Lionel Wilson finished a poor third in the primary election on June 5. Either Wilson Riles, Jr., or Elihu Harris would become the next mayor of Oakland.

With the Raiders deal in limbo, the Oakland Coliseum Board and the baseball Athletics verbally agreed to a new lease in May 1990. The A's would receive the extra $500,000 annually that was discussed when the first Raiders deal was hot. And a "sweetheart" escape clause was inserted into the lease that would allow the A's to break their contract and leave town if they lost a total of $3.5 million over three years. Although the Athletics were riding very high after winning the 1989 World Series, it is possible that their increasing payroll will not keep pace with revenues, especially if attendance drops off. The Coliseum Board, Alameda County Board of Supervisors, and the Oakland City Council all obediently approved the lease, and columnist William Wong of the *Oakland Tribune* did not demand a public reading of the deal as he did with the Raiders.

The reactions out of Oakland should have helped Los Angeles make a comeback. But MCA Inc. decided to bow out of their partnership with Spectacor, which stymied any meaningful discussions. On May 17, the *Los Angeles Times* reported that Davis wanted a $17.5 million upfront payment from LAMCC as a guarantee to stay in the Coliseum. Mayor Bradley would only agree to a $5 million advance and Spectacor would not go higher than $2 million.

In Sacramento, construction started on the stadium that could ultimately be home to a professional football or baseball team. Gregg Lukenbill sold 5% of his interest in the Sacramento Sports Association to partner Joe Benvenuti to raise cash to fund the construction costs.

But it wasn't enough. On July 12, Lukenbill asked Sacramento sports fans to pay a fee of $250 to $1,250 to finance the stadium. They would be guaranteed a seat in the stadium if a major league team ever came to town.

In June, the capital city was awarded a franchise in the new World League of American Football. The team will play its spring 1991 schedule in Hughes Stadium until Lukenbill's ballpark is completed.

On May 31, another California city extended an indirect invitation to the Los Angeles Raiders. Kagen Management Services, a private firm, announced plans to build a 75,000-seat stadium and indoor arena in the city of Fontana, which is about 50 miles east of Los Angeles. The total cost would be about $450 million. Kagen announced that the group would seek existing franchises for their complex. (Wonder who they have in mind?)

The attempt by Oakland to prepare a new proposal was successful. On June 14 a new offer was revealed. All ticket guarantees were dropped and the Raiders would be responsible for selling tickets, which would be priced at the same level as earlier. A $31.9 million loan to the Raiders, to be repaid in two years, replaced the $54 million franchise fee of the earlier proposal. Taxable bonds would be used to finance the reconstruction of the Coliseum. The estimated value of the proposal was $127 million.

If the Raiders sell out all home games during the 15 years of the agreement, Davis would make more money and the City of Oakland and Alameda County less than in the earlier offering. But both the politicians and the media seemed pleased that most financial risks were removed. With Russo, Riles, and the other former detractors supporting the new deal, there was virtually no opposition this time. The Oakland Athletics received additional concessions to their lease that would allow them to move by the end of 1995. But A's president Walter Haas, Jr., insisted that the team had no plans to vacate the Oakland Coliseum.

On July 17, 1990, the Oakland City Council approved the new proposal by a 6–1 vote. Three days later, the Coliseum Board gave its OK and the Alameda County Board of Supervisors voted 4–1 to accept on July 24. The next move was up to Davis, who was given until August 31 to agree to the offer.

*   *   *

The month of August 1990 was filled with rumors that the Raiders return to Oakland would be imminent. But both home preseason games and the opener against Denver were played in Los Angeles. On August 31, Davis and Oakland agreed to a 30-day extension.

The Los Angeles Coliseum put forth a last-ditch effort to keep the Raiders. On August 15, Spectacor outlined a new offer to Al Davis that included $146 million in stadium renovations, $10 million in advance cash payments, and the foregiveness of the $6.7 million "loan" given to the Raiders in 1982 that was never paid back. Al would be required to sign a 20-year lease. Both the LAMCC and the Raiders would drop their ongoing lawsuits. The deal was put in final form on September 6 and Davis was given until September 11 to make a decision.

Oakland representatives were not overly disturbed. "I've never been overly concerned about L.A.," said Don Perata. East Bay officials were hoping that Davis would accept their $168 million deal by the end of the month and perhaps play the final part of the 1990 season in Oakland.

During the period when so many cities were trying to satisfy him, Al Davis had often said he didn't want to be a lame-duck owner. Commissioner Tagliabue said that the league does not want "lame-duck" teams, which indicates that no lame ducks will be allowed to swim in Los Angeles.

Tagliabue didn't have to worry. Davis made the LAMCC deadline and on September 11 announced that he would stay in Los Angeles. The Coliseum will build 150 to 225 luxury boxes and 15,000 club seats. The capacity would be reduced to 70,000.

Los Angeles won the sweepstakes but Sacramento has emerged as a winner in this race, too. Gregg Lukenbill showed the sports world that the capital city will be a serious contender in the franchise game in the future, both for baseball and football. With only one team in the Bay Area, an NFL expansion entry in Sacramento is a possibility. Perhaps Lukenbill will court the San Francisco 49ers. Owner Eddie DeBartolo, Jr., has never been ecstatic about playing in Candlestick Park, and it is possible that the Niners could look to Sacramento someday. But Lukenbill may have to permanently abandon his demands for local ownership to attract Eddie, Jr. Another San Francisco team that Lukenbill could seduce is the baseball Giants. After voters rejected a plan to build the China Basin stadium near downtown San Francisco in November 1989, Giants' owner Bob Lurie started talking to the suburban city of Santa Clara about a new ballpark. Located about 45 miles south of San Francisco, Santa Clara will have to share expenses with other neighboring cities if attempts to secure the Giants are to be fruitful. If they don't succeed, Lukenbill should be waiting in the wings. On September 4, 1990, Sacramento was one of ten cities that applied to the National League for a baseball expansion team.

Whatever became of Irwindale? As of this writing there has not been a peep heard from this city of 1,040, but it seems likely that a legal attempt will eventually be made to get back that $10 million from Al Davis.

Now that they've been given a reprieve as the home of the Silver and Black, the LAMCC must make good on the deal and renovate and maintain the Coliseum as a modern facility. Giving Spectacor a free hand in the management of the Coliseum was a good first step. Now LAMCC must be willing to back their management team with the big bucks that are necessary for an effective operation. Hopefully the agenda of keeping the Raiders in Los Angeles will not change with the ever-changing nine member Commission.

For Oakland, it was "the big fish that got away," not once but twice. Maybe it should be called "Immaculate Reception II." People such as George Vukasin, Lionel Wilson, and Don Perata were sincere in their efforts to lure the Raiders back, but the undermining by petty politics in an election year proved to be fatal. With the 49ers across the Bay, it is doubtful that Oakland will ever receive an NFL expansion team. They now must work to satisfy their existing tenants.

Al Davis has received considerable criticism over the latest installment of "Where Will the Raiders Go?" He was accused of holding all of the competing cities hostage and extracting "ransom" from trusting and gullible politicians. Most of this bashing was not justified. Nobody put a gun to Irwindale, Oakland, Sacramento, or Los Angeles. All four cities saw the large economic gains that would accrue if a National Football League team came to town. Oakland certainly felt the economic losses after the Raiders departed. The politicians were also reacting to their constituents. It would have been very easy for the large legion of Raider fans in Northern California to abandon the Silver and Black after they left town. They could have believed the media, which sided with the politicians and Commissioner Pete Rozelle, and vilified Al Davis when all discussions to keep the team in Oakland collapsed in 1980 and 1981. But it didn't happen. Although the San Francisco 49ers started winning Super Bowls when the Raiders moved to Los Angeles—and it would have been easy to change allegiance—the Raider fan base stayed mostly intact. And despite the Raiders having one foot out the door, 55,000 Los Angeles fans still made it to the 1990 home opener. It may have been the deciding factor. Oakland fans will be devastated by the inability to regain the Raiders, but should take pride in fighting the good fight.

"That terrible Al Davis," the critics said. "He's only

after the money." Sure, he's after the money. But Al Davis would not personally become richer by what was being offered. He was already wealthy when he started coaching at Adelphi College in 1950, when he took over the Raiders in 1963, and when he moved to Los Angeles in 1982. The money that the Raiders receive when an agreement is finally enacted will be used for continuing to make the Raider organization successful. "Commitment to Excellence" is the Raider credo. As long as Al Davis can breathe, the commitment will be there. But it will now take big bucks to maintain the excellence.

But there is a down-side to this episode that borders on the preposterous and the absurd. The three-year search for a permanent home that has included at least five known candidates has been an embarrassingly farcical experience for both the National Football League and the Raider owner. The failure to stick to the Irwindale agreement and then to keep their good-faith money; the embarrassment of the rejection of the first Oakland deal; and the premature erosion of the fan base in Los Angeles—all have painted Davis as a man who has suddenly lost his sense of timing and his ability to make a decision. Wouldn't it have been better to have deferred this entire city search to within a year of the expiration of his lease with the LAMCC and then entertain proposals, making the final decision at the conclusion of the 1991 season? They still would have pursued him in Oakland and Sacramento and supported him in Los Angeles. This is a man who, in his later years, just can't bite the bullet, admit his mistakes, and go on.

When you combine the inability of the Raiders to find a home with the poor football decisions involving Marc Wilson and others in recent years, it must be asked once again if the parade has passed Al Davis by. That question was posed to the many people who were interviewed for this book. One particular response keeps gnawing at the author. When asked about Davis, this football observer had an interesting theory. "The creative life of any artist is about 30 years," he said. "Stravinsky, Shakespeare, and Picasso all produced their best work in roughly a 30-year period," he claimed. "Their efforts later in life did not match the earlier achievements."

He may be right.

INDEX

Also of Interest
to Football Fans:

The San Francisco 49ers—Team of the Decade

The Inside Story of How They Came from Nowhere to Win Four Super Bowls, Revised to Include the 1989–1990 Championship Season

Here's the updated and revised edition of last year's bestselling book on the legendary 49ers including an in-depth look at their incredible championship season and back-to-back Super Bowl victories. It all began in 1979 when Coach Bill Walsh inherited a demoralized and losing team. He wasted no time in building an organization whose roster over the next ten years included the likes of Joe Montana, Roger Craig, Jerry Rice, Dwight Clark, Ronnie Lott, Randy Cross, and Jeff Fuller. The authors have been given unprecedented access to the 49ers. Unusually candid interviews with owner DeBartolo, George Seifert, Bill Walsh, and scores of players and former players bring a sense of excitement to the narrative. The result is a gripping account of a great dynasty still in its prime.